The Pastoral Clinic

The Pastoral Clinic

ADDICTION AND DISPOSSESSION
ALONG THE RIO GRANDE

ANGELA GARCIA

UNIVERSITY OF CALIFORNIA PRESS

University of California Press, one of the most distinguished university presses in the United States, enriches lives around the world by advancing scholarship in the humanities, social sciences, and natural sciences. Its activities are supported by the UC Press Foundation and by philanthropic contributions from individuals and institutions. For more information, visit www.ucpress.edu.

University of California Press
Oakland, California

Library of Congress Cataloging-in-Publication Data

Garcia, Angela, 1971–
    The pastoral clinic : addiction and dispossession
along the Rio Grande / Angela Garcia.
        p.   cm.
    Includes bibliographical references and index.
    isbn 978-0-520-25829-7 (cloth : alk. paper) — isbn 978-0-520-26208-9
(pbk. : alk. paper)
    1. Heroin abuse—New Mexico.   2. Drug addicts—New Mexico.
I. Title.

hv5822.h4g37 2010
362.29'3092368078952—dc22

                                                        2010001811

Manufactured in the United States of America

25 24   23   22   21   20
10   9   8

Para Ruby y Lucía

Memory aches, wherever it is touched.

Giorgios Seferis

Contents

Illustrations

Acknowledgments

My deepest gratitude goes to the many women and men struggling with heroin addiction in the Española Valley who let me into their lives. It was an honor to be trusted with their stories. I thank my neighbors for teaching me what it is to be just that—a neighbor, generous of care. Although I give pseudonyms to those featured in the pages that follow, I want them to know that their lives have left an indelible imprint on my own. I so much wanted the woman I call "Alma" to be able to read this work. It is my hope that her story will one day help others.

I am indebted to the staff of Nuevo Día, especially the executive director, for allowing me to chronicle their work and for welcoming me as a staff member, researcher, and friend. I also thank the many health professionals, activists, and residents in the Española Valley who shared their thoughts and stories with me. Special thanks go to Luis Torres and *High Country News Magazine* for getting me on the path to writing.

This book grows out of research that I conducted for my Ph.D. dissertation at Harvard University. I would like to thank my thesis chair, Arthur

Kleinman, for his scrupulous engagement with my work and for his confidence in this text. His advice to focus on what truly matters ultimately inspired me to return to New Mexico. Byron Good has been a trusted source of support on matters intellectual and practical, as well as a friend; my thanks go to him. I thank Kay Warren for her generous insight, for her support, and for being a true *compañera*. Also at Harvard, I would like to extend my deep appreciation to Michael Fischer, David Carrasco, and Mary-Jo DelVecchio Good. The following institutions made this research possible: the National Science Foundation, the National Academy of Sciences Ford Doctoral Dissertation Fellowship, the National Institutes of Mental Health NRSA Predoctoral Fellowship, a Harvard University Graduate Fellowship, and a Summer Research Fellowship for Health and Social Justice, School of Social Medicine, Harvard University.

I owe a debt of gratitude to João Biehl for reading earlier drafts of this book and for his persistent reminder to stay close to the ethnography. It is a deceptively simple message that strengthened this work in important ways. I thank the University of California Press, especially its astute reviewers, for expressing confidence in this book and Sheila Berg for her skillful editing. I am especially grateful to Stan Holwitz for his enduring support and words of kindness. And I thank Stuart Bernstein for reminding me that I am a writer.

I am also grateful to the following individuals for their crucial advice and support: Leo Chavez, Clara Han, Philippe Bourgois, Joe Dumit, William Maurer, Tom Boellstorff, Julia Elyachar, Michael Montoya, Keith Murphy, Eugene Raikel, William Garriott, Noelle Stout, Omar al-Dewachi, Hosam Aboul-Ela, Chris Dole, and the editors of and anonymous reviewers for *Cultural Anthropology*. I began revising this work during my tenure as a President's Postdoctoral Fellow at the University of California, Los Angeles; my thanks go to Carole Browner, Susan Slyomovics, Jason Throop, Linda Garro, Allesandro Duranti, Chon Noriega, and Otto Santa Ana. I also owe special thanks to Lawrence Cohen and Nancy Scheper-Hughes, my mentors during my undergraduate years at UC Berkeley. It was their work that inspired me to pursue anthropology, and it inspires me still.

Thank you to Jaime Santos, Tali Bray, and Michael Marco for supporting me over the years and for making life such a pleasure.

I end by expressing my deepest gratitude to my family. Rubén Martínez supported me from the very beginning to the very end of this work. His insights, encouragement, patience, and editing skills are woven into every page. Rubén made New Mexico a place that I could call home again, and for that I am especially grateful. Every day I thank my daughters, Ruby and Lucía, for their wonderful appearance in my world and for making every day such a joy. And the Garcia women—especially my mother, Wilma, and my sister, Kristina, who were the first to teach me what it means to care. And, finally, my gratitude to Bear and Chino.

Introduction

The clinic is a house: small, brown, made of straw bale and mud plaster. It sits at the end of an unpaved road ten miles from the nearest town. Fifteen acres of dirt dotted with desert sage surround it and, here and there, clusters of cottonwood trees, dilapidated outbuildings, rusted metal chairs. A netless basketball hoop leans precariously. It looks as though it is about to collapse with the next gust of strong, summer wind. We watch it from our perch by a coffee-can ashtray and wonder when it will finally fall.

John smokes a cigarette and stares blankly at the cloudless blue sky. Though it's 85 degrees, Lupita's thin body is wrapped in layers of sweat-shirts and blankets. She nods off in her chair, her head rhythmically falling and rising, falling and rising. Bernadette complains that her legs hurt, feel knotted and twisted up. "How much longer," she asks me, "till the next dose?"

The three are heroin addicts living at a drug detoxification clinic in northern New Mexico's Española Valley.[1] Since the early 1990s the Española Valley has had the highest per capita rate of heroin-induced deaths in the United States. In a region of just over 30,000 residents, nearly 70 people died from heroin overdose in little over a year—which is to say that within this close network of rural towns and villages, everybody knows somebody who is addicted to heroin or has died because of it.

John, Bernadette, and Lupita are in varying stages of heroin detox, a month-long process that uses medications to ease the pain of withdrawal. Like the majority of patients at the clinic, they are court appointed—or sentenced—to detoxification, the first official step in a longer process of drug recovery and, in their cases, punitive rulings.[2] This is not the first time they have undergone treatment, or sentencing, for their heroin addiction.

I had recently been hired to work at the clinic as a detoxification attendant—a job I took as a means to get closer to subjects in my area of ethnographic study. Like all the other attendants, I received no formal training for the position, although I was required to take an examination that certified my ability to properly distribute prescription medications used in the clinic, especially the narcotic-based *relajantes* (relaxants) that many patients used on the "streets." At the clinic, use of these medications was "legitimate," and patients asked for them with desperation. They were unable, it seemed, to adjust their bodies' addictive demands to the clinical indications of *las pildoras*—capsules such as Darvon and Librium—which on the street are commonly crushed and injected like heroin.

On my own I quickly learned to keep the patients occupied and briefly distracted before their next scheduled dose. On this afternoon, as Bernadette grew increasingly restless, I suggested a walk to the Rio Grande, which formed the western boundary of the clinic grounds. John and Bernadette reluctantly agreed. We left Lupita and headed toward the river.

We walked slowly, the sun hot on our dark heads. I watched John and Bernadette concentrate on their legs and feet as they moved. Their steps were uncertain and deliberate, like the very young or the very old. They stopped for a cigarette break, during which they considered turning back. But by that point we were closer to the river than to the clinic. With my urging, we pushed on, our socks shot through with prickly thorns.

The walk to the river brought forth memories: of apple orchards and dirt bike trails, trout fishing and twelve-packs. John said the river was fuller back then and the crops that drank from the irrigation ditches it fed more abundant. We wondered about the coming monsoon, whether the rains would finally be strong and lasting; the region had been in a severe drought for the better part of a decade. Then, for several minutes, we walked in silence.

"I can smell the water," Bernadette said, her face glistening with sweat.

The edge of the river was lined with a thick tangle of brush. I led the way through it, pushing back angry branches and locating dry footholds along the muddy perimeter. Bernadette followed close behind me, and John followed her. We cleared the brush and then, suddenly, were standing on the east bank of the Rio Grande.

The river was brown and shallow, its surface pebbled. We stared at the muddy water and remembered summer swims.

And then, Bernadette: "This sucks."

Not wanting to admit defeat, I suggested walking upstream where the river widened before heading back. Bernadette lit another cigarette—she'd had it—and fell behind while John and I walked ahead without her. I imagined as we walked that we were looking for something to call forth our memories—perhaps schools of flickering minnows or deep pools of clear water. We walked quietly. After a few minutes, John stopped. "*Mira* [Look]," he said, pointing. Caught in a cluster of rocks lay a heroin cooker made of an old soda can, along with two discarded syringes.

"*Este río está muerto* [This river is dead]," John said.

John lit another cigarette, and we turned back toward the clinic in silence—our shoes heavy with water and mud. When we met up with Bernadette, John again announced that the river was dead. Bernadette looked at him blankly, and the three of us continued without speaking. When we arrived we found Lupita exactly where we had left her—bundled up and nodding off in the sun.

·   ·   ·   ·   ·

Later that evening, just before midnight, John disappeared from the clinic after eight days of heroin detoxification. He left behind his few belongings (muddy shoes, a weathered Bible, and a portable CD player) and walked a series of dirt roads that led to the main highway. From there he hitchhiked to Española, the nearest town, ten miles away. Because his departure placed him in violation of his probation, the attendant on duty was directed to notify the police. John's patient file was labeled "self-discharge against staff advice," although it is unclear whether any of the staff advised him to stay.

The next morning police found John in his pickup truck, parked beside the garbage bins at the Española Dairy Queen. When they approached the driver's window, they found John in a drug-induced sleep—in the passenger seat beside him an empty syringe. John was arrested. Three months later he was sentenced to return to the New Mexico State Penitentiary in Santa Fe, where he was to serve a two-year sentence for drug possession and outstanding warrants. In the eyes of the detox clinic, John was just another patient who had relapsed and failed treatment.

Since his arrest I have often wondered if John's so-called self-discharge was precipitated by our encounter at the river. By all accounts he was doing well with his recovery program and was, in his words, "committed to kicking it this time." Indeed, he seemed to have gotten over the hardest stretch of heroin detox—the first few days when the physical pain is at its worst. And the threat of prison was, he said, "enough to keep me straight." What happened? Did John's intimate recognition of the heroin cooker and syringes we stumbled upon awaken an overwhelming desire to get high? Or were there other, perhaps deeper dynamics of loss and longing during our walk that contributed to his relapse? How would I be able to begin to understand the motivations, force, and meaning of his "self-discharge"?

Shortly after John's arrest, I sat beside a different stretch of the Rio Grande near my house. A discarded Budweiser can, caught between fallen branches, shone brightly, like a medallion in the murky water. I poked at the can with an old wooden crutch that had been abandoned by the river's edge. And everywhere, in the branches of the cottonwoods, among the black-billed magpies, in the weed-choked irrigation ditches, caught on barbed-wire fences, were discarded plastic bags emblazoned with the Walmart logo. *Low Prices. Always.* I recalled John's words about the *río muerto* and wondered if it had ever been alive.

·   ·   ·   ·   ·

When I returned to northern New Mexico in January 2004 to begin researching heroin addiction, hypodermic needles seemed to be everywhere. They were discarded along the tortuous county roads connecting the tiny, ancient, Spanish-speaking villages—Santa Cruz to Chimayó, Córdova to Truchas, La Canova to El Guique. They were tossed in the acequias—the centuries-old labyrinth of irrigation ditches that feed the valley's crops. They were reportedly found in restaurants, schoolyards, and cemeteries. To my surprise, there were syringes hiding under the leaking sink of the house I rented, unused and forgotten.

For weeks, I surveyed my property, looking for sharp objects. I wore thick-soled shoes and moved across my acre of dry land methodically, in square-foot parcels. I didn't find any syringes (except for those inside my house), but I collected dozens of broken beer bottles and other wasted objects. I also soon discovered that my next-door neighbor was a heroin dealer and, along with her boyfriend, operated her business out of her home. After witnessing a series of violent incidents at her house, I stopped wandering around my property and took to sitting in my attic window. For months, I watched cars spitting up dust as they drove up and down our shared dirt road. I watched her customers duck into her darkened adobe house and quickly reappear at all hours of the day and night. I listened for the desperate sound of late-night knocking and the other sounds that often accompanied it: screams and blows and, sometimes, the shattering of glass. And I watched my neighbor's eight-year-old son running out of the house as though it were on fire and taking refuge in the tiny pump house, which sat just below my office window.

The ubiquitous and troubling presence of the syringes highlighted the extent to which heroin had become enmeshed in every aspect of physical space and everyday life. They were everywhere in the landscape, on public land and private, tiny but dense sites in which history and subjectivity merged and, ultimately, disappeared. Anecdotes to a local reality, the syringes were imbued with alienation, desperation, and longing. They appeared to me as a kind of ghostly sign, like the handmade memorials called *descansos* (resting places) that line the highway, marking the site where someone died or was killed in an automobile accident.[3] I understood my task as an anthropologist to conjure up the social life that produced these signs, to give it flesh and depth. Indeed, that is why I went to New Mexico to study heroin—to try to give purpose and meaning to an aspect of American life that had become dangerously ordinary, even cliché.

I grew up in New Mexico, leaving at the age of seventeen for the West Coast and later the East Coast. For years I would speak of New Mexico's distinctive beauty, never of the deep suffering that I knew existed there.[4] I kept memories of New Mexico separate in my mind—maintaining a firm boundary between what could be rendered (its celebrated landscape) and what could not (the uncertain and secreted experience of addiction). But from my moment with John at the Rio Grande, I recognized that the two were inextricably linked. New Mexico's landscape makes visible the existence of addiction, and addiction shapes and is shaped by New Mexico's landscape. Each has its own processes of sedimentation, which are entangled in ways that this book tries to understand.

GEOGRAPHIES OF ADDICTION

John's moment at the river and subsequent relapse provide a powerful introduction to several themes that I explore in this book. First, there is the material and symbolic nature of finding the used syringe during our walk. I had suggested the walk to the Rio Grande precisely because I thought it would provide a respite from the many challenges of clinic life—from the physical pain of detox to the boredom and discomfort that accompany the clinic's slow tempo.[5] My plan seemed to work, at least before we got to the river itself. John's and Bernadette's memories of events that had occurred along the river harkened back to a time before heroin and its personal devastation. But seeing that even the river was, in a sense, contaminated by heroin pointed to just how deeply entrenched the region's addiction problem was and would push me to address how there is ultimately no space—physical or experiential—external to it. Our discovery along the river would force me to address the way in which heroin haunts so many aspects of everyday life in this region, from the most public to the most intimate.

"Our landscape is everywhere spotted with ruins," J. B. Jackson (1994: 15) wrote of northern New Mexico. This book starts from the idea that this particular geography of addiction encloses multiple forms of spatial and existential ruin, sedimented and entangled through time.[6]

As I learned the contours of John's personal history, I came to understand that his declaration that the river was dead expressed a feeling of loss that was intimately connected to the social and political history of the region. This feeling, and the language used to describe it, resonated powerfully with many addicts I interviewed, especially as they spoke of memories of dispossession and loss of land. Indeed, addicts' narratives of heroin use were often related to mourning a lost sense of place.[7] The *presence* of heroin here is closely connected to the multiple and changing ways that this land has been inhabited, labored on, "suffered for," and lost (Moore 2006). A central theme in this book is how loss and mourning provide more than a metaphor for heroin addiction: they trace a kind of chronology, a temporality, of it. They even provide a constitutive power for it.

An important part of this geography of addiction is the growing presence of the public health and legal apparatus. What I want to describe now are the high stakes involved in how these institutions classify and respond to events such as John's relapse and how these classifications shape addicts' understandings of their addiction and, by extension, themselves. In defining John's departure from the clinic as a "self-discharge," certain claims were made regarding his capacity and will to be a "good patient" and "good citizen"—that is, within the realm of the law or, in this case, his

Figure 1.   El río. Photo by the author.

inability to be such. John's "relapse" or "treatment failure"—purportedly neutral terms in a medical sense—would become morally charged by his subsequent arrest and imprisonment. The effects of these competing institutional claims are a central concern of this book. I argue that such claims and the structures of authority in which they are embedded extend into the addict, presenting him or her with a new life script, such as "the patient" or "the prisoner."

By attending to the politics of what I call the *patient-prisoner*, I explore how the local phenomenon of heroin addiction and addicts themselves are constituted not only through hardship and loss but also through the logic, routines, and practices of medical and juridical regimes (Bourgois 2000; Lovell 2006; Rhodes 2004). Such an inquiry extends Michel Foucault's (1979, 1998, 1990) inquiry into how forms of governance become forces for the creation of new forms of subjectivity. I work with a somewhat similar set of concerns in trying to describe how institutional structures and claims are absorbed by the addict, exacerbating a sense of personal failure that contributes to a collective sense of hopelessness and, in turn, the regional heroin problem itself.

In this work, I approach heroin addiction as a human and ethical phenomenon that urgently requires understanding, especially as it can be illuminated through ethnography.[8] I also approach heroin addiction as an analytic in which culture, politics, and history coexist as a site of struggle and whose examination requires close attention to the personal and collective histories that form subjects and their drug use. By viewing addiction as phenomenon and analytic, I hope to show how Hispano addictive experience is closely related to history and not merely cultural or personal pathology, as it is so often described. In doing so, I call attention to both the personal and political stakes of heroin addiction—its phenomenology and its political economy, its intimate and institutional forms.

Anthropologists and others have established that the addict cannot be disconnected from the broader "moral world." My analysis extends this insight by showing how specific geographies of addiction intersect with institutional and historical formations to shape the lives of addicts. In thinking about the connectedness of the heroin addict to the broader moral world, I have attended to the many spaces, roles, and identities "the addict" inhabits.[9] This approach stands as a critique of popular representations of addicts as separated from "traditional" social and intimate bonds, or as isolated from parents, children, and community. Though many addicts do experience isolation, I question the notion of the "isolated addict" and insist on the persistence of intimate and genealogical ties in addicts' lives. I demonstrate how these ties are maintained through everyday modes of care within addicted families and between neighbors—from the family household acting as a proxy clinic for the state, to practices of "gifting" heroin in times of physical need and economic scarcity, to funerary rituals for fatal heroin overdoses, such as "shooting up" the graves of the recently departed.

On the one hand, these practices of care can be interpreted as criminal, perverse, or self-defeating, and they have been incorporated in the "crackdown" strategies of local and state police.[10] Several police officers I interviewed mentioned that drug possession cases can most effectively be "rounded up" at local cemeteries, where heroin addicts frequently mourn loved ones lost to the drug while getting high themselves. On the other hand, these practices can be described as the "burden of care" families and communities must shoulder in the context of poverty and institutional neglect.[11] Both framings risk missing the dynamics of connectedness and longing from which these practices emerge. My goal here is to restore the embodied, economic, and moral dynamics of addiction as they play out in domestic and community relations and to show how these relations enhance, remake, and sometimes reduce the life possibilities of the addicted (Bourgois 2002; Lovell 2002).

This book's orientation to tracing the connectedness of the addict to the broader moral world extends to its consideration of how personal history is interwoven with cultural and political history. Northern New Mexico has always been depicted as a remote and insular region. In reality, it has been the site of colonial exploitation and transformation for more than four centuries. Today, locals passionately express the material and cultural losses that resulted from the region's embattled past—in particular, the loss of Spanish and Mexican land grants—and they are likely to understand its heroin problem as a contemporary consequence. The memory of locals and their personal encounters with heroin (and the international trafficking circuits on which it depends) made it clear to me that northern New Mexico is anything but isolated. It thus became essential to resist taking an isolationist stance in which personal histories of addiction are reduced to individual soma or psyche. Instead, I understand individual histories of addiction as a historical formation and as embedded in an immanent social context. Put differently, I explore heroin addiction as a contemporary modality of Hispano life based in the *longue durée* of Hispano dispossession. This geographic, or pastoral, vision of addiction grounds my analysis of how the historical and continuous processes of dispossession of Hispano property and personhood emerge as a condition of possibility for the contemporary phenomenon of heroin use.[12]

．　　．　　．　　．　　．

At the same time that I foreground the *inseparability* of addictive experience from history and the broader world, I recognize that I am exploring forms of experience—getting high, overdose, suicide—that insist, to a degree, on the *singularity* of the subject. These forms of experience exclude me, and yet they concern me; heroin overdose is endemic to the region (and may thus be considered "collective experience") and yet, in the end, is a solitary act. Such quandaries that this research encounters raise epistemological problems that center on the question of how to think and write an account of experience that is fundamentally foreclosed to the ethnographer, sometimes even to language itself. These are dimensions of experience that often escape clinical and critical analysis and that necessitate working on the margins of knowing and acknowledgment (Cavell 1976).[13]

Rather than bracket these questions, I attend to them as moments of incomprehensibility. I do so with the intent that they be understood as moments that raise fundamental questions for anthropology and for an ethics of care. Where to look, for example, when one wants to understand the experience of *losing oneself,* as getting high and overdosing is so often described? What does this form of self-exile communicate in terms of the (broken) interdependencies of self and other? In foregrounding those moments that appear unknowable, I seek to demonstrate the significance, and sometimes penetrability, of certain limits: the limits of experience, understanding, and ethnography, especially as they form the basis from which we constitute others and ourselves.

On a methodological register, considering the historicity, interconnectivity, and incommensurability of addictive experience has meant attending to seemingly different fields. For example, after John's "self-discharge," I realized that it would be important to follow his movement through the penal system in order to understand what happens to addicts that "fail" forms of medical intervention. And I did follow John and other addicts as they cycled through arrest, hospitalization, and incarceration. While examining these institutional realms, I came into contact with more intimate details of addicts' lives.

In fact, it was at John's drug court hearing that I began to piece together details of his personal life: an estranged father living in a mountain village, a younger brother fighting in the war in Iraq, a five-year-old daughter living with John's mother in Chimayó. I would move accordingly across these different sites—from the clinic to the courthouse to the mountain village to the prison—following the contours of John's life across space and time. As I did, I recognized that these sites were not disparate but a part of the same process of formation: the formation of an addiction and of a life.

Sometimes following the story means hitting dead ends, and I encountered many of them. These included states that I could not access given the nature of my research (such as understanding what it *feels* like to overdose) or situations that I turned away from for fear of reprisal (such as the offer to observe the buying and selling of heroin along a secluded stretch of river). There were also subjects who were lost to "the streets," imprisonment, and death. I argue that it is in these moments where the connections end that the vulnerabilities of drug life—and life itself—are most powerfully visible. Such dead ends provide us with clues to what is most at stake for the subject, a family, and a community.

Although my interest in rethinking addiction is situated in understanding the entanglements of history, sociality, and subjectivity, it is vital, too, to understand the standard approaches to understanding addiction, in particular, in the medical and juridical domains. Each chapter of this book considers how selective institutional interventions (in this case, state-regulated treatment and criminalization) lead to an internalization of new moral codes, which must be negotiated between addicts and within families and communities.

In the section that follows I briefly examine some of the prevailing models for understanding heroin addiction and for "rehabilitating" heroin addicts, commenting on how these models have their own adverse effects, such as "fixing" addicts in certain life scripts whereby they continually return to the system meant to rehabilitate them. This cycle of failure, I argue, is as much a human failing as an epistemological one. It is my hope that this book upsets the acceptability of these standard approaches and the kinds of claims that operate through them, and that it points toward a more critical—and ethical—approach to thinking about and treating heroin addiction.[14]

ADDICTION'S CYCLES

From the point at which heroin enters the bloodstream, the physiological effect—the *rush*—occurs very quickly, usually within twenty seconds to a minute. The central nervous system and the cardiovascular, respiratory, endocrine, gastrointestinal, and genitourinary systems, as well as the skin, are affected. Morphine, the psychoactive ingredient in heroin, causes the state of euphoria, analgesia, and sedation associated with a heroin high. Over time, increasingly larger and more frequent doses of heroin are needed to achieve this state. Using becomes less about achieving a high and more about staving off withdrawal. Heroin is medicine; it relieves the pain its use creates.[15]

There is a complex, even geometrical relationship between the physiological experience of heroin addiction and the explanatory model of "chronicity"—established by scientists and caregivers to understand and treat addiction. Briefly, the model of chronicity likens addiction to a lifelong disease, such as diabetes, asthma, or hypertension (Appel and Kott 2000; Cami 2001; Heymann and Brownsberger 2001). The notion that addiction is a disease—chronic, subject to relapse, rooted in the subject's neurobiology and beyond his or her rational control—corresponds to developments in the technosciences of addiction (such as neuro-imagery) and a distancing from older lexicons of moral failure, stigma, and social causality. With addiction thus viewed as a chronic disease process, or, more specifically, a chronic relapsing brain disorder, its treatment is now conceived as long term and partially effective. Relapse is an expected occurrence during or after treatment episodes, especially where there are underlying physical, psychological, or "environmental" factors (Appel et al. 2000; Volkow 2005).

The chronicity model emerged in the early 1960s, in part as a response to the high incidence of repeated relapse seen among addicts who entered publicly funded treatment programs. It was intended to dispel the long-held assumption that heroin addicts were innately psychopathic and irredeemable (see Acker 2002).[16]

Underpinning this rescripting of addiction was the explosion of drug use in new economic and social settings—out of the "shadows" and into the white, middle-class mainstream. New constellations of disciplinary interests emerged that reexamined the etiological and clinical aspects of addiction. This turn culminated with the introduction of methadone maintenance in the 1960s. The idea was that methadone, a longer-acting drug than heroin, could be administered to prevent withdrawal and stabilize the addict's physiology so that he or she could legitimately engage in life.

The tropes of chronicity and maintenance have become key organizing principles for the kinds of therapeutic work that take place in clinical settings. They have also ushered in a new agenda for addiction research in the behavioral and biological sciences. Recent developments point to the neurological basis of addiction, whereby repeated use of addictive substances, such as heroin, alter the neurological circuitry for dopamine, which triggers pleasure. According to this model, such changes in the dopamine system (described as "adaptive changes" or "habituation") involve states of dopamine deprivation, which produce, among other things, feelings of pain, depression, and a persistent, worsening, and *chronic* need for more of the drug.

One wonders, what assumptions go into the making, interpretation, and circulation of such explanations? How do older discourses about addiction and recovery converge with and contradict those of the neurosciences?

I do not deal extensively here with brains or genes, or how popular discourses of addiction causality and relapse haunt addiction science (Campbell 2007; Courtwright 2001, 2009). I am interested, however, in how the scientific understanding of addiction shapes—or to be more precise, does not shape—local understandings and experiences of addiction. In this sense, this work is quite different from Emily Martin's (2007) insightful analysis of bipolar disorder, in which her interlocutors assume, often in expert fashion, narratives of neurons and neurotransmitters when describing their experiences of mental illness. Such scientific discourse was largely absent in Hispano addicts' narratives, although local community-based treatment programs, such as the one I worked for, adopted the "chronic illness-care model," accepting and even anticipating that addicts who complete the program will eventually return.

According to Nuevo Día's executive director, "We always want recovery to be a onetime thing. But it isn't. It's every day of your life. It's hard to structure a treatment program based on that. So you do what you can all the while knowing . . . yeah, its unfortunate, but 'I'll be seeing you again.'"

.   .   .   .   .

Before brain scans could render the recircuitry of the addict's dopamine system, Gilles Deleuze described the recircuitry that takes place in the context of addiction but in slightly different terms. In his essay "Two Questions on Drugs" (2007), he considers the "turning point" that takes place in drug use—that threshold where the "vital experimentation" of drugs crosses into a deadly one. Deleuze imagines vital experimentation as taking the drug user to new lines of flight. Over time, these lines roll up, start to turn into black holes, and the drug user finds herself "dug in instead of spaced out" (2007: 153). He asks, is this transformation from vital experimentation into deadly dependence inevitable? Is there a point at which pleasure and relations erode and everything is reduced to a "dismal suicide line" (154)? What causes deadly drug experimentation, and is there a certain point when intervention can and should occur?

I argue that is important to consider how certain circuits of experience are rewired, in part, by scientific translations of addiction and the medical and behavioral interventions that are informed by them. For now, let me say that the current vision of addiction as a chronic disease bears contradictions that are both enabling and disabling. It can indeed counter old, reductionist explanations of behavior or culture and potentially relieve the moral repercussions of "relapse," the term preferred to describe the recurrence of drug use after a period of abstinence.

Etymologically, *relapse* denotes one who "slips again" and thus still carries the moral residue of other morally charged terms, such as *regress* or *recidivism*. Like drugs themselves, the framework of chronicity risks altering its own causality by insisting on a schema of return and repetition, whereby each return recapitulates a sense of inevitable demise. In addition, such a framing risks obfuscating other, perhaps more *vital* dimensions that encompass a local sense of what it is to suffer from an unending condition.

THE PROBLEM OF CHRONICITY

There were extremely high rates of "relapse" at the clinic.[17] During the year that I worked as an attendant, it was rare when I would return to work and see the same patients I had cared for during the previous shift. Generally, addicts were admitted, stayed for a few days, and left—most often, like John, in violation of their probation.[18] I witnessed several patients' return within weeks.

The clinic staff seemed unfazed by the quick turnaround. "We're used to it," one counselor said. The staff warned against getting too involved and embraced a "tough love" attitude toward patients, many of whom were friends or relatives. When I suggested to a counselor that the clinic's rates of "self-discharge" were alarmingly high—nearly 90 percent—he quipped that *"excusas"* (excuses) were part of the game. "We can't save someone who doesn't want to be saved," he said. I thought about Marisa, a young addict with two children in state custody.

Marisa told me on admission that she had "everything to lose" if she did not get clean. Within a week she had left the clinic, and her children were eventually placed in permanent foster care. With so much to lose, why didn't she stay? How might the clinic's practices, based on the logic of chronicity, undermine the very possibility of Marisa being "saved"? A central theme of this book thus concerns how the interplay of biomedical and local discourses of chronicity compel the dynamics of the Hispano heroin phenomenon and how addicts struggle to confirm their existence against their shared presupposition of return.

The trope of chronicity is used in other modes as well. Many community and public sector programs, such as the one I worked for, have assumed the chronic illness model for addiction. They have done so partly as a means to challenge the legacy of stigmatizing and marginalizing drug users but also in order to remain competitive in a discipline that is now almost exclusively directed by managed care principles and technologies.

Under the managed care system, "eligible individuals" must meet strict criteria for substance abuse problems, determined by a formal assessment known as the Addiction Severity Index (ASI).

The ASI is a semistructured instrument used in face-to-face interviews conducted by clinicians, researchers, or technicians; however, increasingly, automated telephone self-report is being employed as a new cost-cutting measure. It is designed to obtain recent and lifetime information about medical, social, and psychiatric problems, which guides decisions regarding treatment eligibility, planning, and outcome measurement. In the clinic, severity ratings were calculated largely according to the duration and scale of drug use and the number of times an individual had already been treated for addiction. The more frequent (or chronic) the condition, the higher the score, and the more "eligible" the individual was to receive treatment.[19]

I observed dozens of ASI interviews during my work at the clinic.[20] The interviews were designed to take approximately an hour, and staff members were initially encouraged to thoroughly assess all sections. But the "Family/Social Relationships" section of the ASI proved time-consuming, no matter how simple the instrument's phraseology. Patients' responses to questions regarding "living arrangements" and "family conflict" could not be contained by check boxes and rating scales (which makes the very notion of an automated telephone instrument absurd). Instead, they responded by telling stories and sharing memories or with long stretches of crying and silence. Eventually, the staff was directed to focus on the "Drug/Alcohol Abuse" and "Employment Status" components of the instrument. The most important thing, staff members were told, was to determine immediate treatment need and ability to pay.

Despite the increasing reliance on metaphors of chronicity, the motivating factor behind drug recovery is typically understood in terms of personal choice or will. This is due largely to two factors: the prevailing Twelve Step model of recovery, which emphasizes individual choice and personal power over addiction (made possible by "surrender" to a "higher power"); and the ever-expanding punitive approach to addiction, which emphasizes the addict's capacity to reason and therefore control his or her drug-using behavior. The Twelve Step model and the juridical response to addiction draw their justification and legitimacy from liberalism, which claims personal autonomy for each rational agent and, correspondingly, treats individuals as responsible for their freely chosen actions.[21] Thus while relapse is understandable and even expected (at least from the medical point of view), the relapsed addict is ultimately assigned blame for the relapse and is therefore seen as lacking the will to recover.

But to what extent do choice and will actually determine the fate of the "chronically addicted"? What circumstances and underlying conditions make it harder for some addicts to "choose" recovery? How have the seemingly incompatible discourses of chronicity and choice supplanted alternative ways to understand and treat addiction? And, most central to this book, what are the moral effects of these discourses on the addict, especially one who has been through repeated cycles of recovery and relapse? Might medical and juridical responses to addiction lock addicts into certain forms of subjectivity where the outcome of relapse is not only expected but also produced?

Jean Jackson (2005) has written of the uncertain ontological status of the chronically ill. She describes how this status provokes stigma and forces the patient into deeper modes of suffering. Many of the heroin addicts I interviewed—addicts who, in today's lingo, might indeed be described as chronically addicted—told not of uncertainty but of fixity. They felt that their lives and struggles were "*sin termina*" (without end)—that their very existence was defined precisely by this constant state of suffering. How does the model of chronicity reinforce such feelings? What kinds of conditions and affects are shaped by the medical model of chronicity, especially as it intersects with local discourses of "endlessness"?

PATIENT-PRISONER

Experts in the hard and social sciences, drug counselors and drug addicts, priests and parole officers, propose a range of answers to why heroin addicts return to self-destructive patterns of drug use. Frequently, these answers diminish or contradict each other. Whereas neurobiologists maintain that the sympathetic nervous system plays a primary role in drug relapse, sociologists and anthropologists are likely to point to socioeconomic factors.[22] And whereas the majority of drug recovery programs and informal support systems, as well as legal enforcement, mandate that recovering and probationary addicts absolutely repudiate future drug use, a growing number of psychiatrists, physicians, and service providers suggest the controlled use of substances (methadone and even heroin) as a more realistic and efficacious model of drug treatment.

Despite these competing and contradictory claims, the fields of medicine, law, and social services have been combined into one apparatus—the drug court system—designed to curb and treat drug addiction. The drug court system is the medium through which these disparate knowledge bases and practices come into play. One of the primary sites of my fieldwork—the heroin detoxification clinic—is an outcome of the recent proliferation of drug courts.

The drug court model is a relatively recent phenomenon, first established in Dade County, Florida, in 1989. The Clinton administration allocated $1 billion to the development of drug courts nationally in 1994. There are now over 2,100 drug courts throughout the United States, and hundreds more are planned. Offenders, usually caught in low-level dealing or stealing to support their addictions, "volunteer" or are sentenced to nine to eighteen months or more of intrusive supervision by a judge, including in-patient treatment, random urine testing, group therapy, and mandatory sobriety meetings. Drug courts leverage the threat of imprisonment if the "offending addict" does not comply with treatment.

With the drug courts, the traditional boundaries between the therapeutic impetus of medical and social services and the state's authority to control "criminal" individuals and populations are further blurred, even eradicated. Nearly all the addicts I encountered during my research were sentenced to detox and treatment—a finding that mirrors national statistics of publicly funded treatment programs.[23] Addicts assigned to the drug court system are dually and contradictorily marked; the addict/offender is patient *and* prisoner. The patient-prisoner experiences the weight of a double sentence—to recover *and* to reckon.

At the heart of this book lies the paradox represented in my sketch of John: the more urgent the desire or mandate to "recover and reckon," the more injurious the effects of its failure. Guiding this book are the questions of how such failure is experienced—by the addicted subject, the family, and the community—as well as how it is understood—by the subject and the institutions. My aim is to explore the myriad ways we might read John's "self-discharge"—and the myriad elements of abnegation the term implies.

REMEMBERING, FORGETTING

What is it that John "discharged" himself from? The institution, the discomfort of detoxification, the burden of memory and history, or experience itself? What does this gesture of self-discharge, which inspires both release and reproof, tell us about these subjects, this place, and humanity itself? John described the perverse refuge heroin offered: "The only time I feel good, feel love, is when I'm high. When I'm flying, I don't feel the pain. I don't feel the time."

John's account of love enabled through heroin echoes philosophical writings that explore forgetting as essential to life (Augé 2004; Blanchot 1986). Friedrich Nietzsche (1985), for instance, calls for the abandonment of the past through the "active forgetting" of experiences and memories that are considered disadvantageous for present and future life. From this perspective, "active forgetting" is actually selective remembering—that is, an attempt to rationalize one's relation to the past in order to overcome those haunting elements that disturb the calm of a later moment. What interests me about Nietzsche's proposition is the question of what the process of active forgetting signifies about life. In other words, to what events and experiences do such conscious erasures refer us?

Emmanuel Levinas rethinks Nietzsche's pragmatic perspective on the uses of forgetting. In *On Escape* (2003), he explores the role of forgetting by suggesting that human existence is marked by an essential duality: on the one hand, it is assumed to be at peace with itself; on the other, it is fraught with tension and burden.[24] In order to understand this duality of being, Levinas asserts, one must seek to understand the vital desire and need for escape, which he identifies as an essential aspect both of human existence and of philosophical inquiry. The question of escape becomes "the need to get out of oneself, that is, *to break the most radical and unalterably binding of chains* . . . to break the chains of the I to the self" (55; original emphasis).

During one of our last interviews, John echoed Levinas's formulation regarding the essential relation between suffering, confinement, and self-discharge. He said, "When I'm high . . . everything just goes away."

It is precisely this category of self-discharge, this sign and expression of escape, that I aim to make visible and comprehensible in the context of addiction. I investigate the contemporary conditions and historical struggles that constitute this need for transcendence locally, as well as the expansion of knowledge and practices intended to control or inhibit it. Ultimately, my goal is to show how the desire for escape and its local forms (getting high, overdose, even suicide) delineate a set of vulnerabilities that are common and shared and from which the possibility of an ethical responsiveness can emerge.

BADLANDS

The Española Valley is located in north-central New Mexico, in Rio Arriba County, equidistant between the art-tourist meccas of Santa Fe and Taos. The valley straddles the western edge of the Sangre de Cristo Mountains and runs north-south along the Rio Grande. The river snakes through the valley, brown and slow, framed by tall cottonwoods and verdant fields of alfalfa and apple orchards. Beyond the river rose-colored buttes alternating with *barrancas,* or steep ravines, form the valley's badlands. It is here that ranchers graze cattle and hunters take practice shots before heading into the mountains in search of elk and deer. It is here that addicts make their connections.

The region encompasses the site of the first Spanish colonial settlement in the Southwest, where Española, the largest town in the valley, is located today. Radiating from Española is a network of small, tight-knit villages that were established as Spanish colonial settlements in the early seventeenth century. Many of the residents of these communities trace their ancestries directly to the original Spanish settlers. They thus consider themselves "Spanish" or "Hispano," and Spanish remains the dominant language in many valley households.

Two Native American pueblos are located in the valley: Ohkay Owingeh (formerly San Juan) and Santa Clara. Other than the flashing neon "Casino" signs that glow along the highway at night, the physical boundary between the Hispano and Pueblo communities is largely unremarkable. Indeed, the interior and plaza of Hispano and Pueblo communities closely resemble each other, in terms of both architecture and age. The communities also share a host of social ills—including high rates of poverty, addiction, depression, disease, and suicide—which both Hispano and Native American health activists identify as consequences of mutual histories of conquest.

But there are long-standing divisions and tensions between the two communities, dating as far back as the Pueblo Revolt of 1680, an uprising of the Pueblo peoples against the Spanish colonists. These divisions and tensions continue today in the "casino wars": many Hispanos blame the Native American–run gaming establishments for the deepening poverty among the mostly elderly (and mostly Hispano) casino patrons who at any time of the day or night can be seen betting away their social security checks on electronic games called "Money Man" and "Western Warrior."

These tensions flared up on several occasions during my research in gestures big and small. For example, it was during my fieldwork that San Juan Pueblo officially returned to its pre-Hispanic name, Ohkay Owingeh, with much fanfare, including an unveiling ceremony of a colossal statue of Po'Pay, the leader of the Pueblo Revolt. I was one of the few Hispanics to attend the ceremony and was reminded (how could I forget?) that just up the road, facing the pueblo, loomed a bronze statue of the Spanish conquistador don Juan de Oñate, whose brutality is a key part of Pueblo historical narratives.[25] The symbolic encounter of the two figures that afternoon—a larger-than-life marble Po'Pay holding the knotted cord that determined the start of the Pueblo rebellion and Oñate high on his horse—powerfully dramatized the contested histories of the communities.

But there were smaller contestations between the communities, too, such as the July Fourth celebration at the Ohkay Casino. That afternoon I joined hundreds of locals on the blazing tarmac to listen to the music of Merle Haggard. Haggard was slow to make his appearance, perhaps because of the heat, and by the time his performance began patrons had consumed plenty of alcohol. Shortly into the concert's first set, a spectator who was dancing drunkenly stumbled and collapsed into the temporary fence that cordoned off the crowd from the stage. Haggard stopped midsong to ask if the fallen man was all right. While security staff removed the man, Haggard took the opportunity to discuss his newfound sobriety and half-joked about the dangers of alcohol, especially in the desert heat. Although Haggard remained congenial, the mood turned sour. Hispanos began muttering obscenities about drunk Indians, though it was never clear whether the fallen man was Indian or Hispano, inebriated or not. It was an ironic moment, since the local discourse of addiction is generally focused on Hispano addiction to heroin. Nevertheless, in that instance the trope of the drunk Indian was easily reinstantiated and fulfilled social frustrations that the figure of the Hispano junkie could not.

In addition to a large Native American population, the valley is home to a growing number of Mexican immigrants, whose presence is easily seen and felt. In Española there has been a recent proliferation of brightly colored *tienditas,* little stores that advertise, among other things, "authentic Mexican" foods, music, and novelty items. There are newly opened Mexican *tortillerías,* bakeries, and restaurants. Mexican farmworkers tend fields of corn, chile, and squash along the main highway, which runs through Española.

In recent years these Mexican immigrants have become easy scapegoats for the region's worsening heroin problem. A series of unresolved murders of Mexican immigrants in 2006 are presumed connected to heroin trafficking, although there is no direct evidence of this. In this context the figure of the Mexican *narco* (drug trafficker), like the drunk Indian, gains visibility and force as locals attempt to explain away the sheer complexity of the valley's drug phenomenon, which of course preceded this immigrant presence.

History, memory, and belonging are issues of contention in the Española Valley. Most residents are characterized as mestizo descendants of Spanish- and Mexican-era colonists. Eighty-one percent of the valley's 30,000 residents are "Hispanic or Latino," and 8.7 percent are "American Indian or Alaskan Native."[26] There is also a small but powerful Anglo minority and an increasing number of second-home owners from the East and West Coasts. Despite this relative diversity, approaching the valley from the south, drivers are greeted by a large billboard that reads, "Welcome to OUR Española Valley," signaling that certain cultural and historical claims have been established, though these are continually contested.

.   .   .   .   .

In the 1990s, media and politicians, and more recently researchers, made the Española Valley ground zero for heroin trafficking and addiction in the United States (Burnett 2005; Trujillo 2004; Willing 2005). This is a distinction supported by government statistics.[27] National media coverage—such as a feature on NPR's *All Things Considered* that aired on August 18, 2005—highlight the "bucolic atmosphere" and the "traditional and devout ways" associated with residents of the valley, including the addicts. These characteristics are meant to stand in sharp contrast to popular notions of heroin addiction; in these "urban" accounts, the city is the stage and heroin addicts are cast in the figure of either the downtrodden hustler or the troubled genius, or both.

Even anthropological and sociological studies of heroin addiction (and drug addiction more broadly) use an urban milieu to describe the antecedents and intimacies of addiction (Agar 1973; Bourgois 1995, 2004; Lovell 2002; Wacquant 1993). Ethnographic studies of Mexican American, or Chicano, intravenous drug users have also centered on the urban barrio context, focusing in particular on the *"pinto-tecato"* (ex-con/heroin user) subculture as it unfolds on the streets of the city.[28]

The tendency to study and describe the urban context of intravenous drug use is also evident in medical and psychological studies of heroin addiction. Indeed, longitudinal analyses of heroin addiction—such as the U.S. Drug Abuse Treatment Outcome Studies (DATOS) and Eng-land's National Treatment Outcome Research Study (NTORS)—comprise data culled from urban contexts. This also holds true for long-term heroin studies conducted in Australia, Denmark, Italy, and Spain.

In pointing this out, I do not wish to diminish the contribution of these studies. Rather, I suggest that there are rural experiences of heroin addiction (and addiction more broadly) that have heretofore gone unde-scribed. Certainly there are certain shared experiences of heroin addic-tion across the urban-rural divide. But studying heroin use in a rural milieu—especially a Hispanic/Mexican/Native American milieu—points to significant differences in experiences, circumstances, and representa-tions that are constitutive of addicts' relationship with heroin and the so-cial world. I use the methods of anthropology and the representational genre of ethnography to elucidate these overlooked experiences and dy-namics and to fill in some of these voids. In doing so, I caution against the current hegemony of "the urban" in addiction studies and suggest that place as it is experienced, remembered, and narrativized should be-come a central site of understanding addictive experience—and experi-ence itself.

.   .   .   .   .

My focus on heroin addiction in the Española Valley occurs at a time when drug use has steadily increased across the rural United States. Since 2000 the mainstream media have reported steadily on the problem of methamphetamines in the so-called American heartland, which many now liken to a "rural ghetto."[29] Like the reporting on heroin in the Es-pañola Valley, the articles highlight the unlikely places meth labs have been discovered—from abandoned farmhouses to chicken coops—and the unlikely persons addicted to meth—from retired farmers to Evangel-ical teenagers. Numerous studies and articles have reported that rural communities are especially "vulnerable" to meth because of two primary factors: first, the relative ease of manufacturing the substance (meth is made using common household goods and anhydrous ammonia, which is also used by farmers for fertilizer); and second, the abundance of "wide open spaces . . . and many abandoned buildings such as farm houses and barns on remote roads" where labs can operate undetected.[30] Surprisingly, few of these reports have examined the dynamics surrounding the figures of wide open spaces and abandoned buildings: declining economic conditions, chronic poverty, high rates of family violence, among others.[31] A connection needs to be made among these dynamics, the associated changes in physical landscape, and the increasing levels of despair and addiction.

DIVIDING WALLS

I began ethnographic research in January 2004. My interest at the time centered on the experience of recovering addicts within the Espanola Valley's growing Evangelical Christian community.[32] I wondered how conversion to Evangelical Christianity from Catholicism enabled "a break" with one's past and how conversion could be used as a conceptual tool for thinking through the complexities of Hispano history. I also wanted to understand how this temporal reorientation, and the rituals through which it was managed, shaped the experience of Evangelical addicts and the course of their recovery.[33]

I began by visiting Evangelical churches and Christian-based addiction programs in the Española Valley. Many of these strictly limited my access to services and congregants, and several church members were wary of my intentions. I soon learned that this mistrust was due in part to the recent death of a young addict who had been receiving in-patient treatment at a prominent faith-based recovery program. He hanged himself from a cottonwood on the facility's grounds. His suicide raised an outcry of concern regarding the efficacy of faith-based addiction programs. Such concerns had long been leveraged against publicly funded programs, but this was different. This was, as one local described, "God's territory."

While maintaining my interest in temporality, addiction, and recovery, I refocused my research and began talking to community and state-based treatment programs. The most prominent of these was Nuevo Día, which means "new day" in Spanish.[34] I first visited Nuevo Día on a cold April morning. Located in an industrial zone on the edge of Española, the facility looked like a temporary structure, like the transportable trailers that commonly spill out into public school yards. A large gravel lot surrounded it and was filled with parked cars—mostly Chevy pickups and low-slung Chryslers.

Taped to the entrance of the building were computer-generated notices, mostly in Spanish, that contained details about drug court procedures, DWI school (for convicted drunk drivers), upcoming Narcotics Anonymous (NA) meetings, and payment requirements. Just past the entrance sat the receptionist's office. A thick, Plexiglas wall surrounded the office, forming a transparent barrier between the small waiting area and the restricted interior of the building. Before me, a young woman leaned against the wall, crying. She wore a frayed mini-skirt and a pair of ill-fitting slippers. Blood trickled down her thin legs. Months later I would see her again.

A circular voice box permitted conversation between the two sides of the wall, and, through it, the receptionist threatened to call the police. Although she was only a foot or two away, it seemed as if we were listening to her from a great distance. The distraught woman, whom I would come to recognize as Bernadette, continued to press her body against the wall and cry. Unmoved, the receptionist looked past her, toward me, and asked if I needed help. I told her I had an appointment with the executive director and was immediately permitted to pass through a locked side door.

I followed the receptionist through a narrow hallway. I asked her about the crying woman. "Just the usual," she said.

We entered a large conference room. Windowless and white, it offered no semblance of comfort and smelled strongly of coffee and ammonia. Taped to the walls were handwritten signs in Spanish that read "No Teasing!" "Pregnancy and Heroin Don't Mix!" "Remember Your Roots!"

Within minutes, Andrés, the executive director, joined me in the conference room. He was tall and wore the typical *norteño* outfit: Wrangler jeans, western shirt, and cowboy boots. He greeted me warmly and, as *norteños* are apt to do, quizzed me about my family—asking which Garcias

I was related to, whether I knew such-and-such person. I was prepared for these questions, largely because I grew up with them.

Weeks earlier I had met with a medical sociologist from the University of New Mexico who had conducted research on heroin use in the region. She knew Andrés and told me that he would be vital to my project because he was "one of the caciques" of northern New Mexico (a reference to a tribal form of government in which leaders maintain strict control). She also suggested that he would ultimately support my research not because of its merit but because I was a "native." There was frustration in her voice as she described a situation in which few Hispanos would talk to her or her non-Hispanic research team, of locals being highly protective and suspicious. But she suggested that I would manage because, in her words, I was "one of them."

Numerous men and women walked through the conference room on their way to an adjacent office. Although it was nearly noon, a few were still wearing pajamas; others were dressed in work uniforms. Andrés later explained that they needed to perform their daily urine analyses, to prove to the drug court counselor and their probation officers that they were clean. (Several months later I learned that the drug court coordinator on staff at that time was purchasing heroin from patients and forging documents that asserted their urine analyses were clean when in fact they were not.)

At the time of our meeting, fifteen heroin addicts lived on-site, sleeping in one of two narrow rooms—one for men, the other for women—that were located at the back of the building. Of these patients, half were in active detoxification; the other half were in the ninety-day Community Adjustment Program, designed for addicts who had completed the first phase of detox but who were not yet prepared to leave the program. Andrés described a situation in which addicts who still had heroin coursing through their veins were sleeping inches away from addicts who had accomplished weeks, or even months, of sobriety. In some cases the patients were related; in others, they were former rivals; sometimes they were both.

"We've got people piled up on top of each other, even sharing beds. It's worse than many prisons I've seen," he said. "We've got hundreds of outpatients, and then the in-patients. Clients disappear, new ones show up . . . it's too much." The good news, he said, was that in a matter of weeks the detoxification unit was going to move into a new facility, located ten miles north, in the village of Velarde. It was a project in the making for several years, and one that was long overdue.

As I prepared to leave our meeting, Andrés asked if I would take the job of detoxification attendant at the new detox facility. He explained the basics of the job and that my hours would be from six o'clock in the evening to seven o'clock in the morning, the graveyard shift. I would be the only staff member present during my shift. The best way to understand heroin addiction, Andrés said, was to be with addicts in the throes of withdrawal.

Sensing my hesitation, Andrés said that Nuevo Día had seen its share of social scientists and Ph.D. candidates. He asked me whether I wanted to "observe" or whether I wanted to "work." I understood this distinction between "observation" and "work" as a call for me to make myself useful, to take on the condition of what I wanted to study—to get my hands dirty.

That afternoon I took an exam designed for home health aid workers and underwent a background check at the nearby police department. To my surprise, I was not required to take a drug test. I would be paid $8 an hour, a wage I knew was more than most people in the region earn.

When I left my meeting with Andrés, I saw Bernadette, still pressed against the plastic wall, crying. She was squatting against the building, her skirt riding high against her dirty thighs. Her long black hair fell across her face, and I could see that her underwear was stained with blood.

OVERVIEW

This book's narrative and temporal orientation finds expression in the pastoral, a multivalent conceptual frame that allows me to explore two related themes. First, my interest in the pastoral includes its use as a literary and artistic style attentive to the changes in a rural landscape—such as the trope of nature and of the abandoned.[35] Georgia O'Keefe, Ansel Adams, and others have rendered northern New Mexico as a kind of pastoral ideal—as a bucolic landscape, usually without people. Yet landscape is both working and peopled, as Raymond Williams reminds us in *The Country and the City* (1975), his powerful critique of the pastoral mode. Reading the material history embedded in images of the English countryside, Williams reveals the story of the capture of land, people, and history and exposes the violent relations of agrarian capitalism and the alienation that results. I hope to contribute to the critical trajectory established by Williams by thinking through the ways of seeing, representing, and experiencing the Española Valley and by analyzing how heroin figures into the historical and contemporary experience of dispossession—an experience covered over (or mystified) by the New Mexican pastoral imaginary.

My exploration of the pastoral thus endeavors to evoke the lived realities of heroin-addicted Hispanos who have long called this landscape home. Descriptions of the Rio Grande, villages, roads, and homes are intended to provide a spatial language for the deep-rooted and complex nature of addiction. These "landscapes of affect" make visible the multiple and interlocking geographies of self, community, and environment (Moore, Pandian, and Kosek 2003).

Second, my interest in the pastoral stems from its use as a form of care that is salvation oriented and that promotes new forms of subjectivity. Indeed, as a form of spiritual counsel, the pastoral is increasingly prevalent in treatment (and through the establishment of "faith-based initiatives," authorized and expanded by the state) that invites addicts "to suffer, and to handle the realities associated with the tragic structures of existence" (LaMothe 1999: 102). In this context, such tragic structures of existence involve the tension between, on the one hand, the desire for transcendence of the body and history and, on the other, the persistence of embodiment and social ties. I explore the emerging role of pastoral care in the negotiation of such conflict, and the way it provides an alternative therapeutic frame through which diverse processes of "recovery" are understood, desired, and experienced.

Foucault (1984: 214) asserts that pastoral power, like pastoral care, "cannot be exercised without knowing the inside of people's minds, without exploring their souls, without making them reveal their inner-most secrets. It implies a knowledge of conscience and an ability to direct it." In recent years the Española Valley has come to embody more than a little of the spirit of Foucault's inquiry, with this interiorized sense of the pastoral taking on a tangible presence. Here, houses become spiritual meeting places, and evangelizing takes place along rural roads. These activities provide a continuous form of "pastoral" care that connects material and psychic landscapes and that blends faith, public health concerns, and the legal apparatus (Foucault 1979, 1983). A classic Foucauldian interpretation of this dynamic might be that such incitements to care have the panoptic effect of creating individuals who are increasingly willing to make themselves vulnerable and controllable. But based on my research, I must wonder if, far from excluding the possibility of pursuing ethical ideals of caring, pastoral power might actually instantiate such an ideal?

Ultimately, both Williams and Foucault draw attention, albeit differently, to the pastoral as a productive site to reflect on and learn about the power effects of seemingly benevolent representations or action. *The Pastoral Clinic* blends their analyses of the pastoral into one critical vocabulary that aims to convey the intricacies of addiction. Among Hispanos, this approach means being attentive to the dialectics of materiality and subjectivity, memory and forgetting, despair and longing.

The heroin detoxification clinic where I worked and where much of the ethnographic material for this book was gathered is the central site in which these dynamics came into play. It is the pastoral clinic, but the subjects and effects of the pastoral—as representation, mystification, experience, power, and care—exceed the clinic's bounds. My hope is that this approach will lead to a rethinking of old assumptions that operate through standard approaches to addiction, as well as present possibilities for understanding addiction as a reflection of our broader world.

·   ·   ·   ·   ·

Chapter 1 situates the heroin detoxification clinic in space and time and demonstrates how the clinic's institutional vulnerabilities reflect the world outside. Daily life at the clinic is presented as key to understanding what is at stake for heroin addicts within and beyond its walls. This chapter also introduces the question of how—in the context of day-to-day vulnerability and isolation—an ethics of social commensuration is possible.

Chapter 2 examines the relationship between specific histories of loss, addiction, and subjectivity. I draw heavily on the narrative of Alma, who I followed closely during my research and who recently died from a heroin overdose, and that of a recovering addict named Joseph. My interest is in showing how certain forms of loss in the Hispano milieu are compelled by a set of repetitive social and historical situations. These losses, I argue, have led to a culturally prevalent form of melancholia through which heroin addiction can be read as a kind of contemporary consequence. More broadly, this chapter addresses possibilities and problems in thinking about addiction in the framework of melancholia and asks if such a framework might unwittingly lock addicts into a permanent melancholic state, foreclosing the possibility of recovery.

Chapter 3 explores the phenomenon of intergenerational heroin addiction among Hispanos. Specifically, it examines the social and familial context of heroin use, focusing on certain economic, historical, and affective burdens that become factors in the use of heroin between generations, especially among women. Through the documentation of feminine patterns of heroin use and the examination of addictive experience for mother-daughter pairs, it frames addictive experience and the constitution of the addictive subject not through alienation or autonomy, as it is so frequently represented, but through history and in heteronomy—of and between generations of women.

Chapter 4 examines the tragic and increasingly common phenomenon of suicide by heroin overdose. It conceptualizes heroin-related suicide as a "form of life" situated within a complex weave of intimate, physical, and institutional dependencies—not as an action or event exiled from them. Returning to the theme of commensurability, I argue that the internal structuring of intentional heroin overdose makes clear the simultaneous aloneness of the addict and her connections to the larger world.

Most ethnography is based on fieldwork that happens in a condensed time—a year or two of "being there." The first four chapters of this book are similarly based on a sustained period of fieldwork. But as this book argues for temporal depth in terms of thinking about addictive experience (and experience more broadly), a return to the field, and to the lives that I was writing about, seemed especially important. Chapter 5 is based on a second round of research conducted nearly two years after leaving the field. The focus here is on the closing of the detoxification clinic and the relationship between neoliberal economic processes and shifting dynamics of treatment. By examining "informal" medical spaces and practices that emerged after the detoxification clinic's closure, this chapter ethnographically documents how the narrow economic focus of health reform dangerously shifts public responsibilities for care into intimate domains. In addition, it reveals the conflicting sentiments that pervade "informal" acts of care that family and communities must provide in the absence of other forms of therapeutic support.

Chapter 5 also represents an ethical and methodological response to one of the strong arguments of this book: to examine addictive experience most effectively, we must not artificially lock our query (or representation) into one particular time frame or narrative. It is an extension of my attempt at an ethnography that is temporally deep in order to render—however imperfectly—the *process* of addiction, recovery, and of living a life.

I conclude with a description of my most recent return to the field and explore Nuevo Día's initiation of a "land-based" recovery program after the closure of its detoxification unit. It is here that I return to questions regarding the role of material and cultural dispossession and its relation to addiction and, perhaps, to recovery.

.   .   .   .   .

The chapters that follow tell a story about the entanglements of temporality, materiality, and subjectivity as they bear on heroin use in the Española Valley. It is an ethnography of addictive experience and an ethnography of place. I believe that there is much to learn from this seemingly isolated region and its "epidemic" of heroin use, especially in terms of the connectedness of the addict to the broader moral world and, ultimately, the connectedness of one to the other.

ON WRITING WITH CARE

This book is concerned with the possibility of caring for one another in the context of extreme difficulty and vulnerability. The way that this book is written is an extension of this concern. To write with care in this context is not only a matter of changing names or identifying details in an effort to prevent harming those about whom I write, although I have done so. Indeed, changing names and details is not enough—a lesson I learned when an article I published was inappropriately linked to a heroin-addicted couple I came to know during my research. Although the couple's story was not included in what I had written, the editors of the magazine that published my article included revealing photographs of them with my text. These images originated from a different article on the topic of Hispano heroin addiction and were obtained from the Associated Press. They were superimposed on what I had written without my permission. My article would be reprinted in other venues, and with my words, the same set of photographs. Through its repeated circulations, the photos (and my article) took on a social life of their own.

With each circulation followed certain intimate and institutional consequences—not for me, or the photographer or venues that published the work, but for the addicted couple. They found themselves locked into a kind of "photographic present"—a tense that would eventually lead them into deeper modes of despair. This regrettable experience highlighted for me just how important it is to choose one's words and images carefully. To that end, many of the episodes presented in this book have been modified in an effort to mitigate their injurious potential.

Writing carefully is not only about writing cautiously; it is also about craft. Along these lines, I have written this book in a particular way, foregrounding Hispano heroin addicts that shared with me their lives. Conversations, encounters, recollections, and incidents—between them, between us—form the heart of this book and make it move. They capture the humanity, vulnerability, and hopefulness of lives I came to know and care about. It is my hope that this feeling of care makes possible a deeper understanding of the close relationship between addiction and treatment and its symbiosis of local history and unequal political and social relations.

In putting these moments and feelings to analytic work, I have tried to be reserved in my use of theory as such. I believe that ethnography can be constitutive of theory and knowledge production (Borneman and Hammoudi 2009). I have also been reserved because so much theory forecloses the possibility of letting things be vulnerable and uncertain—states of being that I want to engage and evoke. I am similarly cautious about making definitive conclusions about the nature of addiction wrought from historical, anthropological, or epidemiological analysis. This cautiousness, again, stems from my concern about "fixing" identities to a specific state, especially since so many of the subjects herein describe their ongoing struggles with feeling or being perceived as always already caught within them. The challenge, then, is to evoke this sense of being fixed without permanently locking the subjects into such a state.

.   .   .   .   .

The people, places, and relations I describe in this book can all reach back to particular moments—from don Juan de Oñate's arrival in the Española Valley in 1598 to the Mexican War of Independence in 1821 to the signing in 1848 of the Treaty of Guadalupe Hidalgo and the failure of the United States to live up to the spirit and letter of its law.[36] Throughout the writing of this book, I struggled with the question of what to do with this vast and complex history, which is omnipresent in the region's social and political vernacular. Over a period of four years, I consulted dozens of books on New Mexico's colonial history and its postcolonial land grant movement. I pored over documents at the New Mexico State Archives in Santa Fe, researching specific villages and the changing health and economic indices of their residents. Through the study of textual and visual media, I became familiar with representations of the landscape and its people—texts produced largely by "outsiders," which is how Hispanos tend to imagine and identify the legions of writers and artists who have arrived from afar.

Rather than try to provide a comprehensive historical account of all this material, I try to evoke how certain forces have been interacting over many years to shape this contemporary condition called addiction. In representing this, I take my cues from Michel de Certeau's analyses of everyday practices, in particular, his sense that we often encounter the past where we least expect to find it.[37] My references to historical documents, family genealogies, novels, and visual media, along with focused descriptions of the changing Hispano landscape, are intended to show a range of concerns related to thinking and representing the past. Through these works I have tried to sketch a critical historiography constructed of multiple voices and emotions. For those wishing to explore further, I have included notes pointing to additional resources.

This book is about Hispano heroin addicts—women and men—who have found their lives inescapably entangled with institutions designed to apprehend and/or care for them. It should go without saying (but must nevertheless be said) that not all Hispanos have addictions and some manage to kick their habits, including heroin. In addition to meeting locals who had never used drugs, I came across an occasional "success story"— an addict who managed to "clean up" and improve his or her life, whether through education, work, faith, or sobriety alone. These stories are powerful, especially because, in this context, they are so rare. This apparent exceptionality is in part an effect of my work in the clinic, where I was in constant contact with addicts as they cycled through arrest, hospitalization, and incarceration. The addicts I came to know were more likely to die of heroin overdose than to overcome their addiction. But even outside the clinic—in homes, churches, and community centers in the valley—"death stories" were far more common than "success stories." I am sadly confident that the picture I present here is a realistic reflection of addicted life among Hispanos. It is my greatest hope that this book offers insight into how this came to be, how "successes" might become more common, and how, in the face of so much failure, we might redefine the very nature of these impoverished terms.

ONE Graveyard

The heroin detoxification clinic lies at the end of a typical road in the Española Valley. Little more than a path, the road is unpaved, deeply rutted, and strewn with shards of broken glass. Pack dogs roam along it and are prepared to chase—for a few moments at least—the occasional passing car or three-wheeled ATV. Crumbling adobe houses line the road, abandoned for newer trailer homes. The adobes and the trailers sit adjacent to one another, marking a transition between generations. Both are set on small plots of land once used for cultivating squash, chile, and corn. Like the adobe, artifacts of a prior agricultural life remain: there is the ubiquitous tractor, broken down and stripped of its tires; the empty storage shed, once brimming with apples. Both appear to be sinking into the land from the force of years, sun, and neglect.

The road to the clinic is like any other. Except for a small hand-painted sign that reads "Nuevo Día," there is no obvious indication of institutional presence or, for that matter, of heroin.

.   .   .   .   .

The clinic spans several buildings. First, there is the cluster of small adobe houses, whose curved, earth-colored walls closely resemble the traditional architecture of the region. These surround a much larger, central building, whose gray-painted exterior and crisp lines suggest an institutional aesthetic. Like the adobe and the trailer, the juxtaposition of the clinic's structures suggests a transition from tradition to modernity, intimacy to order. During the early stage of its operation, the detox program was fully located in one of the adobe houses and was affectionately referred to as "la casita," the little house. However, as the program expanded to accommodate an increased patient load, it was moved into the larger building, and the term *la casita* fell out of use.

In the past the clinic was a state-run residence for mentally ill adolescents named Juniper Hills. Its patients were primarily from the Española Valley, and they suffered a range of afflictions—bipolar disorder, depression and schizophrenia, physical and learning disabilities, substance abuse. Many had a history of physical or sexual abuse, and some had had run-ins with the law. Despite its idyllic name, Juniper Hills led a troubled existence. It was underfunded, short-staffed, and overcrowded. The structure displayed scars wrought by its previous inhabitants: fist-sized holes in plaster walls, obscenities etched into windowsills. By the time I arrived, it was hard to tell to which institutional generation the scars belonged.

According to a former patient attendant at Juniper Hills, the sheriff's department was frequently called in to settle fights, or to take away the most unruly or the suicidal. Most of the kids would return after a few nights in juvenile detention, or "5150," the code for involuntary psychiatric evaluation. The sickest patients, the attendant said, "stayed inside like chickens," pecking at themselves and at each other, while the healthier patients sought refuge outside, spending long hours wandering the facility's expansive grounds.

The attendant was eighteen years old when he worked at Juniper Hills—the same age as many of its patients, some of whom he'd known since grade school. During his period of employment, he said he felt that he was "going crazy" himself, a feeling he attributed to the institution's unsettling environment. He recalled the lure of the Rio Grande, on the western boundary of the facility. Patients often escaped to the river like stowaways, wandering upstream or down. Most of them would return within a few hours; they had nowhere else to go. Usually, they would set off again, until a tall chain-link fence topped with barbed wire was erected along the perimeter of the grounds.

It is said that a young girl diagnosed with schizophrenia set fire to one of the Juniper Hills buildings. According to the stories, she died in the fire and the facility closed. Numerous people recounted the story to me in similar order and detail, which went something like this:

> The girl was depressed, crazy. One night she locked herself into a room and started lighting matches. Her clothes caught fire and so did the room. But the girl didn't make a sound. She stayed quiet, even while she burned. Clearly, the girl just wanted to die, you know what I mean? Eventually, the other patients smelled the smoke, but by then it was too late . . . no, I don't remember her name.

I consulted police reports and newspaper archives looking for "evidence" of the story. There was only the building itself; its walls were still scorched from the long-extinguished flames. For months, I visited the building as if I were visiting the grave of an estranged friend. Staring at its blackened walls, I imagined that the fire was still raging, that the girl inside was burning, and that the flames she started had spread to me.

Over time I began to understand the story of the girl who immolated herself as an allegory for the precariousness of Hispano life and as a means to situate the multiple and overwhelming wounds of past and present.[1] Flowing through locals' recounting of the fire were sentiments of sorrow, helplessness, and rage. The story of the girl seemed to enable locals to talk about their deep ambivalence toward the very presence of the institution along the Rio Grande and their collective failure to have cared for such a girl, whatever her name may have been, or will ever be. Like the Mexican folktale of *La Llorona,* the Weeping Woman, the story's continued circulation seemed to insist that *we* must all be more careful next time—that we must listen more closely for the girl's silent cry.[2]

After its closure Juniper Hills was again transformed, this time into a *picadero,* or shooting gallery. Several addicts described it to me as a perfect setting for heroin binges. Parts of the facility were relatively intact, providing shelter from sun, rain, or snow. There were beds, forgotten medical supplies, and bathroom mirrors, the latter of which enabled addicts to inject heroin into areas of the body that were otherwise impossible to see. Juniper Hills remained a popular *picadero* even after the rodents, mold, and asbestos set in. Eventually, county officials considered condemning the building, but a 1999 special congressional hearing on the region's heroin problem identified it as a potential site for a much-needed drug treatment center.[3]

Five years later Nuevo Día's detoxification clinic opened its doors.

.   .   .   .   .

The opening of the clinic was celebrated with much fanfare. Musicians performed traditional *rancheras* as journalists and state politicians toured the facility, carrying with them paper plates heavy with tamales. County representatives spoke movingly about the opportunity to stem the endless tide of heroin overdose, and many recounted their own struggles with alcohol and drug addiction. A prayer for healing was murmured. With the cutting of the yellow ribbon, the troubled memory of Juniper Hills was laid to rest and Nuevo Día was born.

The year Nuevo Día opened there were forty fatal heroin overdoses in the Española Valley, testament, in part, to the inadequacy of addiction services in the region. At the time those services included two residential recovery programs with a length of stay ranging from two years to less than thirty days, several outpatient programs that rely on Twelve Step Fellowship principles, and a harm reduction program specializing in needle exchange and methadone maintenance. At one point there was one residential alcohol detoxification facility in the valley. The center experienced several temporary closures between 2003 and 2006. It was closed permanently in 2007 as a result of conditions that placed the health and safety of patients at risk.

Despite the many psychological and emotional issues that are often broached in the context of drug addiction, mental health was not an integral component of these programs.[4] Nor were educational or vocational rehabilitation services. Also lacking were detoxification facilities explicitly for drug addicts; heroin addicts were referred to facilities in other parts of the state, many of which had waiting lists ranging from three to six months. Significantly, these referrals were court ordered—that is, they were made in the context of an addict's legal troubles, most often stemming from a drug-related offense. In many instances prospective "patients" were forced to remain incarcerated for a longer time than necessary in order to facilitate their entry into a residential recovery program.

Given such dire circumstances, the opening of Nuevo Día's detoxification clinic was significant on both practical and symbolic registers. It was the first detox facility in the region specifically for drug addicts that focused on heroin addiction. It was also the first to promote and use a medical model for detoxification by offering anti-opioid medications and what it considered a "clinical setting." The clinic's "modern sensibility" signified certain cultural, economic, and medical advancements that were celebrated in a historically impoverished and drug-weary region. Behavioral health workers and locals in general embraced these developments as a major step forward. The wound of Juniper Hills finally seemed healed.

The timing of the clinic's opening was fortuitous. I had just returned to New Mexico to begin ethnographic fieldwork on the region's epidemic of heroin addiction and felt lucky to be among the first people hired to work as a detox attendant. My shift was the "graveyard"—six o'clock in the evening to seven o'clock in the morning—and I hoped that by working at the clinic I would be afforded an "insider" view of the intimacies of addiction, recovery, and institutional life. I wanted to gain a deeper understanding of the acute physical and psychic aspects of heroin addiction and recovery, especially as they are experienced in an institutional set-ting. Given how deeply entrenched heroin had become in the valley, I wondered if the workings of institutional life reflected or differed from the world "outside." Could the clinic provide enough of a counterpoint to the pressures of addiction and everyday hardship to enable addicts to begin the process of recovery? What might such a process look like? Or was the very idea of an alternative to the harsh realities of addiction naive, even counterproductive?

The night before my first shift a heroin addict named James advised me that I should quit before I even started, that "detox attendant" wasn't the kind of job that afforded the luxury of time to "think," which is how he understood my role as an anthropologist.[5] I met James at a Narcotics Anonymous meeting. He was a *"veterano,"* or longtime heroin user, a re-spected status that implied he'd witnessed and experienced the harsh re-alities that accompany addicted life. Over the course of my research, I of-ten turned to James for advice with my project. He was a practical and protective man and discouraged me from working the graveyard shift. What are you going to do, James asked, when an addict from the village of Chimayó gets in a fight with another addict from the village of Hernán-dez? *Or,* what are you going to do when you're the only "authority" in the middle of the night, and someone breaks into the clinic in a desperate at-tempt to deliver a heroin-filled syringe to a detoxing lover? *Or,* what are you going to do when someone jimmies the lock to the medicine cabinet, swallows a bunch of pills, and starts convulsing? The scenarios James of-fered (which were, he said, based on years of "experience") were endless, and with each he warned: There's no time to *think,* Angela. *What are you going to do?*

It turns out that James was both right and wrong. He was right that ur-gent situations arose requiring immediate and unconsidered responses. But these situations, and how I responded to them, would form the basis of my thought. In what follows I sketch the first emergency that I en-countered, one that James did not anticipate but that nevertheless offers an entry for considering the structures and fractures of clinic life.

PRIMAL SCENE

There was no indication of turbulence that afternoon. At home, the cottonwood leaves shivered in the breeze and the dogs lay belly-up in the sun. Reluctantly, I drew the shades to shut out the bright June light. Dr. Bustos, the clinic's medical director, had suggested a midday nap to store up energy for the long night ahead, but my body was unaccustomed to these new hours, and I found it impossible to sleep.

I arrived at the drug detox clinic at 5:30—just as Maria, the day-shift attendant, put away the evening meal. She offered me a bowl of pinto beans and warmed a tortilla. The beds were full, she said. There were four women and six men, eight heroin addicts and two alcoholics. As she washed dishes, Maria reported that nothing unusual had happened on her shift and that the patients had retired to their rooms.

I signed into the Daily Log—a wide-ruled spiral notebook that detailed the events of the day. It was my first shift, and I didn't know what I was supposed to write, so I flipped through previous entries for clues. Copying the language of earlier entries, I wrote, "June 9, 2004. 5:45 P.M. A. G. assumes shift from M. G. M. G. says there is nothing unusual to report. Patients resting. Facilities secure."

Maria led me into the nurse's station—although at the time and during much of my employment there was no nurse, only minimally trained detox attendants such as myself. We reviewed the medication schedule. Two tablets of the muscle relaxant Robaxin and four tablets of Vistaril, a medication for panic disorder, were to be given at midnight and 6:00 A.M. Residents in Dorm One were to receive fifty milligrams of the sedative Librium at 10:00 P.M., followed by doses at 2:00 and 6:00 A.M. Five patients were to receive three milligrams of the antipsychotic medication Haldol at 9:00 P.M. and 6:00 A.M., and all patients were to be given their respective SSRIs, prescribed for the treatment of depression, anxiety, or both.

Maria showed me a corresponding graph of the medication schedule. Patients' names and ages were in one column, and in another, medication, dosage, and dosing hours. Some indications were notated in milligrams, others descriptively—by the color and shape of pills. The graph was incomprehensible and sent me into a panic. What if I incorrectly dosed patients? Maria told me not to worry, that the patients knew exactly what they needed; they were experts in their own treatment.

"Just don't let them fool you," she said.

.   .   .   .   .

The night attendant's station was an L-shaped desk located where two hallways met—one led to the men's dormitory, the other to the women's. Beneath harsh fluorescent lights, the hallways glowed like highway tunnels. I instinctively felt the need to shield my eyes when I walked to and from the rooms.

The hallway lights washed over the attendant's desk, where I was to remain throughout the night, monitoring the patients and recording events in the Daily Log. During my orientation, I was warned that sleeping was grounds for termination. I wondered how an attendant could possibly sleep with the shock of those lights, especially after hearing the famous "graveyard stories" and their gruesome details: patients jumping out of dormitory windows; rival gang members stabbing each other in bed; desperate addicts overdosing on stolen bottles of rubbing alcohol. I wasn't worried about falling asleep.

Within seconds of Maria's departure, closed doors opened, and patients emerged from their rooms. From my station I watched men and women shuffle down the hallway in slippered feet. They moved toward me unsteadily and met my greetings with silence or high-pitched requests for *"algo,"* "something"—something to take the pain out of legs, arms, and backs contorted by the absence of a fix. Even before introductions were made, I could tell the heroin addicts from the alcoholics by the way clothes hung from bodies. My initial assessments were confirmed on closer inspection—by the fresh track marks and swollen abscesses on arms, hands, ankles, and necks.

For the next three hours I deflected growing demands for *something* by filling bowls with vanilla ice cream and permitting the use of a boom box. Soon, the sounds of Tejano and hip-hop music filled the clinic. Though the volume was turned up high, the music inspired no movement, no recognition. The patients sat motionless on tattered couches, their eyes fixed on a clock hanging high on the wall. At one point a young addict named Yvette said that she felt like we were stuck on a deserted island. Together, we waited for the dosing hour like the arrival of a rescue plane.

By 12:30 in the morning everyone but Peter had received enough medication to bring about a thick veil of sleep. Peter sat with me in the common room, nervously extending and closing the leg rest of an old reclining chair. Although he was only twenty-nine, his body looked shrunken by time and pale against the chair's rough orange fabric. I watched him grab his thighs and punch his arms with shrunken fists. The spasms in his limbs were clearly worsening. Peter cried out in pain, cursed God, and apologized for the vulgarities.

"I can't help it," he said.

"It's okay," I answered.

We both knew it would be hours before he could get another dose of a sedative. In any event, the last dose hadn't offered any relief. Peter described the pain as razor blades ripping through his legs, electric bolts coursing through his spine.

"I can't take it anymore," he cried.

I went into the men's bathroom and drew a bath, sprinkling Epsom salts into a current of warm water. In the absence of more effective anti-opioids, the clinic's part-time doctor encouraged salt baths. But patients were reluctant to take them, dreading the sting of stripping naked in brightly lit rooms, of cold porcelain against burning skin.

Sitting on the edge of the tub, I watched the water level rise. Dried vomit and diarrhea caked the rim of the toilet. A pair of soiled underwear lay crumpled in the corner of the room. Windowless, the bathroom had a strong odor of feces and cheap air freshener. Another deterrent from bathing, I thought.

Suddenly, the lights went out.

Blackouts in the northern villages were fairly common during storms, but there were no rains that night. I shut off the faucet and turned toward the hallway. The emergency lights and the outdoor floodlights were out, too, and the clinic was encased in darkness. Staggering around furniture,

I opened the blinds in the common room and the nurse's office to let in the glow of the receding moon. A swath of milky light cut across Peter's legs. I was relieved to see that he was still sitting on the reclining chair because, for a moment, I wondered if he had intentionally cut the power.

·   ·   ·   ·   ·

At night the villages of the Española Valley are dark enough, even with electricity. There are only a handful of streetlamps, and these are a dim yellow—like the streetlights I'd seen in Mexican barrios or South African shantytowns. And these village lights illuminated only the most danger- ous intersections—State Route 582 and County Road 1040, for instance— a junction marked by shattered glass and handmade memorials, *descan- sos,* that plead, "Rest in Peace." Even with electricity, one is guided by the memory of curves and ruts, by the glow of car headlights, by the wash of moon.

That night, the entire village had lost power. There were no candles or flashlights—I quickly discovered that the clinic had no emergency sup- plies whatever—and it would be at least five hours till morning.

"I can't take this anymore," Peter cried. "I can't fucking take the pain in my legs no more."

The bath was now out of the question. I approached Peter and lightly touched his calf. He grew still. Tentatively, I pressed the palms of my hands against his thigh, wrapped my fingers around his legs and squeezed. I had seen strung-out addicts touch each other in the same way.

Peter's thighs felt brittle beneath his thick sweatpants. His knees were swollen and stiff. Peter wept as I massaged his legs. He apologized for his weeping. He asked me to squeeze his feet and hands, and he apolo- gized for those requests, too. He apologized for his pain.

·   ·   ·   ·   ·

The darkness obscured the wall clock, and I couldn't tell what time it was. I told Peter this. "Take me outside," he said. I helped Peter from the recliner, careful not to pull his arms too strongly. The stars and the moon gave off a hazy light. We could see the blackened outline of the cotton-wood trees that lined the Rio Grande and the chairs that patients sat in during the day, shivering in the sun. Peter looked up and, after a few moments of silence, announced that it was about two in the morning. I wondered if he really knew this or if he said so because he knew that two o'clock was the dosing hour.

"You can tell by the stars," he said, pointing upward with his hand. "The one useful thing my father taught me." The tip of a cigarette glowed like a firefly between his fingers. Peter's father had introduced him to heroin fifteen years ago, when Peter was fourteen years old.

I looked up, but I was unable to make sense of the night sky. "We should go back in," I said.

"Let me smoke my *frajo* [cigarette] first."

We stood together in the predawn light. I listened to Peter as he muttered quiet obscenities between drags on his cigarette.

Fortunately, I had measured out the 2:00 A.M. doses in tiny paper cups before the blackout occurred. Still, the darkness of the clinic was absolute, and I struggled to carry the medication and water from room to room. I opened doors, shook shoulders, and called out names. *Yvette, Pauline, Lupe, Marcos, Andrés, Mikey, Arnold.* The patient's hands reached across the darkness for their small cup of pills. "Where the fuck is it?" Yvette asked as she grabbed at the air. Everyone but Peter returned to sleep. When I returned to the common room, he was squatting on all fours, groaning.

"It's all my fault," Peter cried. "It's all my fault. It's all my fault."

"Come outside with me," I said.

"It's all my fault."

I touched Peter's back. His shirt was drenched in sweat.

"Would you do it again?" he asked. He wanted me to touch him.

"Come outside with me." I didn't want to touch him anymore.

Peter crawled to the door. Outside, I placed two chairs alongside each other, facing the river. It was cold, and we huddled beneath a bedspread for warmth. Every once in a while I asked Peter to look up and tell me the time. We did this until dawn, when the first light streaked orange-red across the sky.

Figure 2.   Waiting room. Photo by the author.

QUESTIONS OF COMMENSURABILITY

> The incommensurable relation of one to the other
> is the outside drawing near in its separateness and
> inaccessibility. Desire, this pure impure desire, is
> the call to bridge the distance, to die in common
> through separation.
>
> Blanchot, *The Writing of Disaster*

I spent the better part of my first graveyard shift in absolute darkness. The blackout had a dramaturgical effect, amplifying the precariousness of the life of the addict, the vulnerability of institutional life, and the instabilities and anxieties of subjects caught within. It also amplified the precariousness of my relation to Peter and the uncertain nature of our responsiveness to each other. The tempo and feeling of our subjective positionings could not have been more different. Yet the situation that we were thrown into made me question whether singularity and difference can be productive of care, even commensuration.

Thirteen hours after I began my shift, I finally prepared to leave. Because of the blackout, I had not recorded the details of the night in the Daily Log. When the day-shift attendant came on duty she noticed the hours unaccounted for and asked me to "fill in the blanks" for the sake of record keeping. I wrote:

> June 10, 2004. At approximately one A.M., the clinic lost power. No power until morning. Peter D. experienced severe withdrawal symptoms. All other clients appeared to sleep comfortably and were treated as indicated.

While such a summary was sufficient for the purpose of clinical record keeping, it was a woefully inadequate representation of the complexity of that night. It did not mention the cries or the touching, the confusions and anxieties. Instead, I struggled in my field journal to reconstruct the night's unfolding of events and emotions. "They all cried for *some-thing*," I wrote. "*Some thing* to take the pain away, some thing to help pass the time." And: "I did not ache the way I imagined they did, but I ached nonetheless. The ache was caused by their stares, spasms, and resentments. By time itself."

What does it mean for a patient and attendant-anthropologist to remain in each other's presence from within such radically different sites of experience? And what does it mean for the institution to find itself, again, bereft of the power to provide one of our most basic needs—the light by which to see?

Though we were all together—stuck, as Yvette suggested, on a deserted island—what I think we shared most was a terrible feeling of aloneness. This aloneness, or singularity, operated on many levels. Perhaps most significantly, for patients, it is most powerful in terms of the bodily experience of detoxification itself. Science has shown that addicts who are physically addicted experience detoxification as an "all-consuming pain"—one of the consequences of the changes in the nervous system induced by long-term heroin use.[6] This "hyperalgesic state" has both physical and mental effects, including violent abdominal cramping (often leading to uncontrollable diarrhea), the sensation of burning in the arms and legs, severe headaches, physical agitation, and feelings of anger and depression. In the early stages of withdrawal, patients experience uncontrollable physical and vocal disturbances that closely resemble the symptoms of Tourette's syndrome. They may hit themselves, pull their hair, and scream vulgarities. An addict I spoke with who emerged from this state described those first days as "the worst possible hell, especially since you know you can just *fix it*." Perhaps that is why the request for *something* has such an urgent appeal; it represents the possibility of something else, something beyond the pain.

Although patients may collectively feel pain, they do not share it. The pain forms a kind of inconsolable solitude. Jean Cocteau's diary of opium addiction, composed while he was undergoing "the cure" in a Paris clinic, contains drawings that come close to expressing the inferno of pain that detoxification entails. There are images of screaming mouths, contorted limbs, and decapitated bodies. "I am describing a wound in slow motion," Cocteau (2001: 18) writes of his detox experience. In his images and words, he is entirely alone.

Within the clinic the question of shared pain was more than physical. It concerned the possibility of an ethics of commensuration among dispossessed and singular subjects who are consigned together under the sign of "recovery."[7] Can singularity and dispossession produce commensuration and healing? Or are these states best interpreted as irresolvable symptoms that are produced, in part, by the institutional contexts in which subjects are made to live?

I was first confronted with the need to imagine a sociality based on incommensurate experience and subjects the night of the blackout, when Peter and I sat beneath a blanket, waiting for morning. The separateness of Peter to myself, the darkness of each hour, the tension in his limbs versus the tension in mine—all of it was, for lack of a better word, utterly *human*. In the clinic I would also witness such expressions in the fleeting moments between patients—in the way addicts touched each other's aching limbs or the way they regarded each other's tattoos. I witnessed it when a group of women gathered around a mother who had just learned that her daughter, also a heroin addict, had died of an overdose. They were moments of rupture and of shared singularity. These were moments when I could imagine the possibility of a new kind of care.

A PURGATORIAL ZONE

> Have I been here before? Oh God, I've been here before.
>
> Lucretia Martinez, on her first day of heroin detox

I have provided a detailed recounting of my first night as a detox attendant because it stands out as an early and formative event in the course of my fieldwork that operates as a sustained reflection on the terms of clinic life. My use of the Freudian notion borrows from its interpretive strategies wherein events or memories that have made certain claims on us—but that are not entirely clear—are rendered visible through processes of recollection and elaboration.[8] I work with the idea that the "primal scene" described above—its staging and its subjects—is illustrative of the many material and personal vulnerabilities of institutional life. Of particular interest to me in this regard are the effects of the clinic's technical instability vis-à-vis an enduring pastoral setting, the prevailing sense of uncertainty that pervades the everyday, the commensurability and incommensurability of experience between subjects, and the ways these features structure the interpersonal and the therapeutic domain.[9]

I view the clinic as a kind of purgatorial zone—an interstitial and provisory place where patients are made to wait and reflect on life before, during, and beyond their institutionalized present. My use of the term has resonance with Roman Catholic doctrine, where *Purgatory* denotes a place and condition of suffering inhabited by the souls of sinners who must expiate their sins before going to heaven. The idea here of redemption and salvation provides a powerful metaphor for clinical life: patients experience an anguished state of "waiting" during which they are encouraged to look back at their past. This process of looking back is not for purposes of interpretation, in a psychoanalytic sense; rather, it is to make amends and to break with one's past life in order live a more healthful, and moral, future.

I saw patients protest against the purgatorial zone in which they were placed. In words and gestures, they insisted that the past was forever in their present and always already embedded in their future. How can one imagine a "future life" that depends on a radical break from these infinite temporal flows (Bergson 2000)?[10] Could the clinic's attempts to disaggregate time make possible a "temporality of second chances" (Das 2006: 101)? How might the *other* spaces and conditions in which patients were entangled, such as those on intimate and juridical registers, affect such a possibility? Finally, how do the needs of the physical body, which is a central part of both Catholic and therapeutic modes of redemption, disrupt the possibility of "salvation," or in this case, recovery.

To think of the clinic as a kind of purgatorial zone, it is important to examine life beyond clinic walls, to integrate previous social contexts and events through which the institutionalized present takes form. The analytic and ethnographic mode I use here is therefore dynamic. It moves in and out of different temporal and physical settings and introduces different patients that I came to know during my work at the clinic. The point of this movement is to map the multiple and intersecting forms of vulnerability in everyday life and to show how these forms reflect and mediate the experience of vulnerability within the clinic itself.

.   .   .   .   .

What contributed to the clinic's purgatorial sensibility is that it was a part of a larger governmental apparatus, one that bridged psychiatric and penal systems, and was thus structured by the concerns of these sometimes conflicting, sometimes parallel domains. Although most of the addicts receiving treatment were court appointed and referred to as "patients," they often identified themselves as "prisoners." They were aware of mental and behavioral health's symbiotic relationship with the law, just as they were aware that their addiction was linked to the ways that "gatekeepers" in both fields imagined addicted lives and which influenced their futures. The stakes, then, for the patient-prisoner were exceptionally high, and there was an implicit understanding that, depending on what happened during the course of one's "program," life could either be made or unmade. The formal consequences for treatment termination, or self-discharge, included prison, institutionalization in another treatment or psychiatric facility, and the loss of child custody. The informal consequences generally included a return to drug life (and its attendant intimate, economic, and social wreckage), which might involve a precipitous increase in drug use, sometimes leading to overdose or death. Significantly, the outcome for patients who had "successfully completed" their treatment programs was similarly grim. According to one program analysis, nearly 90 percent of so-called successes resumed heroin use within two years of program completion, and more than half of these individuals returned to the clinic one or more times for additional treatment.[11]

The clinic provides fertile ground for exploring the question of how to live in purgatorial spaces, as well as the question—expressed frequently and openly by patients—of whether a "future life" was worth living. I want to take a detour now and introduce Lucretia, a woman whose failed return to the clinic after "losing everything" suggests how some patients come to incorporate the very idea of purgatory into their drug narratives as a means to forever suffer that which was lost.

A DIFFICULT PATIENT

One summer afternoon, one of the clinic's counselors, Beto, called me at home to ask for help admitting a "difficult patient." Without giving specifics, he said that the presence of a female attendant was necessary. Within minutes I was driving down the stretch of dirt road that led to the clinic, which was a mere mile from my house.

When I arrived at the clinic, Beto was waiting outside, smoking a cigarette. Lucretia hadn't arrived yet. Between drags on his cigarette, Beto told me matter-of-factly that Lucretia was his half sister and that he had been through this routine with her too many times. Inside the clinic, patients talked about Lucretia's imminent arrival. They all seemed to know who she was, and they all anticipated that she would be in terrible shape. She was.

Lucretia was escorted into the clinic by a police officer. She was without shoes, and her feet were coated with dirt. A terrible odor surrounded her. "She shit her pants," the officer said.

A solicitous female patient named Marcy quickly offered a pair of her extra sweatpants. As she ran off to the women's dorm, the circle of spectators that had gathered around Lucretia began to break away. Beto stood there for a moment and stared wearily at his sister. Then he asked me to take her to the bathroom and prepare her a bath. I extended one of my arms around Lucretia's narrow shoulders and guided her down the hallway. "Who are you?" she asked me, a mess of black hair covering her eyes.

As we walked to the bathroom, Lucretia began to violently cry out, "It won't work, it won't work." She said she knew where she was, and, no, it just wouldn't work. I sat her on the toilet seat, turned my back to her protests, and prepared a bath. To my relief, Marcy joined us and helped me remove Lucretia's soiled clothes. We eased her trembling body into the bath. The water quickly turned brown, as if colored with drops of dye. Marcy poured water over her back and head. All the while, Lucretia shivered and repeated her cry of hopelessness.

I stayed at the clinic that night, checking in on Lucretia every few hours. She stayed in bed the whole time and refused conversation, meals, and medication. The following morning, as I prepared to leave, I wrote in the Daily Log, "Concerned about L. M." When I returned for my next shift, Lucretia was gone. Her patient file contained a note that she left beneath her pillow. Written in uneasy block letters and presented here verbatim, the note read:

> same room same bed it dont work
> i no what I need. just let me go.
> i miss angel and my daughter but they are gone
> 4-ever dont you get it?
> i dont want to go thru this no more.
> life is hell just let me go.

I tried to talk to Beto about his sister, but he said that they were estranged and that his contact with her was limited to her stretches as a patient at the clinic. "You know as much as I do," he said.

It was through her patient file that I learned Lucretia had twice been sentenced to the clinic for drug detox in 2004, both times in lieu of being sent to jail for drug possession. I consulted the Daily Log during the dates that corresponded to her residence. One entry noted that she had again refused food and medication, another that she refused to take part in group counseling sessions and demonstrated a deepening "pessimism." In these clinical accounts the language of failure and refusal seemed to characterize Lucretia. I wondered about the multitude of "failures" and "refusals" she had suffered outside of the clinic.

Several home addresses were listed in Lucretia's patient file, and I recognized the street names and the villages. I did not imagine that I would ever visit her in these homes and doubted that she was even aware of my presence at the clinic that night; our encounter had been so brief, and she was so distraught. However, months later I ran into Lucretia in Española, and I took the risk of reintroducing myself. As expected, she did not remember me, but she invited me to her home, provided I give her a ride.

We drove to an address that I did not recognize, to a trailer she shared with two other women. During our ride, I told her that, in addition to working with Beto as a patient attendent, I was a "researcher," studying heroin. She asked me if I could write her a prescription. When I answered "No," she grew quiet. Then she chuckled and said that she could tell me a thing or two about heroin, if I was interested in her version of things.

When we arrived at her trailer, Lucretia asked if I wanted to get high. Then she asked if I cared if *she* got high, and then she laughed, announcing that she didn't care if I cared. I excused myself and went to the bathroom for an interval of time that would allow her to fix. When I returned Lucretia was relaxed. We sat quietly for several minutes, until she was ready to talk. In a slow, muted tone, she began to unravel what she described as *the beginning of the end*, the death of her husband, Ángel, and the loss of her daughter.

We both fixed that night, after Angelita [her daughter] was sleeping. We tried to be good about that, you know, for her not to see. Well, we fixed, we watched a little TV and fell asleep. I always fell asleep first. Ángel used to say I slept like a baby when I was high. It was the only time I really could sleep, you know? *Pero cuando me levanté, Ángel se murió* [But when I woke up, Ángel died]. He was dead.[12]

Lucretia turned her back to me and with great effort lifted her long black hair, revealing her husband's name, tattooed in vertical letters along her upper spine. Then she let her hair fall like a curtain. She stood unsteadily and walked into the living room, which seemed to serve as her makeshift bedroom. When she returned she carried a wallet-sized school portrait of her daughter, Angelita, who was named after her husband. She handed me the image, which I held in the palm of my hand. Angelita wore black-rimmed glasses and smiled purposefully. "She's a good girl," Lucretia said.

After Ángel's death came a series of events that led Lucretia to the detox clinic and, eventually, to prison. The first event was losing the subsidized one-bedroom apartment she shared with her husband and daughter as a result of her inability to pay the rent. At that time she was "trying to make it straight," and there was no one who could take her in who was not using heroin. I asked her about her brother, Beto. He was clean, wouldn't he help? Lucretia simply shook her head.

In the days that preceded her eviction, Lucretia resorted to selling the majority of her belongings, including her husband's beat-up car and, when times got really tough, the apartment's stove, for which she was arrested. With her few earnings and belongings, she and her daughter moved into a room at the Western Scene Hotel, located on the outskirts of Española. Lucretia remembered the room's bowed mattresses and stained carpet. "I paid $25 a night for that shitty room. Some days I didn't eat."

At that time Lucretia said she wanted to get help for her addiction, but she didn't have the $50 addicts who admit themselves are required to pay. If she had been arrested she would have been admitted to the clinic free of charge. She actually *wanted* treatment but didn't have money then. Nor does she now. "It makes no sense," she said.[13]

Lucretia recalled a small window in the hotel room that offered a view of the Jemez Mountains—a place she fondly remembered as a child. The view of the mountains helped, she said. Plus, her stay at the hotel was designed to be temporary, until she got back on her feet. But living there day to day, hungry and unable to sleep, Lucretia returned to heroin.

> A friend of Ángel's found me at the hotel. "What are you doing here?" he asked. He was like, shocked, because he knew me before, with Ángel. We had a good life. It was a hard life, but it was good. Well, he felt sorry for me, I guess, and he took me and my girl to Sonic [a fast-food drive-in restaurant]. He asked me if I needed anything, and I started crying right there in the car. I told him I hadn't slept in like a month, that I couldn't eat nothing. I missed Ángel. He was being all caring-like. He told me he missed Ángel, too.
>
> He didn't want to take us back to the hotel, but I made sure he did. I didn't want no funny stuff with him. I didn't want him in my room either. He told me I looked tired, and he offered me a *gorrita* [measure of heroin]. He gave me the works [syringe]. I hadn't touched the stuff since Ángel died. I didn't want to take it, *pero* I took it.

Lucretia shot up alone that night after putting Angelita to bed. As before, she fell asleep. And as before, she awoke to the sounds of her daughter crying—this time at the sight of police officers standing before her mother's drugged body. Angelita was promptly taken away by child protective services and Lucretia arrested. She was sentenced to thirty days of heroin detox at Nuevo Día—which she had previously sought out on her own but could not afford. Lucretia didn't have to pay this time around.

Lucretia's relapse and loss of her daughter were thus, in part, a consequence of technical procedures: as a self-referring addicted mother, she was turned away from treatment because of her inability to pay a $50 registration fee; as an "offender," she was sentenced to treatment, with all fees reimbursed by the state. But in her transformation from addict to offender, Lucretia had lost the roles and loves that were most meaningful to her. She no longer had a reason to undergo treatment. She no longer had hope.

That afternoon in her trailer, I began to understand the nature of her "failures" and "refusals"—why she was a difficult patient. Her desire to recover was gone. She felt betrayed by the various institutional arrangements that had initially caused her to be turned away from treatment, then demanded it. Recalling her last stint at the clinic, she said, "I didn't want to sit through no bullshit and to pretend like it was gonna get better. Ángel was gone. Angelita is now, too. I knew it wouldn't ever get better."

THORNS

The blackout that occurred during my first shift at the clinic lasted for nearly seven hours. By 6:30 in the morning, the electricity had been restored, and the clinic was flooded with the light of sunrise. And yet the darkness—its prevailing sense of uncertainty—persisted. Peter returned to the orange chair, his body still contorted with pain. The other patients began to emerge from their rooms and resumed their requests for pills, coffee, sugar—all the *somethings* that provide temporary relief from the pain of withdrawal. I took refuge in the nurse's station and arranged the morning pills in small paper cups. At seven o'clock I announced it was "medication time." The dispensations were ritualistic. The patients lined up quietly just beyond the door of the nurse's station and, one by one, swallowed their pills, an action I recorded in the medication log.

Before breakfast, a group of patients assembled for an informal Bible study. I prepared breakfast—scrambled eggs and tortillas—while Yvette read awkwardly from the Gospel of Matthew: "And some fell among thorns; and the thorns sprung up, and choked them."

"What?" someone asked.

"Thorns are sin," Pauline said gently. Pauline was forty-two years old and had recently found God.

"Check out *these* thorns." Marcos lifted his shirt above his head. Spread across his back was a tattoo of a Jesus. Blood dripped from where the spiny crown pierced Jesus' temples.

"Jesus got my back," Marcos said. "Otherwise, I couldn't take this shit."

The five days and four nights Marcos had spent at the clinic were little different from the years he spent on the "outside," a childhood of foster families and a recent five-year stint in prison for drug trafficking. A dirty urine analysis sent the recently paroled Marcos to the clinic, where, in his mind, everything resembled something else—a prior time, a prior place.

"The clinic is just like *la pinta* [jail]," Marcos invariably said when talking about conditions of everyday life there—the food, arguments, and restrictions on movement or telephone use, feelings of boredom and frustration. Prison was Marcos's constant reference. Eschewing a linear narrative, he applied the feelings and experiences of his incarceration to deepen his portrayal of his life before prison, especially his early childhood. About that time he said it was "like being behind bars. Everybody on watch and nowhere to go." Or, "In *la pinta*, you gotta have a game-face, you know, don't let nobody know what you're thinking. When I was a kid, same thing. You don't want people to know nothin' about you, 'cause *en la mañana*, someone come to take you away. Game-face."

According to his patient file, Marcos had bipolar disorder and dyslexia. He was also described as having "trust issues"—a frequently uttered gloss for any kind of behavior or attitude deemed suspicious or reserved. Marcos's adamant refusal to sleep in a dorm with other male patients was taken as a symptom of his "trust issues." (Some staff members attributed it to possible rival gang affiliation, although there was no evidence that he was in a gang.)

At night a mattress was placed in a utility closet for Marcos, where he slept soundly among mops and brooms, thus earning himself the nickname *"el portero"* [the janitor]. Months after our first encounter at the clinic, Marcos told me why he slept in the closet. We were sitting face-to-face in a plastic dining booth at the fast-food restaurant in Española where Marcos worked. It was three o'clock in the afternoon and the restaurant was empty. Marcos told me that a male relative raped him when he was eight years old. In hushed tones, he described a terrifying childhood—the days and nights spent hiding from his perpetrator. The sexual abuse continued until the age of ten, when he was sent to a foster home. So began a series of temporary living situations with unfamiliar families across the state. "The first time, you don't know if its gonna save you or be just more of the same," he told me. "You hope it's gonna last, you know, that you got *una nueva familia, nueva casa* [a new family, new house]. But it don't."

Toward the end of the interview, Marcos expertly assumed a *"gabacho"* (Anglo) accent and said that he managed to "slip through the cracks" when he was sixteen. After years of being tracked by the state, he

Figure 3.   Trinity. Photo by the author.

said, "I was on my own, with nobody following me." At twenty he was arrested for possession of heroin with intent to sell.

"I'll tell you what. Being in prison is the worstest thing in the world for someone like me," he said. That's why he tattooed Jesus on his back—not as an act of bravado, as it was so often assumed, but as a desperate attempt to protect his body. "I didn't want no one touching me," Marcos said.

.   .   .   .   .

Over breakfast Marcos congratulated me on surviving my first night. You have no idea, I thought. But of course he did. There would be more of the same on my graveyard shift. Perhaps it wasn't a power shortage (although during the monsoon rains the clinic lost power repeatedly) but a shortage of beds, medication, staff, money, food, and activities to keep the patients engaged. This shortfall led to an increase in the already high rate of patient discharges. Some were sent to jail, and others were kicked out or walked out, only to begin using again—and on more than one occasion overdose and die.

The clinic operated in a constant state of instability. The administration struggled to make ends meet, the attendants struggled to keep patients comfortable and in line, and the patients struggled to stay. Day to day, moment to moment, there was little continuity, little security. Life at the clinic vacillated between chaos and boredom, just as patients ricocheted between states of agony and relief. Indeed, the quality and tempo of life at the clinic mirrored that which patients lived *afuera*, on the outside, at home or on the streets. Many patients left the clinic, reasoning that they were no better there than they were anywhere else.

The turnover also applied to detox attendants. Most quit after a single shift, and during the course of my employment, at least one was fired when it was discovered that he was dealing and using drugs on clinic grounds. The administration reported that one of the greatest challenges with hiring attendants was not that they were undereducated or undertrained; it was that often they were relatives of patients and had a history of drug addiction themselves. Like many rural mental health or drug rehabilitation centers, the pool of clinic employees came from the very communities and families of addicts they served. They shared neighborhoods and homes and knew intimate details of one another's lives. Hence, despite the few symbols and rituals of technical distance—such as the attendant's log, our thick ring of keys, and access to locked medicine cabinets—there was little personal or professional distance. The proximity of institutional and intimate life reflected just how deeply entrenched the heroin epidemic was.

"Blood is thicker than bureaucracy," the clinic's executive director liked to say. This "thickness" of relation between staff and patients did not necessarily encourage trust or understanding—principles that the clinic espoused. Family favors were as common as family feuds, and the presence of family members at the clinic, as in Lucretia's case, added to the sense of the inexorable familiarity of family life and drug life. Within the clinic, various social, familial, and medical identifications and relations inter-twined.

Whereas many ethnographies of institutions foreground the deliberate division of these areas (e.g., Desjarlais 1997; Rhodes 2005), in this setting institutional life was an extension of a broader realm of sociality, especially of family. The incorporation of these forms of social life into the structure of the clinic—an incorporation that reflects specific economic, historical, and social realities—produced a very different configuration of "institu-tional power," as well as different possibilities and challenges for "rehabil-itation" or "recovery." While patients in the clinic talked frequently about *"la vida afuera"* [life outside], there really was no such place. Life outside thrived *within* the clinic's walls. It established the tempo of the clinic and played a large part in determining the futures of its patients.

As an institution, the clinic operated not rationally or coherently but symptomatically—always as a response to unforeseen or unmanage-able events. This symptomatic structure contributed to the clinic's over-whelming feeling of instability, the most obvious contributing factor of which was its financial constraints. The telephones located in the nurse's and attendant's stations rang ceaselessly. Yet a receptionist was out of the question; there was no money for administrative support, or for a desig-nated cook, or for "real nurses," or for "first-line therapies" such as the highly effective anti-opioid medication buprenorphine, popularly known as the "magic bullet."[14] Even with the lack of financial, administrative, and medical support, there was an endless waiting list of patients—often reaching as far back as five months. Attendants were told to tell them to call back, knowing that the likelihood someone would actually answer their calls was slim.

The instability involved more than just money and staffing. Though this was a medically monitored treatment program, there was little con-sistency in the treatment itself. Detox patients were regularly given (or unknowingly took) the wrong type or amount of medication, at least twice with near-fatal consequences. With no apparent justification, medications were abruptly stopped, replaced, or newly assigned to patients. These changes were noted in the medication log lightly if at all. And evidence of mishaps was sometimes erased from the log altogether.

Adding to the irregularity was the fact that many of the patients were transferred from mental health facilities or jails. Medications for psychosis, depression, diabetes, and HIV were often "lost" in the transfer. Newly admitted addicts frequently experienced weeklong drug interruptions, a problem exacerbated by the rural location of the detox clinic, its distance from well-stocked pharmacies, and the lack of trained medical staff to assess and follow up on a variety of critical prescriptions.

Indeed, patterns of "legitimate" medication use in the clinic mirrored the use of illicit street drugs. With a limited supply of second-class therapies, attendants "made do," treating not so much as needed but as able. Treatment was intermittent, even experimental. Patients familiar with newer, more effective therapies for heroin withdrawal, such as Suboxone, asked for the medications by name and complained that this or that drug was not available to them. They were told, "Beggars can't be choosers," and, according to patients, medication was sometimes withheld as a form of reprimand. In this setting, the provision of medication was not a neutral act (Biehl 2005).

The request for medication at nondosing times was constant, and the attendants who dispensed medications, including me, were sometimes called dealers. Although the clinic was presented as a rehabilitation center, the drug economy of the streets persisted within it.

LA VIDA AFUERA: LIFE OUTSIDE

Before admission to the clinic many of the patients had moved between prison or psychiatric hospitalization or from one failed drug rehabilitation program to another. This erratic movement between institutions followed the patients' movements across diagnoses and drug regimens. For three years, Peter received methadone at another drug treatment program. Like Marcos, he was diagnosed as bipolar and prescribed the antipsychotic haloperidol, as well as numerous medications for depression, muscular rigidity, and insomnia (all side effects of haloperidol). Throughout this period of "licit" drug use, Peter also used heroin. When he could not get heroin he took "benzos" or drank excessively—anything, he said, "to maintain."

By the time I met Peter at the detox clinic, he had been incarcerated twice and court appointed to drug rehab three times. In 2003 he was admitted to the University of New Mexico Psychiatric Center for "crisis stabilization," the result of multiple overdoses and emergency treatments with injections of naloxone, a medication that fights the life-threatening depression of the central nervous and respiratory systems during heroin overdose. "Everyone thought I had a death wish," he later explained. "Maybe I did."

Peter's father died six months before Peter was admitted to the Psychiatric Center. "The thing is," he said, "I didn't ever really know him. We never lived together or nothing. The only way I knew him was *chiva* [heroin]. The way he came to be my father, it was *chiva*."

He described his introduction to heroin as we sat together on the clinic grounds:

> The first time, I said no. I was in his house, over in Chimayó, right there by the Sacred Heart [Catholic church]. We talked about when he was young, and all this family on his side that I didn't know. He told me he was sorry for not being in my life. It was making me kinda upset. He kept saying he was sorry, and he pulled out a joint. It tasted funny, and my dad laughed [and] said it was laced with heroin. I started freaking out. *I've got heroin in my system?* He told me to relax. It was okay. It felt good, *no?* I relaxed into it, and we just chilled.
>
> In a little while, he pulls out like an ounce [of heroin.] He puts it on the kitchen table and says, *Wanna do a shot with me?* I told him no thanks. He loads it anyway. He cooked it in a spoon and was cooking it right in front of me and telling me he was sorry and we should go fishing. He liked to fish trout. I told him yeah, that would be nice, and he's cooking it nice and slow right in front of me. He asked if I'd ever seen this [preparing heroin]. I said sure, but I lied. He smiled and loaded it.
>
> He told me to lie down on the couch. Close my eyes and give him my arm. Honestly, I didn't want to do it, but I figured I already got it [heroin] in me. He shot me up. That was the first time, and I was like, wow! It took all the feelings away, you know? He did it, too, and we stayed there together.
>
> It was a long time ago.

Peter's memory of his introduction to heroin is one of the few he has of his father. Soon after he introduced his son to the drug, he moved to

Los Angeles. Peter never saw him again. Over the course of ten years, there were only a handful of telephone calls, the content of which Peter can barely recall. Peter learned of his father's death several months after it occurred, and though he was never told the official cause, he suspects it was heroin related.

This pattern of familial, intergenerational heroin use—common in the Española Valley—stands in sharp contrast to the mainstream notion of heroin addicts as isolated from family or community. In this milieu the biological family is often the primary domain of heroin use, as well as the primary source of support and care. Most cases of heroin overdose are "handled at home" by relatives, never coming to the attention of health workers.[15] Family members, especially parents, are known to buy heroin for their loved ones who are undergoing *las malias*, the pain that accompanies heroin withdrawal. This characteristic of the heroin problem has even been given a name, or symptom, *"m'ijto-itis"*—as in, "I'll do anything for *m'ijo* [my child]."

This rewriting of domestic norms should not be read as pure pathology or bad parenting. In a later chapter I explore intergenerational heroin use as a contemporary modality of kinship that simultaneously articulates and enables the fragmentation of Hispano social and domestic life and embodies a distinctive sense of one's being in relation to another. For now I want to mark this issue as a practical response to a pattern of "intensified disengagement" of social and medical services (Biehl 2005). The paucity of local services, the endless waiting lists for the few that exist, and the provision of blatantly suboptimal care have forced families to perform a kind of social and medical triage. Parents and children work as substitute psychiatrists and first responders. They obtain medications, such as narcotics and psychopharmaceuticals, through means legal and not. They adjust prescriptions as they see fit, often decreasing doses in an attempt to make medications last longer or increasing doses to bring about a stronger effect. They attempt to revive loved ones who have overdosed.

Among the free monthly trainings offered by the local police department is a naloxone injection class. One winter evening I observed one such training, held in the parish hall of a local church. A dozen or so people attended, all of whom identified as parents, children, or spouses of heroin addicts. A police officer opened the training with the painful acknowledgment, "It is you who will be in the position to save a life. More than likely, by the time we get there, it will be too late." Most of the attendees already knew this. They had already felt the devastating sense of helplessness that accompanies an overdose. Using adult-sized dummies, we practiced administering naloxone, an opioid antidote that if administered in time revives the body's respiratory and central nervous systems.

This monthly training does more than symbolize the gravity of the region's heroin phenomenon. It also demonstrates how practices of care become reconfigured through heroin, intensified at the kinship level. This intensification of kin relations is concurrent with processes of intensified disengagement at the state level. The expansion of these types of "consumer-centered" or community" trainings occur precisely at the moment when public funding for mental and behavioral health programs are being drastically cut and when publicly funded clinics are being privatized or closed.

One of the obvious problems with the family shouldering the burden of care is that it, too, is unstable. The narratives of Peter, Mikey, and Lucretia point to the fact that the family, like the clinic, is marked by vulnerability. This wasn't always the case, as many valley addicts like to point out. More than once, I heard addicts insist, "There was a time . . ."—a time when families didn't use, when they "kept it together."

Ironically, the practice of family members using together, of trying to keep the problem of addiction close to home, arises in part from the profound significance family has in Hispano culture. The phenomenon of heroin use *within* the family attests to the endurance of these ties, as distorted as that may seem.

WHAT REMAINS

On day 23 of his program, Peter and I sat in the very spot that we had huddled together the morning of my first graveyard shift. There was color in his face, and his body had filled out slightly, in proportion to his

growing appetite. He told me he was going to make it—that he was
going to complete all thirty days. But it wasn't because he was "recovering." He wanted heroin just as badly as before, and he had no illusions
that he was going to remain off the drug once he left the clinic. But he
was going to make it, he said, because he had nowhere else to go. He had
nothing else to do.

> That's what you never think about. You don't think, *what's this person
> gonna do when they get outta here?* It's stupid. You guys are stupid. It's not
> like it *stops* here. It never stops. You get out and it's the same. You go to
> the same place, even if you have this idea that it'll be something else. It's
> not. As soon as you get there, someone starts knocking on your door
> with it [heroin]. You don't have to go to it. It comes to you.

I asked Peter to comment on the relation between life *afuera* and life
inside:

> What do you think! Look around you. It's all addicts here, no? It's just
> like outside. I mean, if you guys were really serious about helping me
> out, you wouldn't put us in a room with someone who is strung out. The
> look of it . . . it makes you want to get fucked up. No. The first thing you
> gotta do is get rid of all the *tecatos* [heroin addicts] in order to save one.
> Otherwise we're all just reminding each other of what we need.

Peter's response was a challenge on many levels. The detox clinic,
while filling an important void in the Española Valley's addiction services, would not be the force for healing it had been celebrated as at the
opening ceremony. Given their insufficiency and the lack of continuity,
addiction services were to remain decidedly unstable—just like life itself. Indeed, without the radical transformation of *la vida afuera* the detox
clinic would be just another rung in a repetitive institutional machine
that addicts like Peter would ceaselessly move in and out of.

Ultimately, the bigger challenge Peter posited was not about the fail-
ings of institutional life but about an ethics of care. His comment on the
presence of other addicts as being a crippling reminder of his *need* presents
us with the opportunity to consider an ethics of care based on the idea of
commensurability. Within the clinic the idea that the other's suffering is

our own is not abstract; it is visceral. How might those in the throes of pain help to heal each other? How might the suffering of others and the painful forms of recognition it evokes be a force for care and not a crippling force, as Peter suggests? In other words, how might the recognition of shared pain transform the nature of our need?

I thought of Peter and the night of the blackout—the uncomfortable intimacy forged between us that would remain unfathomable. I would never fully understand the nature of Peter's pain or of his need. And although I could not understand it, I still endured something alongside him; and Peter allowed me—perhaps even needed me—to be by his side.

That night represents to me the tremendously difficult process of commensurability—of remaining in the face of one another's unshared vulnerabilities. These vulnerabilities cannot be resolved any other way but by remaining close to one another. I write *commensurability* and not *incommensurability* because, over the course of those dark hours, what emerged between Peter and me was a *common* vulnerability. And it is through this common vulnerability that we can begin to understand the possibilities for a kind of care, one in which the parameters of the clinic and of the patient are not so easily defined. Perhaps *we* are the patient, and the clinic—intended as a space for healing—is all around us.

TWO

The Elegiac Addict

These pleasures, Melancholy, give
And I with thee will choose to live.

Milton, "Il Penseroso"

ALMA

On the cusp of her twenty-ninth birthday, Alma Gallegos was discovered lying in the parking lot near the emergency room entrance at Española Hospital. Like many patients that present at this ER, she was anonymously dumped by acquaintances who likely feared she might die or was already dead. According to the physician who treated her, Alma was close to death: her breath was shallow; her heart rate was barely discernible; and, despite the intense summer heat, her skin was cold to the touch. On quick inspection of her swollen limbs, the physician determined that Alma had overdosed on heroin, and she was treated with naloxone, which, if administered in time, revives the body's central nervous and respiratory systems. Alma's vitals were soon stabilized, and she remained in the hospital until the local drug court mandated that she be transferred to Nuevo Día, the very drug treatment facility from which she had recently discharged herself.

Four days after her overdose, Alma emerged from the women's dormitory. Having privately suffered through the initial torments of heroin withdrawal, it was expected that she "join the program"—that is, participate in all aspects of clinic life, including bathing, cleaning, journaling, and daily counseling. I accompanied Alma to her first mandatory counseling session. The transition from private suffering to putting addictive experience into a social and linguistic frame—an exercise central to the clinic's therapeutic process—was a challenge for her. Alma pulled at her hair uncomfortably. Her body twitched, and pebbles of sweat collected on her brow. For several minutes she looked around the counselor's small, windowless office and then asked in the Hispano manner (more statement than question), "¿Yo estuve aquí una vez, no? [I've been here before, haven't I?]."

Indeed, it was Alma's second admission to the detoxification clinic in a year and her sixth admission to a drug recovery program in just five years. Addicted to heroin for half her life, Alma's affective world—from her embodied pains to her cravings to the quietude she experiences during a heroin high—was as familiar to her as the institutions intermittently charged to apprehend and/or care for her. It was a familiarity achieved through certain recurring fractures, indexed by long stretches of heroin use, arrest, mandatory treatment, and an eventual and ongoing return to heroin use, arrest, and treatment.

Though in clinical parlance returns to detox, such as Alma's, are considered a "relapse," a framing that correlates to an understanding of addiction as "chronic disease," Alma understood her presence at the clinic less as a relapse—which connotes a period of remission—than a "return." It is a return to living "once more and innumerable times more" (Nietzsche 1974: 274) *this* aspect of Hispano life: these weary limbs, this room, this familiar and anticipated question posed to her by the drug counselor: What happened?[1]

Alma plainly answered that nothing happened. The counselor persisted. She asked Alma about her relationship with her husband. Weren't her friends and family supportive of her recovery? Why did she lose her part-time job as a teacher's aide? Was her living situation unstable? Each of the counselor's questions pointed to identifiable events that the counselor imagined might establish a foundation for Alma's relapse, and for her memory, ready for recounting.

Alma shook her head at each of the counselor's questions, even when her mouth sometimes answered, "Yes." Between gesture and voice, she seemed to say that everything and nothing happened. The counselor was confused. Alma turned to me in exasperation and, in a language the counselor couldn't understand, said, "*Es que lo que tengo no termina* [It's just that what I have has no end]."[2]

Two years later Alma was again rushed to the same hospital emergency room, where she was pronounced dead after overdosing on heroin.

.   .   .   .   .

This chapter examines what I am calling melancholy subjectivity in the context of addiction. My interest is to show how certain forms of loss in this milieu are compelled by a set of social and historical situations. These losses, I argue, have led to a local ethos of melancholia through which heroin addiction, and heroin-related death, can be read as a kind of contemporary consequence. I focus first on the narrative of Alma, who powerfully described her condition as *"sin fin"*—without end—which I now understand as her insistence on the centrality of unfinished grief as an ineradicable truth of heroin addiction and Hispano life. Hers was a sentiment that is shared by many other addicts I came to know. I then turn to the narrative of Joseph and to an analysis of how his historically situated pains shaped his experience of addiction. But let me now return to Alma.

Between 2004 and 2006 I closely followed Alma as she moved within and between institutional and intimate domains: the clinic, the drug courts, her home, ancestral village, and church. My dual roles as front-line clinical staff member and anthropologist enabled an understanding of the strong relationship among them, and as the discursive forms and practices associated with them worked toward constituting Alma as recovering or *not*, a picture of return emerged. Outside of the clinic, Alma was a part of a local world that readily used heroin to "treat" the recurring pains associated with the ongoing history of loss and displacement that had come to characterize Hispano life. Within the clinic, she was expected to prepare the grounds for her "recovery," even if the model of chronicity, on which the clinic's practices were based, alleged that her condition was, by definition, unending.

Embedded in these simultaneously opposing and conspiring worlds, Alma struggled to confirm her existence against their shared presupposition of inevitable return: a return to certain historically situated pains, a return to using heroin, a return to the clinic. It is my central argument here that the interplay of these biomedical and local discourses compelled the very dynamics of "endlessness" in which Alma felt herself caught and set the groundwork for her fatal overdose.

A WORK OF MOURNING

Anthropology has shown how following the life history of a single person can illuminate the complex intimate and structural relations that constitute a life, a community, and a social world (Biehl 2006; Das 2000; Desjarlais 2003; Pandolfo 1998). In following the plot of Alma's life, I also engage in this form of inquiry. I do so while recognizing that there are many elements of Alma's story that I do not know, and other elements that could be told in the voice of many other subjects I followed during the course of my research. All were caught in the same cycle of trying to live their lives without heroin and succumbing their lives to it. I thus present Alma as embodying a condition that is more than hers alone.

While certain refrains occur in Alma's experience and the experience of Hispanos more broadly, one of my commitments here is to convey Alma as she appeared to me—generous, reflective, and deeply engaged in trying to find a way to live. In relating Alma's life, and in trying to reckon with her death, I am presenting a kind of "work of mourning" but in terms that differ from recent anthropological works on violence and subjectivity, which examine discursive practices that seek to make possible the repair of injury and of the everyday (Das 2000;

Das and Addlakha 2001; Seremetakis 1991). Rather, this constitutes a work of mourning in another tradition—the Hispano tradition—which commemorates the singularity of death while insisting on the inevitable repetition of it.

Consider the ubiquitous *descansos* that are placed at or near the site of death. The *descanso* does not seek to reinhabit the site of loss, or repair the everyday, but insists on death's essential relationship to life. Over the years heroin-related *descansos* have gathered on the Hispano landscape. Frequently adorned with the used syringes that contained the lethal dose of the drug, they highlight just how enmeshed heroin has become in physical space and everyday life and pose the question of whether and how "mourning as repair" is possible or even desired in the face of unrelenting loss. Rising along the edges of dirt roads and scattered among the valley's juniper-dotted hills, the undisturbed presence of the *descansos* constitutes a kind of ethical commitment to that which was lost; they keep vigil over it; they coexist.

. . . . .

One day, while sitting together in my parked car in front of the Española Public Library, a certain memory flashed up for Alma, urgent and unannounced. It was a cold afternoon, already dark despite the early hour. I turned on the car's ignition and was ready to return Alma to the halfway house in which she resided after thirty days of heroin detoxification. To my surprise, Alma grabbed my hand and told me to wait; she wasn't ready to go back.

For a few moments we stared quietly at the library's iron-barred windows, our breath visible in the chilly air. Alma broke the silence and told me that her older sister, Ana, whom she had never mentioned to me before, loved to read. Ana had been killed by a drunk driver four years before. She had been on her way to work, Alma recalled, driving along the winding, two-lane highway that connects Española to the village of Chimayó.[3] "She loves reading," Alma said, stressing, it seemed, the present tense, as if Ana were still alive. We both stared at the tattered romance novels that sat on Alma's lap.

Following local custom, the Gallegos family put up a handmade *descanso* in the spot where Ana was killed. Alma told me that afternoon that it still marks her sister's death, and she asked if I'd seen it. She described the plastic yellow flowers and the fading family portrait that adorned Ana's wooden cross. I told Alma that I knew the *descanso*, and I offered to drive her there. Alma shook her head no, adding that for years she would have to turn her head and look away every time she passed the cross on her way to Chimayó to meet her dealer. She confessed that she still turned away from the sight but was able to conjure the image of the *descanso* in her mind. "Ahí está," she said, "mirándome [There it is, looking at me]."

In his examination of the English elegy, Peter Sacks (1985) notes that the traditional forms and figures of the genre relate to an experience of loss and the search for consolation. The passage from grief to consolation is often presented in the form of repetition—the recurrence of certain words and refrains. According to Sacks, the elegy's repetitive structure functions to separate the living from the dead and forces the bereaved to accept a loss that he might otherwise refuse.[4] In this way, the repetition creates a rhythm of lament that allows grief to be simultaneously conjured forth and laid to rest. But what if the structure of repetition creates not the working through of grief but the intensification of it? How might the structure of repetition become a constitutive force for a kind of mourning that does not end?

Passing her sister's roadside memorial on her way to score heroin, Alma created her own rhythm of lament—a counterpoint of yesterday and today, memory and forgetting, dead and living. Like her sister's *descanso*, the elegiac character of Alma's narrative offers a continuous double-take on thinking about the relation between history, loss, and the present: what is lost *is* what remains. In Alma's words, it is *sin fin*, forging the patterns of her experience.

THE MELANCHOLIC SUBJECT

In "Mourning and Melancholia" Freud writes (1989: 586), "Mourning is regularly the reaction to the loss of a loved person, or to the loss of some abstraction." It designates a psychic process to loss where the mourner is able to gradually work through grief, reaching a definite conclusion whereby the lost object or ideal is essentially let go and the mourner is able to move on. Melancholy, by contrast, designates a kind of mourning without end. It entails an incorporation of the lost person or ideal as a means to keep it alive and thus suggests that the past—that is, the lost past—remains persistently present. Regarding its somatic features, Freud describes the sleeplessness of the melancholic, suggesting that it attests to the steadfastness of the condition. "The complex of melancholia," he writes, "behaves like an open wound" (589).

In Freud's conception, the melancholic's sustained devotion to what is lost is pathological. He warns that the intensity of the "self-tormenting" condition can culminate in the melancholic's suicide (588). More recent efforts to examine Freud's exploration of melancholia have been critical of his understanding of it as a strict pathology and have offered important modifications to his theory.[5] An important area of such work concerns the productive possibilities of melancholia, in particular, in terms of subjectivity, art, and politics (Butler 2004; Cheng 2001; Eng and Kazanjian 2003; Kim 2007). But here I want to pursue Freud's original suggestion regarding the danger to life melancholy may pose. In *The Ego and the Id*, Freud writes that the unrelenting nature of melancholy transforms the subject into one who mourns—transforms her, first and foremost, into a melancholic subject. But what if we conceive the subject of melancholy not simply as the one who suffers but also as the recurring historical refrains through which sentiments of "endless" suffering arise?[6] How to attend to these wounds?

The melancholic subject here is Alma, and the structures in which her fatal overdose took root. And it is the all-too-familiar experiences of loss, articulated now as addiction, that have been shaped, in part, by the kinds of attachments that the logic of chronicity assumes. The recent work of anthropologists shows us how medical and technical forms of knowledge and intervention shape the experience and course of illness and, more broadly, affect subjectivity (Biehl 2006; Cohen 1998; Petryna 2002; Scheper-Hughes 2000; Young 1995). In the context of addiction, chronicity as knowledge and practice has become the ground for a new form of

melancholic subjectivity, one that recasts a long-standing ethos of Hispano suffering into a succession of recurring institutional interactions.
As Michael Fischer (2003: 51) writes, "We are embedded, ethically, as well
as existentially and materially, in technologies and technological pros-
theses," and these take us into new models of ethics in which "our older
moral traditions have little guidance or experience to offer." In the context
of emerging technologies, Fisher aptly describes us as being "*thrown* . . .
to new forms of social life" (51; emphasis added). But I want to suggest
that the Hispano ethos of suffering is a social referent for addiction's recent biomedical turn, and the disparate technologies in which this turn
is embedded (drug treatment centers, drug courts, NA meetings, etc.)
deepens this ethos of suffering in unexpected, even dangerous ways. In
the context of its preceding Hispano forms, I want to examine how these
technologies not so much throw us as *bury* us beneath the weight of that
which does not end.

A PERSISTENT MEMORY

I'm thirty years old. Ana died five years ago. She never did drugs. She
never caused nobody harm. She was twenty-six when she died. My
mother said to me, *It should have been you.* She cried and said she was
sorry for saying it, but I told her it was okay. She was right. There were so
many times I should have died. You can't imagine the situations I've been
in. Situations where you think nobody can survive that. Nobody should
survive that.
    Sometimes I'd shoot up and be sure it was like the last time, that I
wouldn't be around to see the day. The needle'd be in me and I'd be
pushing the plunger in thinking, *this is it! ¡se acabó!* [it's over!]. But I'd
wake up and life for me . . . [pause] it doesn't stop. Even when it should,
you know? There's no reason to live a life like this. Not one like this. Do
you know what I mean?

It was 2:45 in the morning when I recorded these words. Alma was
coming off a four-day heroin binge, which culminated in being sent back
to Nuevo Día after testing "dirty." I was surprised when I saw her walk
in the clinic door; she had just successfully completed a ninety-day heroin

detox program, followed by a short stint at a halfway house. We had been at the library together only a week before. Things seemed to be going well.

It was now Alma's third admission in one year. The counselor asked why she "sabotaged" her recovery yet again. Alma responded that there wasn't anything to sabotage; that this was her life.

I had just fallen asleep on one of the sagging couches in the clinic's common room. Technically, I wasn't allowed to sleep while on duty, but I justified a short nap because I was, once again, covering for a no-show. I set my watch alarm for 2:00 A.M., the next dosing hour, and tucked the keys to the medicine cabinet deep in my jeans pocket. I turned off the fluorescent overhead lights and turned on a dim floor lamp beside the couch. My shoes remained on, and I carefully positioned my body so that I could easily monitor hallway and bathroom activity—just in case the patients woke up from their drug-induced sleep. I'm a light sleeper, I thought— "hyper-vigilant," I'd been told by a therapist who treated me during a bout of insomnia. If someone wakes or something happens, I'll surely know.

But somehow I had slept through my watch alarm and woke up only to the feeling of Alma anxiously shaking my shoulder. She was kneeling down beside me, her face inches from my face. ¡Dios mío! She cried. She told me she thought I was dead. I jumped up from the couch and began making my dosing rounds—first giving Alma her medication and then serving the other patients, whom I had to rouse awake. Afterward I made a fresh pot of coffee and splashed water on my face at the kitchen sink. When I returned to the common room, Alma was still there.

"I can't sleep," she said.

I sat on the couch across from Alma and suggested that the Robaxin, a muscle relaxant, would soon take effect and hopefully she would be able to sleep. Alma said that although her body surely ached, the problem wasn't her muscles; she hadn't slept well her whole life, and she wanted to talk.

Up to this point, I had formally interviewed Alma a handful of times in my capacity as a researcher. None of these interviews was particularly fruitful; when my tape recorder was on, she answered my questions with,

"Well, what is there to say?" and then said nothing. When my tape recorder was off, she was equally vague. On this night, however, Alma had a lot to say, and she allowed me to record her. We sat at a small table in the common room, tape recorder between us. She began her story.

> I think I told you before I grew up in T.A. [Tierra Amarilla]. That's where my family is from. They've been there forever. There's nothing up there no more. Nothing but memories. My brother moved to Denver and works construction. Me and Ana moved to Española, 'cause what are you going to do? There's nothing up there no more. In my opinion, there never really was, but at least there was family. It's a lot of *viejos* [elderly people] now. I still have memories, some of them good. You been there?

Yeah. That's where Tijerina had his rebellion.

Sí, pero no existia [Yes, but I wasn't alive then]. And that was a long time ago. You know [Tijerina] wasn't even from T.A.? . . . Anyway, *es inalterado* [it's the same]. Ana used to talk about doing stuff, you know, different things: moving to Denver, going to school. Joe, he's like that, too. *Pero* I never talk about stuff like that. Never did. Why is that? How come some people can imagine things and others can't? In my opinion, *es como un abismo* [it's like an an abyss].

What is?

> The future. Life. It's the same thing every fucking day. I went to Escalante [the high school in T.A.]. In my junior class, there were like thirty students. I think maybe half of them are dead now. Probably more.
>   They're dead from drugs. Boredom. In my opinion, *pa' nada* [for nothing]. *Pues,* then there are people like Ana who die even though there's no reason whatsoever. Did I tell you she was pregnant when she died? Nobody fucking knows that but me. It weighs heavy on my heart, you know? She told me like two days before and was all optimistic about it even though it was a bad situation. She kept saying it would be okay and said it was a good reason for me to clean up. She was always looking for reasons for me to clean up. *Pero,* I told her, *what about the reasons I'm fucked up?* She didn't like to hear that. In my opinion, nobody does, not even the counselors who ask you straight up. [Telephone rings.] Who the hell is calling at three in the morning?

I left Alma at the table and answered the phone in the nurse's station. It was Lara's boyfriend, Manuel. Lara had been admitted the previous evening for heroin detox. When she arrived at the clinic, she had a black eye and a broken wrist and was wearing urine-stained jeans. Manuel said it was an emergency. I told him that Lara could not come to the phone but that I could relay a message. He shouted obscenities at me and hung up.

I sat at the nurse's desk, exhausted. I could hear Alma talking into the tape recorder in the other room. I heard her say, "Angela, it weighs heavy on my heart." It was as if I were still sitting beside her.

.   .   .   .   .

Several weeks later I began the process of transcribing Alma's recorded narrative. She spoke of her sister, of Tierra Amarilla, of memories that were her own and memories that she had inherited. At one point in the recording, she paused for a long time, and then she said, "It all keeps me awake at night." And minutes later: "It weighs heavy on my heart." Alma repeated the phrase "It weighs heavy on my heart" throughout the recorded narrative. I kept rewinding the recording and replaying it, trying to locate all the events that explained such heaviness. But Alma's admission of *feeling*, her moving descriptions of her embodied pains, were usually temporally disconnected from specific recollections of the past. For example, in one segment of her narrative, Alma talked of her sister's death, then digressed into a recent trip to Albuquerque, and *then* talked of a heavy heart. Throughout, phrases of pain dangled precariously, isolated utterances that seemed to speak, as it were, for themselves.

I tried to understand the nature of this seeming disconnection between feeling and event. Perhaps it was a consequence of heroin withdrawal, during which orientations to time shift according to the process of detox and to the organizational structure of clinical life.[7] Perhaps it was an effect of the predawn hour and the dimness of the room, which created an otherworldly environment. Or perhaps it was me—I was so exhausted that night—maybe I wasn't putting the pieces together, wasn't asking the proper questions.

Whatever the reason for this apparent disconnectedness, one of the themes that Alma kept returning to was the sense that nothing changes, that life and its ensuing pain is unalterable and without end. Indeed, it was in such terms that she explained her relapse and at one point acknowledged that she *knew* she would return to the clinic, as if her relapse and readmission were simply part of the order of things, simple cause and effect. Referring to the so-called responsibility and challenge of staying clean—which is stressed by counselors at the clinic—Alma said, "It's not that I wasn't *ready* . . . it's that there's nothing to be ready *for*."

One of the things Freud's conception of melancholia offers—especially in his later construction—is a way of thinking about how loss and melancholy attachments possess the power to shape the subject's psychic life in a fundamental way. In *The Ego and the Id*, Freud writes:

> We succeeded in explaining the painful disorder of melancholia by supposing that [in those suffering from it] an object which was lost has been set up again inside the ego—that is, that an object-cathexis has been replaced by this identification. At that time, however, we did not appreciate the full significance of this process. . . . Since then we have come to understand that this kind of substitution has a great share in determining the form taken by the ego and that it makes an essential contribution towards building up what is called its "character." (28)

I began to understand Alma's reflections on the inalterability of life through Freud's elaboration on melancholy and subject formation. I began to see how her experiences of loss—those shared and not—became permanently embedded in her. I began to understand that her heart was heavy with the residue of these accumulated losses and that, perhaps, her inability to sleep resulted from her own kind of vigilance: she was keeping watch over this loss. Seen in this way, Alma's melancholy, her insomnia, her heaviness of heart, and her insistence on the inalterability of life were a kind of ethical commitment to that which was lost. And this commitment was altering her "psychic economy" and perhaps determining her future (Ruti 2005: 643). "I knew I'd be back," Alma said. "What I have has no end."

And yet this apparent determinism bothered me. Though Alma's identity was certainly deeply entrenched, I did not like to think of it as immutable or ahistorical.[8] Furthermore, the question of the relation between the psyche and the social remained. Aside from the experience of loss itself, what social constraints were weighing heavy on Alma's heart and shaping her horizon?[9]

YELLOW EARTH

Shortly after transcribing Alma's narrative, I drove up Highway 84 to Tierra Amarilla. It was mid-fall and the cottonwoods along the Chama River were in full yellow bloom. As I climbed higher into the San Juan Mountains, tall, full-bodied ponderosa pines flanked the road. Set back from the highway were clusters of adobe houses and trailers and, adjacent to these, neat stacks of firewood ready for the coming chill of winter.

As I entered Tierra Amarilla, Alma's words began to echo in my mind. I imagined that she was in the passenger seat beside me, accompanying me with her memories. What memories might she have of that empty lot, or the burned-out trailer next to it? Did she know who scratched out Reies Lopez Tijerina's name on the historic marker that welcomes visitors to the infamous mountain village? Only a generation ago the residents of this village lived primarily off the land—ranching, farming, and working the forests. Now, each weekday morning, the village empties out and becomes a virtual ghost town as locals make the eighty-five-mile drive to Los Alamos or Española for work. Among the abandoned lumber mills, dilapidated corrals, and boarded-up houses, I imagined events Alma might have participated in or witnessed: parties, marriages . . . overdoses, deaths. She had spoken to me of some of these things that night at the detox clinic; told me, for instance, about the suicide of a trusted schoolteacher who had tutored her in reading. "She slashed her wrists in the woods and didn't leave a note," Alma said. "My brother's friends found her when they were out partying. The only thing we could think is that her son died in Desert Storm."

Tierra Amarilla: Yellow Earth. Perhaps more than any other *norteño* New Mexican village, it is the symbolic ground of the Hispano history of dispossession and longing for land and times past that has inspired decades of political struggle—by turns mainstream and underground, through means violent and not. Tierra Amarilla was first settled as a land grant in the mid-1600s. Like all land grants in northern New Mexico, Spanish and, later, Mexican settlers were allotted land for an individual home, an irrigable plot for personal farming, and the right to share common land with other settlers for pasture, timber, and hunting. According to the deeds, personal allotments could be sold as private property, but common lands could not. The commons were just that—collective property—and were to be used and preserved for the community's economic and ultimately cultural well-being.

Since 1848, when New Mexico became part of the United States, generations of land grant heirs have found themselves in an uphill struggle to regain lost lands. Even today they continue to argue that the United States broke the Treaty of Guadalupe Hidalgo, which was intended to protect titles secured before the war, thereby preserving the economic and cultural integrity of Hispano people. Indeed, over the years the majority of land grants were usurped through chicanery that was at best on the margins of the law. The heirs of the Tierra Amarilla land grant alone lost over half a million acres, much of it now part of the Carson National Forest. But the "commons" of a national forest comes with strict land use regulations that tourist and local alike must abide by, even if the latter's forebears were once the rightful owners.

The idea that the land was "lost" is no mere exercise in nostalgia; over generations it has given rise to a constant stream of rebellion, most famously in Tierra Amarilla forty years ago when Reies Lopez Tijerina and a group of armed insurgents stormed the local courthouse, a symbol of an "outsider" authority that drove a wedge between the people and the land. The Courthouse Raid, as it is now known, prompted the governor to activate the National Guard and send in tanks to suppress the rebellion. A five-day manhunt by five hundred law enforcement agents ensued. Tanks and small aircraft were used to search the forest and nearby villages for the fleeing insurgents. Eventually, twenty individuals involved in the incident were indicted on various felony charges. The incident captured national media attention but was not taken as a serious social justice issue as other civil rights movement causes were. Instead, the media largely depicted the event as anarchy in the Old West.

Figure 4.   General store. Photo by the author.

The rebellion was nevertheless successful in symbolizing how deep passions run on the issue of the land and who has rights to it.[10] In an interview after the raid, Tijerina exclaimed, "These people will always remember how they lost the land. . . . They have not forgotten after hundreds of years. . . . They will never forget.' "[11] Indeed, the land grant movement continues apace. Every February 2, the anniversary of the signing of the Treaty of Guadalupe Hidalgo, land grant activists stage a demonstration in the state capital that draws heirs from around the state.[12]

Memories and sentiments regarding land loss remain powerful tropes among elders and youth alike, in that locals draw a connection between land loss, poverty, and addiction. The ultimate irony is that which was "lost" is still *there* for Hispanos to see: it's all around them in the mountains, rivers, mesas, and buttes. One wonders how Freud's conception of melancholy can be extended to address such material losses, losses such as land that remain present but out of reach, especially in a context in which land is constituent to cultural identity and economic survival. How might Freud's reflections on *individual* experiences of loss apply to community and intergenerational experiences? In the Hispano context one sees that experiences of loss and melancholia emerge through specific political and historical contexts. To ignore these would be to privilege theory at the expense of history and politics.

As I drove through Tierra Amarilla on that fall day—through the plaza anchored by the infamous courthouse—Alma's narrative was fresh in my mind. I couldn't help but wonder what role "the land" plays in memories of women like Alma; women who, in her words, "didn't exist" during the most militant phase of the land grant movement; women whose lives have been dominated not by the loss of land but by the loss of people. Certainly these forms of loss intersect in powerful ways. Alma's insistence that there is "nothing there," "nothing but memories," speaks to tragedies of earlier generations, tragedies indelibly linked to the present. And the material legacy of land loss in northern New Mexico is the very stage for losses associated with heroin use. Indeed, the first time Alma shot up was deep in the forest, in a crumbling adobe on a large parcel of land that once belonged to *"la familia Mascaranes."*

For generations, the Mascaranes were shepherds, pastoralists. Like many families, they lost land use rights when much of the common land was designated a national forest, a transformation that erased their livelihood. Today the Mascaranes live in the village of Tierra Amarilla and no longer raise sheep. Their old adobe remains locked in the forest. It is the site of many of Alma's heroin-related memories.

> I remember the first time I went in there I felt bad. I felt like I was trespassing. The windows were all busted out. You could see like the bricks and wood from inside the walls. It was a mess, but it was like our spot, our *chante* [house]. But we called it *los Mascaranes. Vamos a los Mascaranes,* we'd say. And that's where we partied. That's where I got high. The first time I saw somebody overdose was at *los Mascaranes.*

I wanted to talk to the Mascaranes family, but I didn't know how to find them. I thought of asking a clerk at the general store, but the general store no longer existed; it was boarded up. I drove to the county offices—a newer complex painted the color of adobe and the only building in the plaza that wasn't in a state of complete disrepair. Despite being a weekday afternoon, even it was closed.

And, as I drove home that afternoon, I thought of Alma's words. "There's nothing up there no more. Nothing but memories."

INTOLERABLE INSOMNIA

Alma left the heroin detox clinic three days after our predawn interview. According to the detox attendant on duty at the time of her departure, she simply "walked out" at approximately two o'clock in the morning. I asked to see her discharge papers, which patients are required to sign in acknowledgment that they had received counseling on the potential consequences—legal and not—of leaving detox before "successful completion." Alma signed her name in bubbly, childlike script. In response to "Reason for Self-Discharge," she wrote, "CANT SLEEP."

Jorge Luis Borges (1998: 98) writes of the "unbearable lucidity of insomnia." He describes sleep as a state in which one is able to forget oneself. When one awakens, however, time, places, and people return—the self returns. One of the many words in Spanish for "to awaken" and which Borges regularly employs is *recordarse,* which translates literally as "to remember oneself."[13] In this sense, when one awakens, one remembers oneself. By extension, in the absence of sleep, the self never leaves, never forgets, and thus remains vigilant over itself and its memories. Borges understood that this vigilance can lead one to a state of despair. In his short story "The Circular Ruins," a man who suffers from insomnia walks miles through a jungle in the hope of tiring himself, losing himself to sleep. "In his perpetual state of wakefulness," Borges writes, "tears of anger burned the old man's eyes" (98).

According to the attendant who was on duty the night of Alma's departure, no one picked her up at the clinic, which suggests that she would have had to walk fifteen miles of dark highway to reach Española. I called the only telephone number that I had for Alma, which was for the trailer that she shared with her on-again off-again husband: there was no response. Over the next week I tried to call again and again. Eventually, a recorded voice answered, curtly informing me that the number I was trying to reach had been disconnected.

Several weeks after my visit to Tierra Amarilla, Alma called me. She wanted me to know that she was okay and that although she knew what people must have thought regarding her discharge, she hadn't "screwed things up yet." Her tone was casual, even happy. She told me that she found a job at the local Subway sandwich shop. It was easy, she said: boring, but easy. She also told me that she had begun to attend services at a growing Evangelical church in Española. She liked the music, she said, as well as the upbeat message of the pastor. I asked Alma about her living situation: was she with her husband, Luis? Where was she? After a long pause, Alma reported that Luis had left. "I'm living alone now," she said, and then asked me to come by the following afternoon after her work shift. We planned an early dinner at a place of Alma's choosing.

I drove to the trailer that Alma had shared with Luis. When she answered the door, she was still wearing her work uniform: baggy khakis and a green pullover. Although it was still light outside, it was almost completely dark inside the trailer. Alma invited me in, informing me as she did that her home currently lacked phone service and electricity. But she quickly added that she was confident that her utilities would be reinstalled within the week, thanks to help from the Fellowship. I asked Alma if she was warm enough, worried that winter was on its way and the trailer would get terribly cold. Did she need anything? Alma told me that she was okay and laughed that her recent weight gain—a benefit from quitting heroin and eating on the job—was helping to keep her warm.

Votive candles flickered on a small coffee table in the living room, where I waited for Alma to change out of her work clothes. Aside from a threadbare couch, the coffee table, and a large wall hanging depicting the Virgin of Guadalupe, the living room was completely bare. I wondered if this was a consequence of Luis's departure or if it was simply amplified by the absence of heat and light. I looked at the votives and the Virgin of Guadalupe. Alma had not entirely let go of her Catholic roots, her ties to the past. I was curious about her foray into evangelicalism and wondered about her desire to be "born again," for a future. I wondered how Alma's transition from Catholicism to evangelicalism might be understood as a reflection of her complicated relationship with her own past and of a desire to forget.

SECOND CHANCES

Positioned between a discount grocery store and a mobile home showroom, the Rock Christian Fellowship is a sprawling cinderblock complex located in the center of Española. It can be spotted from some distance by an enormous neon billboard depicting the face of Jesus, which reads, "Rock Christian Fellowship: Making Disciples." In addition to traditional church services, the Fellowship offers a child care center, a men's recovery home, a "spiritual university," and a restaurant. The Solid Rock Café sits on the northern edge of the complex. Alma suggested we go there for a light dinner. When we arrived, the café was nearly empty. We sat at a small table near the window and watched the evening rush hour traffic gather along Riverside Drive. To my surprise, Alma pulled out two Subway sandwiches from a backpack. I ordered each of us a soft drink, and we ate our sandwiches, which had grown soggy with time, in comfortable silence.

"This place is helping me out a lot," Alma said. "I don't know what I would do, you know, without it." It was the first time since we reestablished communication that Alma acknowledged that things had been difficult. I asked her about the night she left the clinic.

> I shouldn't have gone back. I'll tell you something: that place don't work. Its focus is all wrong. They want you to always be thinking about what you did, why you did it, how you're always gonna be an addict and you got to stay clean, fight the temptation. Your always 'ceptible to heroin, and there's no cure. . . . [That's why] I like it here [the Fellowship]. They're not always looking back, you know? The pastor talks about the future; he says that's what counts. The future—so you can be blessed and go to heaven.
>   At Nuevo Día, with Twelve Steps . . . it's like with Luis, always reminding me of the fuck-ups, you know? The things I've done. It's like, you

don't have to keep reminding me! I know better than anyone else what I've done and where I've been. I can't forget. But don't keep pushing me down there, you know? I have a hard enough time dealing with my demons.

Alma's account of being "pushed" into remembering that she is at perpetual risk of relapsing into addictive behavior provides a powerful critique of contemporary medical and community models of drug treatment that liken addiction to chronic illness. Although this relatively new approach to drug dependence began as a well-meaning attempt to dispel the moral implications of being a drug addict—in other words, to not view drug addiction and relapse as a moral failing—Alma's framing suggests that there are, in fact, moral and psychological repercussions to approaching addiction as a chronic, unending process.

Jean Jackson (2005: 332) has written of the ambivalent status of the chronically ill, of being seen to "confound the codes of morality of sickness and health." According to Jackson, the uncertain ontological status of the chronically ill—depressed, asthmatic, or addicted—can incite stigmatizing reactions. This is true in Alma's experience, though I would add that the idea that her addiction is chronic—that is, its chronicity, its unendingness—may provoke other moral responses, including depression and a sense of hopelessness. And while some might read Alma's appeal for "the system" and her husband to stop "pushing [her] down there" as "denial," an alternative reading may be that it is a genuine plea for a new understanding and approach to addiction.

I began to understand Alma's turn toward evangelicalism as an attempt to carve out such a response for herself. "I don't want to go through this anymore," she said of the seemingly perpetual cycle of treatment and relapse. Perhaps it was in evangelicalism, and the promise of being born again, that Alma was able to envision putting an end to chronicity as such and to seek for herself a true and lasting recovery.

Indeed, that evening in the restaurant, Alma quietly swore to me that she hadn't used heroin since she left the clinic, crediting the Fellowship and her new, forward-looking perspective for her sobriety. The only problem, she said, was that she still couldn't sleep. I could see in her eyes that this was true. Bloodshot and watery, they conveyed the culmination of too many sleepless nights. She told me she hated nighttime because she worried, even before getting into bed, that sleep would not come. I asked her how many nights it had been since she slept. "Nights!" she laughed. It had been so long that she didn't even remember what sleeping felt like. She described her insomnia:

> It's not just being uncomfortable, you know, like sleeping but waking up because your body hurts or you'd have to go to the bathroom or something. I'd watch the other women at night [in the clinic's women's dormitory]. They all slept, but in the morning they'd all complain like babies, *"No puedo dormir."* [I can't sleep.] But they did sleep! I know because I watched them! I was awake all night watching them!
> I'd love to sleep like that.

Alma is right. True insomnia is not merely tossing and turning on a bad night. Rather, it is sleeplessness night after night, a mind and a body in revolt against themselves. Alma described wanting sleep like a hungry person wanting food; her insomnia was a kind of starvation, or another kind of withdrawal. It had gotten to a point where normal patterns of wakefulness and sleep no longer made sense, or seemed permanently unavailable to her. During the hours that preceded her departure from the clinic, Alma said her mind started "playing tricks":

> I kept going over things in my mind, you know? I'd tell myself to stop, but I couldn't. My thoughts were like separate. I can't control it. It's always been like that for me.
> [That night] I was thinking about my parents and how they're getting old and are probably going to die. How I messed things up and, like, my mom hates me now and she's up there in T.A., and I don't go there no more. I don't. I don't even like to call. But mostly, I kept thinking about Ana and how fucked up everything is, how she died with her baby inside of her.
> This is what I kept thinking that night.

"Insomnia," the Romanian philosopher Emil Cioran (1998: 140) writes, "enlarges the slightest vexation and converts it into a blow of fate, stands vigil over our wounds and keeps them from flagging." Night after night, the same thoughts appeared to Alma. She asked me why that is—why, during the day, she is able to get by, but why at night the same thoughts and memories swell up, always in the same way.

Alma wanted a physician to write her a legitimate prescription for a sleep aid. In the meantime, she resorted to buying prescription meds—mostly tranquilizers—off the street. But it's too expensive, costing up to $10 a pill, and the effect too temporary. The thoughts, Alma told me, always return. They are, in her words, without end.

> The only time I can sleep is with *chiva*. That's the only time, and it's the best sleep, you forget everything. There's nothing, just this quiet. I can't explain it to you. It's the best medicine.
>
> *Are you ever worried that you'll start again? That your sleeplessness will lead you back there?*
>
> Always. It's always on the back of my mind.

PERPETUAL PEACE

Alma's estranged husband found her lying on her couch, alone and unresponsive. Within minutes she arrived at Española Hospital, a short distance from the trailer they once shared, and was pronounced dead. A toxicology examination performed by the Office of the Medical Investigator determined that her cause of death was a lethal combination of heroin and the prescription medication diazepam (Valium). Her death was classified an "accidental poisoning," the standard classification given an overdose with no corroborating evidence of intent.

Less than a year after Alma's death, I returned to the Española Valley and visited Luis. We sat together in the living room of the trailer he once shared with Alma, which was aglow with a scattering of decorations left over from Christmas. Luis recalled the month preceding Alma's death—how he and Alma were trying to reconcile after being separated for nearly two years. For the past decade, Luis, like Alma, cycled through arrest, hospitalization, and incarceration. Unlike Alma, he conveyed no misgivings about his heroin use, describing his repeated institutionalization as simply "part of the territory."

According to Luis, "Alma was always the one talking about getting clean, not me. This is who I am. I told her you go do *your* thing, but this is me, a *tecato*. I stayed away when she was cleaning up. I respected that she was trying to live another way. But you know Alma, she couldn't maintain. So we'd get back on it together. That's how we lived together."

The morning of Alma's death Luis was in a neighboring village, with his children from a previous relationship. He said that he had encouraged Alma to spend the morning with her parents in Tierra Amarilla so that she wouldn't be alone, and promised they'd meet up in Española later that afternoon. But Alma refused to go home because she couldn't deal with her parents' judgment and grief. I asked Luis whether he invited Alma to join him. He shook his head and said, "It was just supposed to be for a few hours. It wasn't supposed to be a big deal."

When Luis returned to the trailer that afternoon he thought that Alma was sleeping. He described the chain of events preceding his recognition that something else had occurred: he went directly to the kitchen and began cooking his heroin, wondered if he should also cook hers, knowing she'd want some, and that her need might interrupt *his* moment. So as he prepared both their fixes, he noticed that heroin was missing from his stash. He again counted the *papeles* that contained the drug to make sure he hadn't counted incorrectly the first time; when he realized he hadn't miscounted, he called out Alma's name, and he continued to call her name as he went to her.

Luis told me he didn't want to talk anymore, that he wanted to take a drive. We piled into my rental car and headed north, along Highway 84. Ten, twenty miles passed, and, with the distance, the snow level began to rise. With his eyes half-closed, Luis told me to keep going. The *norteño*-style music on the radio turned to static.

As we entered Tierra Amarilla, Luis pointed out a small, A-frame house set back from the highway. It was his parents' house, the one he grew up in. I asked if he wanted to stop, and he shook his head no, gesturing with a hand for me to keep going. Less than a mile away, he pointed out another house, its chimney releasing smoke the same color as the sky. Luis told me it was Alma's home, the one she grew up in and where her parents still lived. "We grew up together," he said.

We kept on, into the forest that surrounds Tierra Amarilla, the cheap rental car skidding and jerking along a rutted dirt road. Finally, at an intersection with another forest road, Luis asked me to park the car. I watched him from the driver's seat as he walked into the trees, which stood like exclamation points against the snowy ground. About twenty-five feet in, Luis turned to me and gestured for me to join him. The snow crunched loudly beneath my boots. When I reached him, he pointed downward with his cigarette. It was Alma's *descanso*.

Her memorial was a cross made of tree branches, woven together with bits of rusted wire. Overlaying it was another cross, this one made of intersecting syringes. Etched into her *descanso* were the following messages: "ALMA; R.I.P."; "Siempre" [Forever], and "No te olvides" [Never forget].

Luis told me Alma's father made the wooden cross and had etched into it her name, the day of her death, and the command to never forget. And it was Luis who later added the cross of intersecting syringes. Standing in the forest, the *descanso* voiced the losses of Alma's parents, losses that she had inherited and had affirmed, again, through death. At the same time the cross of intersecting syringes affirmed *her need* to forget. It was a need produced by the collision of history and chronicity, a need that took hold of her life and that finally ended in her what had become endless.

THE ENTANGLEMENTS OF TIME

In thinking about the temporal dimensions of loss and sentiment, I have found Raymond Williams's concept "structure of feeling" especially useful. It refers to actively felt sensibilities derived from lived, material histories. According to Williams, at any given time there are multiple structures of feeling in operation, corresponding roughly to the generations living at that time. Each generation creates its own structure of feeling in response to the world it inherits—taking up or abandoning the sensibilities of its predecessors. His way of thinking about "the living substance of perceptions and relationships" (1977: 34) thus has a temporal dimension that helps elucidate the interlocking nature of experience and affect.

Consider, for instance, expressions often repeated among elder Hispanos: "Todo es historia" [History is everything]. It is a saying that simultaneously acknowledges the loss of times past and the longing for continuity in a precarious and changing world. Another: "La historia es una herida" [History is a wound], which is frequently evoked in the context of expressing the material and cultural losses that resulted from the region's past. And another, repeated by the addicted: "Chiva es el remedio para todo" [Heroin cures everything]. Thus, while elders worry that the younger generation is all too willing to forget the past, the young are just as likely to understand the heroin problem as a contemporary consequence of it, while still offering heroin as a remedy for the pain that accompanies the past. In this way, young and old insist that to meaningfully address the heroin problem, one must also address the region's deep historical scars.

There are other kinds of scars, such as those on the skin. The needle marks and abscesses that map an addict's body—open wounds in the literal sense—powerfully attest to how addiction is also a historical formation and an immanent experience. These are wounds in which the future, the present, and the past commingle through the force of recurring need: the need to score heroin, the need to get high, the need to find a vein. Alma once described it to me like this:

> The thing about being hooked is you're always thinking ahead, thinking about your next fix, how and where you're gonna get the money, who owes you money, who owes you heroin, who'll help you out. It goes on and on and on. And now, I've been using so long, nothing ever lasts. The high . . . it's over before you know it and you're back to it, thinking about the next fix, making calls. It never stops.[14]

Hispano heroin addicts and Hispanos more generally are not the only ones to engage this structure of "endlessness" when describing their lives. Indeed, academics have long relied on it to explore the poverty, isolation, and cultural and temporal "rootedness" of northern New Mexico, and artists have engaged the trope in their own imagined constructions of the region (Kosek 2006).[15] One of the earliest and most influential scholarly articulations of this can be found in George Sánchez's 1930s study, *The Forgotten People,* in which he celebrates the "traditional culture" of Hispanos—resulting in part from an intrinsic "unwillingness to change" (1996: 28). But Sánchez ultimately argues that the unrelenting poverty and cultural and geographic isolation of the region has made Hispanos "pathetic in [their] hopelessness" (28). Only with the influence of modernization, Sánchez argues, will Hispanos finally be "freed from cultural bondage and from the despair of dire poverty" (98). Later studies echoed this sentiment, fluctuating only in tone.[16]

Of course, this reading of Hispano New Mexico would become a driving force for generations of artists and writers who moved to the region seeking an alternative to modern, capitalist America (for example, D. H. Lawrence, Georgia O'Keefe, Willa Cather, and contemporaries such as John Nichols). Their idealized renderings of the region and its "enduring traditional culture" continue to propel the notion of the region as a space of cultural endlessness, the place that time forgot. This imagined regional geography would also become the basis of the region's growing tourism industry, which promotes the idea that the traveler—in visiting isolated Hispano villages or pueblos—is able to literally "Exit the Present" to encounter a way of life that has never changed and presumably never will.[17] The cultural politics of this *imagined* geography are crucial to the work of dispossession and displacement of Hispanos (Rodriguez 1987).

These discursive practices intersect in unexpected ways with sentiments articulated by land activists and "old-timers" who frequently lament cultural loss. They worry that the younger generation—especially those who are addicted to heroin—are all too willing to forget the past. In this context the act of remembering the past—in particular, the continuing struggle against dispossession from the land—provokes an alternative idiom of continuity and longing that, for many, is vital to the community and individual identity. Reworking the trope of timeless cultural ties and an idealized past articulated by earlier generations of artists, one land activist said, "Our past[,] . . . our connection to the land and to our heritage *is* our future. The problem is young addicts are lost without it. That's why they use. They don't have a tie to their history." Many other locals whom I spoke with echoed this sentiment.

But what about women like Alma—women who want nothing to do with the village and the land in which she was raised, land that has been the site of conflict over claims of ownership and belonging? The traffic between these varying "structures of feeling" points to the differing ways Hispanos relate to the past and the differing emotional resonances associated with it. It suggests that it is also people's *specific* histories with the past—and not some idealized or inherited notion of it—that leads to a sense of attachment to, or alienation from, it.

MEMORY AGAINST FORGETTING

The question of why the past, especially in its painful incarnations, reenters or is memorialized in contemporary life is a concern of many scholars. Idelber Avelar (1999) argues that images of ruin—that is, the anachronistic object, the museum piece, or, in Alma's case, the *descanso* that marks the site of her sister's death—are crucial for memory work, for they offer anchors by means of which a connection to the past can be reestablished. These images become especially powerful and urgent where there is an incessant replacement of the "old" with the "new." Similarly, Andreas Huyssen (2000) links "contemporary memory cultures" to reactions to dramatic political or social change. "The turn toward memory," he writes, "is subliminally energized by the desire to anchor ourselves in a world characterized by an increasing instability of time and the fracturing of lived space" (28). Memory is a kind of survival strategy against the increasing fragmentation of daily life. According to Huyssen, memory can also be viewed as being in the "grips of a fear, even a terror, of forgetting" (28).

The fear of forgetting is a powerful sentiment in the Hispano context. In the realm of addiction, many addicts described to me their fear of forgetting loved ones who died from a heroin overdose, as well as their fear that they might die from the drug. Both forms are embedded in the repetitive experience of having lost so many friends and loved ones to heroin. In other words, heroin-related deaths are so common that they culminate in the worry that the specificity of each loss will be forgotten. A young heroin addict named Marisa matter-of-factly told me, "I can't even remember how many people have died [because of heroin]. It's that many." In this constellation of heroin-related death, loss, and forgetting, addicts fear that their *own* deaths will be forgotten as well. Marisa admitted that sometimes she foresees her death and wondered, "Will anyone even know if I'm even gone?"

Hispano northern New Mexico represents a contemporary memory culture insofar as there is a pervasive and articulated fear of forgetting history concurrent with public and private strategies of cultural preservation and memorialization. In the realm of tradition, there are yearly reenactments of the Hispano colonial past, including ceremonial dances, such as Los Matachines, that blend the region's Moorish, Spanish, and Native American roots with centuries-old Catholic processions. Agricultural practices with Spanish colonial roots, such as the acequias, remain vital to the cultural and economic survival of some villages. And language itself speaks to the past, as the unique Spanish dialect of Hispanos is still peppered with archaisms that date back to the original *pobladores*, or townsfolk. But these traditions and practices, which Hispanos claim have been around "forever," are also being abandoned.

Many ancient acequias that once brought water to the fields now sit dry as townsfolk increasingly leave agricultural work for low-wage jobs— largely a consequence of nearby Los Alamos National Laboratory (LANL). The laboratory, and the cultural construction of national security, became a fulcrum for land dispossession (Gusterson 1996). Many locals bitterly recall that the land on which it sits was "stolen" by the federal government in 1943 by invoking the power of eminent domain.

The presence of LANL has profoundly reshaped the Hispano landscape, ushering in an epochal transition from local autonomy and sustainability to dependence on the state. LANL is now the largest employer of Hispano valley residents; Española's Super Walmart is the second. A report by the Rio Arriba Department of Health and Human Services (2000) also considers LANL a contributing factor to the region's declining cultural integrity and worsening heroin problem. Some locals describe Los Alamos as *"una herida,"* a wound.

LOS ALAMOS INTERLUDE

During my research, I was invited to participate in a consortium of researchers and treatment providers working on northern New Mexico's drug problems. The consortium included individuals and agencies from the state-defined Region Three: Santa Fe, Los Alamos, and Rio Arriba Counties. As a concerned community member, my task was to represent and advocate on behalf of the needs of heroin addicts in Rio Arriba County, by far the poorest county of the three and the one with the most entrenched drug problem. I looked at serving on the consortium as a means to acquaint myself with the tensions and contrasts between Los Alamos and Rio Arriba Counties and to explore what many residents of the Española Valley had said to me—that Los Alamos is the very opposite of what *norteño* culture *means,* that it is the ultimate Other of Hispano life, and that the relationship between Hispano New Mexico and Los Alamos is one of dependency and distrust.

From the beginning of the consortium there were problems that resonated with these claims. First, Los Alamos was chosen by a majority of members to be the site where the regional meetings would be held. Organizers from Rio Arriba County immediately objected, arguing that Española should play host, especially since it had the severest drug problems. Further, they expressed concern that housing the consortium in Los Alamos would reinforce the already unequal power relations between the two counties. A heated debate centering on "convenience" ensued, and, by majority rule, the meetings remained in Los Alamos. Fittingly, they were held at the Fuller Lodge, a high-ceilinged log building that was once home to the Los Alamos Boys Ranch School. The Boys Ranch was established in 1917 to help sons of the East Coast elite become strong young men through rigorous outdoor activities in addition to a classical education. In later years the Fuller Lodge would be converted into guest quarters for the Manhattan Project.

Participating in the consortium meant that I joined the flock of Hispano commuters who left their small villages early each morning for the "nuclear city" that overlooks the Española Valley from its perch at the base of the Jemez Mountains. At seven o'clock on one such morning, the highway that connected my village, Velarde, to Española was already bustling with commuters. A parade of pickups and dented sedans whizzed by at speeds ten to twenty miles per hour over the speed limit.

A cautious driver, I wasn't able to even enter the highway from my narrow county road for several minutes. Finally I joined the torrent of traffic and drove with relative ease down Highway 68, until I hit San Juan Pueblo, just north of Española. The traffic came to a crawl. I was surprised to see that the parking lot at San Juan's Okhay Casino was already filled to capacity, likely from commuters drawn in for the famous 89-cent burrito breakfast. Others, I imagined, had likely been there all night, fueled by free coffee and imagined fortunes.

As always, I averted my eyes from the adobe, now boarded up and heavily inscribed with graffiti, that sits directly across from the casino. The story goes that three years before, a young man addicted to drugs and desperate for money broke into his grandmother's house. Caught by the matriarch who had raised him, he stabbed her to death in a drug-induced psychosis while his deaf grandfather slept peacefully in an adjacent room. The recollection of the house haunts me still.

In Española the traffic came to a halt. Stressed commuters punched their car horns or pulled out angrily from the choked lanes in search of alternative routes. Slowly, I passed the Super Walmart, liquor stores, fast-food restaurants, discount tobacco shops, and Mexican *tienditas* that make up Española's main drag. It took twenty minutes to reach Santa Clara Pueblo, a mere four miles from Española's center. I passed the Tribal Clinic, surrounded by dilapidated trailers.

Santa Clara: a pueblo renowned for its micaceous pottery, pieces that are sold in high-end Santa Fe galleries. Santa Clara: a community that barely survives on an average per capita income of just over $9,000. As I passed the pueblo the road narrowed, but the traffic, paradoxically, quickened. Now San Idelfonso Pueblo was before me, resembling Santa Clara, though it has a new cluster of cement-block houses (sponsored by the Bureau of Indian Affairs). Santa Clara Pueblo expects that it, too, will soon be able to move its residents out of trailers and into similar accommodations. But the stretch of land in which the pueblos are located share the troubling problem of groundwater contamination, mostly from radioactive waste that seeps into the aquifer from LANL. Thus radioactivity was the great equalizer in the region: the families in trailers and the ones in cement-block homes were equally at risk. Both pueblos are in the radioactive shadow of the nuclear city and suffer unusually high rates of cancer, especially of the thyroid.

From San Idelfonso to Los Alamos is undoubtedly the most picturesque stretch of the commute. My car slowed as the road began the steep climb. I shifted into third gear as anxious commuters sped past me. I passed through Bandelier National Monument and the juniper-dotted canyons of the Pajarito Plateau. The highway twisted and turned. Every hundred feet or so, I would spot a *descanso* on the side of the road and couldn't help but imagine my own demise. I imagined how easy it would be for my car to slip on a stretch of wintery ice or for my brakes to fail. Envisioning my fall over one of the treacherous cliffs that hugged the highway, I slowed down further, amazed and intimidated by the commuters who continued to pass me with such focused speed, seemingly unaware of the danger. Or, perhaps, the commuters were intimately aware of the danger and sped along with it, along with the idea of risk and loss.

As I entered Los Alamos via Trinity Drive, I recalled the remark frequently made by local Hispanos regarding how incompatible the city was and how it clashed so violently with the rest of northern New Mexico: Los Alamos "didn't belong." The statement was more than just a commentary on its neat wood-framed houses. And it was more than the fact that the land on which LANL sits—acquired or "stolen" by the U.S. government in 1943—belonged to Santa Clara and San Ildefonso Pueblos, as well as heirs of the Spanish Vígil Land Grant. All were relocated to the valley below. It was the people themselves—94 percent Anglo and among the wealthiest and best educated in the country; *they* didn't belong. At least not in a region that is overwhelming Hispano and Native American—a majority population that is nonetheless considered a "minority."

Ultimately, I was late getting to the Fuller Lodge, and the consortium meeting was already under way. I took my seat next to a community activist and great-grandfather from Chimayó who has lost two children and a grandchild to heroin overdose. He leaned over and whispered to me, "Get ready for a fight."

INTIMATE ENEMY

Despite all the symbolic contrasts, the sense of disconnection between Los Alamos and the Hispano villages that surround it only goes so far. Nearly all the Hispanos I interviewed were intimately connected to Los Alamos in some way—usually through a job but also through landscape, imagination (how each imagines the other), and memory. They were also connected to Los Alamos through certain "wounds." Sometimes these wounds were of a corporeal nature, such as the ones suffered by Abel, a retired LANL inspections employee. For more than thirty years, Abel ventured deep into the "Vault," where he monitored containers of hazardous waste. Flashlight in hand, he looked for signs of deterioration or leakage. In the process he was exposed to neuron radiation that far exceeded the "allowable" rate. Abel suffered from stomach cancer, an illness that he and everyone else at the clinic attributed not so much to "the job" as to Los Alamos itself.

At other times the wounds are perhaps more abstract, such as the wounds of colonialism. David, a thirty-five-year-old community activist and agriculturalist, was one of the few Hispanos I knew who grew up in Los Alamos. He "went back to the land" after enduring what he calls a "colonial childhood."

I visited David one late-summer day at his current home in Taos, hoping to talk about his "colonial wounds," but his interest seemed to lay elsewhere. He wanted to talk to me about acequias and their increasing abandonment, which he considered a "cultural scar." As we toured the three-acre property that he inherited from an uncle, David said:

> A generation ago people took pride in working the land. The acequia represented our culture and survival. It was like a parent. We needed the acequia, and the whole community nurtured it. We loved and depended on the acequia. Now, you see them neglected and full of trash. Beer cans, needles, dirty diapers. It *hurts* to see that.

I found it interesting that David would liken the acequia to a parent and talk about need, given that a single mother raised him "off the land." In fact, David's mother made the decision to leave the land and move to

Los Alamos, where she worked, because the commute was too taxing. Plus, she wanted to give her son the benefits of living there: a safe neighborhood and a good public education. Less than 15 percent of Rio Arriba County residents have a bachelor's degree or higher, and one in two students drop out of high school. Los Alamos, by contrast, has the highest rate of Ph.D.'s in the world, and more than 90 percent of its high school graduates go on to receive a four-year college degree.

Like a commuter, David grew up shuttling between his "first world home" in Los Alamos and his "cultural home" in the valley. In Los Alamos he was subjected to racial stereotyping and admits to having felt ashamed of his Hispano roots and his mother's low-level job. But life wasn't much better when he was in the valley, where was made to feel *pocho*—a half-breed who didn't fit in anywhere. The conflicted, subjective state David described was reminiscent of the situation Frantz Fanon (1963: 25) describes, where the constant, painful deliberation of the self in the form of the question, "In reality, who am I?" becomes a crucial battleground for the maintenance of colonial control.[18]

For eighteen years David asked precisely this question of himself as he moved back and forth between these seemingly disparate worlds. He told me he understood the sting Hispanos feel when they leave their communities each morning to work at the laboratory. It's based on necessity, he said matter-of-factly—a more effective way to make ends meet, even if one faces exploitation and stigma on either side of the economic and cultural divide. On the other hand, David resented this necessity, citing, like so many Hispanos do, the psychological and cultural wreckage that ensued. He spoke of his own "broken connection to the land," and he suggested that the figure of the abandoned acequia was symptomatic of the ongoing and unequal relationship between the valley and Los Alamos. "Up there, it's manicured lawns. Down below, things fall apart."

David is now part of a small movement of Hispanos helping youths "get back to their roots." It was a path that he himself took after years of drinking and drifting—living, in his view, the life of a typical Hispano male whose connections to the land were broken by circumstance. "I always had *querencia* [love of the land]," he said.[19] "But I had no idea how to *work* it. I had to learn as an adult because there really wasn't anyone left in my family who could teach me. But it was here." He pounded his heart with his fist as he said this. Today David looks to the past that he was in some ways denied—not as a "relic," but as an engagement with the future. He knows it's a hard sell for many Hispano youths, especially those who are two or more generations removed from agricultural life.

In the afternoon, David guided me through his sprouting rows of garlic and corn and tender bunches of native spinach called *quelite*. We watched the water from the community-controlled acequia form slow-moving streams between his crops. The rows of water glistened in the setting sun. David leaned against a hoe, beer in hand, and contemplated his crops. "The thing is, they're [acequias] etched in the ground here, all over the place. Even when they're full of trash, they're still here."

Across the Española Valley, the abandoned acequias—like the abandoned adobes or the decaying *descansos*—are an image of ruin occasioned by the forced abandonment or loss of a former life. Their ubiquitous presence represents a past that is also the present: absent but remembered, lost but still loved. Whether one calls them relics, scars, or wounds, they represent a permanent awareness of that which was loved and lost in the course of history and may never be returned to, however strong the yearning. And yet the will to reminisce and carry these scars into the present is powerful. David remarked that even in its neglected form, the acequia maintained a certain beauty, maybe even possibility.

MOONRISE

On an early fall afternoon, Joseph announced to me that it was going to be a dry winter. He could tell by the air, he said, by how dry and warm it is, and by how little rain there was over the summer. He pointed to the tiny garden plot that Ricky, his five-year-old son, planted in late spring. The plot was no bigger than a bathtub, but Ricky had big hopes for it. He planted tomatoes and squash, but neither did very well. "It's the land here," Joseph said, as his son lingered within earshot. "It's too dry and rocky. It's not meant to grow." Ricky approached me and asked if I have

Figure 5. Feeding the crops. Photo by the author.

a garden. I told him I did but had the very same problem—too much concrete mixed in with the soil. I could see the look of disappointment on Ricky's moon-shaped face. But he brightened when he told me that his father was going to buy him chickens next year, so that he could gather eggs. "Chickens can live anywhere," Ricky said.

Joseph and Ricky lived in a trailer park on the outskirts of Española. During this visit, Joseph sat on a metal folding chair, his face to the sun. The door to his trailer was ajar, and the strains of northern New Mexican music wafted toward us from the radio inside. It was a Saturday, and, like every weekend, Ricky was in the care of his father. He ran in and out of the trailer, bringing me objects from his bedroom: a tarantula encased in a glass dome, a book about spiders, a leather baseball glove nearly as big as his arm. Joseph suggested that next time he went inside he should bring us a couple of beers.

The telephone rang in the neighboring trailer, less than twenty feet away. I couldn't help but listen as a young woman made plans to meet a friend at a restaurant in town. Joseph tossed his cigarette into an empty beer can and lamented the lack of privacy. Though he had lived in the trailer park for three years, he hadn't gotten used to living in such close quarters. "I didn't grow up like this," he said. "I grew up with a lot of space to run around in, you know?"

Joseph grew up in Hernández, a village about five miles northwest of Española. The photographer Ansel Adams memorialized Joseph's village in what is perhaps his most famous work, *Moonrise, Hernandez, New Mexico.* I described the image to Joseph—the brightly illuminated clouds, the glowing church and cemetery. Joseph shook his head; he was unfamiliar with the photograph, but he knew the cemetery; several of his relatives are buried there. "I used to get high there," he said as he took another sip of beer.

I met Joseph at Nuevo Día's men's support group, a weekly meeting composed of men in various stages of drug recovery. I was allowed access to the meetings in my capacity as a researcher, and I sat as unobtrusively as possible in a back corner, where I was generally (but not always) ignored. The meetings were in a barren room that smelled strongly of cheap coffee. Like the women's group, the meeting was always filled to capacity, sometimes standing room only. Most attendees were under the age of thirty and court appointed. Dressed in "cholo" attire—baggy work pants, sleeveless white undershirts, and flannels—the young men tended to out-talk their elder counterparts—often expressing the challenges of young fatherhood, their disdain of "the system," and the difficulty of staying clean in an environment where heroin seemed to be everywhere. Rarely did the older cohort of men speak up. When they did, it was usually only at the prompting of the meeting facilitator, at which point they would generally describe feeling worn out, tired of having worked a long day, frustrated at not being able to make ends meet at home.

At forty-six, Joseph was equally reticent to speak on his own accord. When he did speak, he held the attention of the younger men. It wasn't until much later that I learned he was a legend of sorts, renowned as much for his voracious heroin habit as his acts of bravado. It was rumored that he killed the man who abused his sister and that he saved another man from a burning house. (Indeed, he had the leathery burn marks on his arms and face to prove this tale, but when I once asked about his scars he changed the subject.) One young addict described Joseph to me as a "badass *tecato*" who, by all accounts, defied Española's drug life by having managed to stay alive.

When I met Joseph he was four years clean and among the group's few "long-term survivors"—that is, he had managed to kick his habit and remain clean. He noted with irony that Hispanos reserve the distinction *"veterano"* for lifelong junkies. But Joseph considered himself a *veterano* in another way. After too many close calls and a tremendous amount of loss, Joseph survived what he calls his own *war*—his war with heroin.

Joseph warned me before my visit to his home that he liked to drink beer, which was not something that he hid from the recovery program. In fact, given his struggles and his commitment to staying off heroin, Joseph frequently told staff members that he *deserved* to drink. On the morning of our interview, he called and asked me to bring him a twelve-pack; not the hard stuff or the fancy stuff, he said, just Bud or Miller Light, whichever was cheaper.

When I arrived at Joseph's trailer, twelve-pack in hand, I immediately noticed a pot of pinto beans simmering on the stove. Leafy plants hung in the narrow windows, and photographs of Joseph's children—ranging in age from five to twenty-seven—were arranged neatly on a handmade bookshelf. Looking around the tidy trailer, I asked Joseph if he lived with anyone else, imagining that the domestic touches were the work of a girlfriend or a wife. Joseph knew what I was thinking and, challenging my stereotypical assumptions, told me there hadn't been a woman in his life since he split with Ricky's mother four years earlier.

I try to make this place nice for my son for when he's here. And for me, too. . . . When I was in *la pinta* [prison] there was nothing. Nothing green except the piss blanket they gave you for your bed. There was no comfort. *Nada, nada.* Most of my life was like that, you know. *Hard.*

Joseph continued:

When you're a junkie you don't care about these kinds of things. You don't think about your kids or your home or nothing like that. Your only comfort is heroin. But when you kick [quit heroin], you need something else. I'm not talking beer or pills or whatever keeps you from going insane. You need a life. This is what I got right now. Here, *like this* [referring to his trailer]. It's not where I want to die. But it is what it is. It's what I got.

Joseph and I spent the afternoon outside, sitting side by side in the green canvas chairs he used for camping. He told me that he only recently began to spend time in the outdoors again, hunting and camping with his eldest son, Ray, who he was estranged from during his drug years, which amounted to most of Ray's life. Staring at his son Ricky, Joseph told me he regretted the years he missed with his older children and that he regretted not being a father to his children in the way that *his* father was to him: present, disciplined, and unyielding in his values.

But life "back then" was easier, Joseph reasoned—easier, even if it was extremely hard. His entire family struggled to make ends meet, yet there was cohesiveness in that struggle—a sense of purpose and unity in caring for each other, for the house, and for the land. There was always so much to do, Joseph recalled: sow the fields, gather firewood, patch the adobe walls, in addition to odd jobs in town. There wasn't time for drugs.

Joseph absent-mindedly knocked on the metal wall of his rented trailer with his bronze-colored fist. And then he began to describe his home in Hernández, where he lived from the time he was born until he was twenty; the home his grandfather built. He recalled how, from one of the deep-set windows in that house, he could see a portion of an adobe wall from the *original* house his ancestors had lived in. Joseph remembered his grandmother nagging her husband to tear the wall down. But his grandfather refused, saying the wall was a part of history.

There is something of his grandfather's refusal in Joseph's recollections of life "back then," for, occasionally, when he talked about the past, he slipped into present tense—as if his deceased relatives were still alive, as if he still lived in Hernández, on the land. But more often than not, Joseph emphasized *then* and *now* with authority. His story, like those of many of his generation, was full of temporal signposts, many of them pointing out the way the land had changed. *The road back then was unpaved. That store didn't exist. There used to be an apple orchard there.*

In Joseph's case, the signposts were more than spatial; they also related to his drug history, one intimately linked to a changing familial, political, and economic landscape. "I started shooting about thirty years ago. Thirty years," he said in disbelief. "It was the mid-seventies, I guess. Some of my buddies came back from Vietnam, the real *veteranos.* That's how I started. That's who showed me."

During the Vietnam War, Hernández and the surrounding villages of the Española Valley, depleted by the draft, resembled ghost towns. Joseph's older brother was among the nearly 850,000 young men chosen during a "draft lottery" in 1969. Less than a year later, he would die in the American incursion into Cambodia. Joseph was eleven years old at the time. He told me his brother wasn't soldier material; he was groomed for traditional agriculture and fixing cars—for shooting elk, not men.

While most of the Hispano men who left for Vietnam eventually returned, each village experienced some loss relating to the war. Soldiers who returned had a difficult time resuming life as it had been, not only because they had been deeply affected—psychologically and sometimes physically—by their experiences during the war, but also because life back home had changed, too. Indeed, it was during the war that many Hispano families, such as Joseph's, began parceling off and selling land. Joseph described a scenario in which selling land wasn't merely related to the fact that there was an economic need and fewer people to work the fields; there was a shift in the experience and meaning of family life. "It was a hard time," Joseph said, alluding to the many miseries a family suffers with the loss of a loved one and the loss of livelihood and tradition. He added with bitter irony that from the late 1960s through the mid-1970s many of the people who began buying these familial lands were "draft dodgers" or "hippie types" who had come to northern New Mexico seeking refuge from Vietnam and its political and cultural repercussions.

But there was no refuge for Joseph, or for the Vietnam *veteranos* who would become his drug buddies. Joseph was reticent to talk about those early years of drug use, perhaps because they were so intimately tied to Vietnam and memories of his splintering family and lost brother. But it was through those experiences that Joseph would come to be a *veterano* himself. It is a local distinction that he remained deeply ambivalent about. He told me that he doesn't understand why Hispanos continue to valorize the *tecato*, adding disdainfully that it doesn't take bravery to shoot up, overdose, and die.[20] And yet he understood powerfully and viscerally how heroin addiction—much like war—can take over one's life, as well as the life of one's family and community. I suggested that perhaps that's why we make *veteranos* out of addicts—to give that experience a framework of meaning. "Maybe," Joseph shrugged.

Though he was reluctant to give me much detail, Joseph said that for more than twenty years he lived what he called the "hard and useless life" of a *tecato*. He had three children, none of whom he fathered in any meaningful way. He held odd dead-end jobs, all of which he quit or was fired from. His relations with his family were nearly nonexistent during those years, mostly because of his own doing. He says he never had a death wish, but neither did he care about his life. In a way his addiction to heroin prevented him from feeling anything—not even the knife wound in his side or the burn of fire on his skin.

> Those years [1980s and 1990s] were tough. I could tell you a bunch of stories, but what's the point? I will tell you I spent a lot of that time *en la pinta*. There wasn't no drug court then. If what you did was bad enough, you just went to jail. For a long time, I got away with stuff, but at some point your luck runs out. Well, my luck ran out.

Joseph was sentenced to the New Mexico State Penitentiary in Santa Fe for burglary in 1994. When I asked him about this period, he looked at me wryly and replied, "What's there to say? I was locked up," as if the fact should speak for itself. Eventually he told me that throughout his six-year sentence his heroin use continued, though it was more intermittent, given the irregularities of the prison drug trade.

His breaks from heroin offered him a period of reflection, though always short-lived. One of the things he acknowledged thinking about during these interludes was his family's home in Hernández, which his mother sold in 1998, after the death of his father. From his prison cell, Joseph could remember everything about that house—each fissure in the adobe wall, each creak of the floorboard. I asked Joseph if since his release in 2000 he ever returned to the family home in Hernández. "What's the point?" he said. "It's not ours no more."

And yet Joseph called to his son Ricky to bring out the photograph of "the house in Hernández." Ricky ran back into the trailer and returned with a small, well-worn photo, which he gingerly placed in my hand. The photograph felt like silk. I studied the yellowing image of Joseph, his two brothers, and their father standing before a large woodpile stacked neatly against an adobe wall. "How old are you here?" I asked Joseph. He popped open another beer and, without looking at the photograph, told me that he was ten years old.

MEANING IN MELANCHOLIA

Despite the advances made in the study of melancholia since Freud, there remains an implicit understanding that the melancholic subject is trapped in affect and incapable of sublimating the pain of past loss so that he may live meaningfully in the present. Even melancholia's contemporary interlocutors tend to agree that such sublimation can occur only through the process of narrativization—such as in analysis or art—through which the past is resurrected but with the intent to vitalize the present (Ruti 2005; Silverman 2000). In this conception the past, though unearthed for its potentiality in the present, is simultaneously laid to rest. To tend to the past as such, to remain loyal to it without this presentist perspective, is to remain its prisoner and to live a life as a partially realized subject.

This seems to me a rather liberal view of how loss and the past structures subjectivity. The idea that the past must be relinquished and/or appropriated to serve as the foundation for the present echoes Nietzsche's work on the liberatory uses of forgetting. In his work "On the Uses and

Disadvantages of History for Life," Nietzsche writes that when the past "attains a certain degree of excess life crumbles and degenerates" (1997: 67). He calls for the abandonment of the past because it "returns as a ghost and disturbs the peace of a later moment" (61). Much like contemporary theorists of melancholy, Nietzsche suggests a critical discourse on the past that would be attentive to the needs of the present and proposes that one "actively forget" those haunting moments—again, so as not to disturb the potential of the later moment.

To a certain degree, the narratives of Alma and Joseph attest to the tensions of trying to live the past in the present. There are moments when both attempt to relinquish certain aspects of the past for the sake of a more livable (though not necessarily more meaningful) life. However, the past remains a fundamental force in everyday experience, and it is not a force that is "appropriated" in the goal of defining a future or that teaches how to self-actualize or even heal. Rather, their past, which is undeniably filled with the sorrow of loss, is experienced *as such*: painful, heavyhearted, and sometimes seemingly endless. Does it mean that to be passionately engaged with the past on its own terms, one necessarily sacrifices the potential for a present and even sacrifices the self? Can one live a melancholy life that is meaningful on its own terms?

Alma's and Joseph's commitment to the past and to certain losses in particular has not precluded them from living in the present. It is through the experience of melancholy that Alma and Joseph are, in my view, living a moral life—that is, a locally and interpersonally engaged life, however precarious these engagements may be. "Seeing the world as dangerous and uncertain may lead to a kind of quiet liberation," Arthur Kleinman (2006: 10) writes, "preparing us for new ways of being ourselves, living in the world, and making a difference in the lives of others." I would add that seeing and experiencing the world and the past as painful—and to not appropriate, forget, or sublimate this pain for other purposes—is likewise a way of living in the world. In other words, there is meaning in melancholia, meaning in wounds that haven't healed, perhaps may never heal.

THREE Blood Relative

On a warm summer evening, a dozen women gather in a community center in the village of Chimayó. There are ten support group participants, the facilitator, and me. The participants are heroin addicts who have been court appointed to attend this group as a condition of their drug sentence, which in most cases stemmed from a possession-related offense. We sit on tattered couches positioned in the form of a triangle. The facilitator asks the two new members to introduce themselves. Of course, they are not really new. As it is with most of the women gathered together on this evening, they have been court appointed to this same group on more than one occasion.

By way of introduction the younger of the two women, Bernadette, rolls up her shirtsleeve and exposes the track marks that line her forearm.

She traces the constellation of injection sites with a finger, lingering on her tenderest wounds. A few of the marks have sprouted swollen, purplish peaks—*coronas* (crowns), as heroin-related abscesses are sometimes called locally. "I was born with these," she says of her scars. The woman sitting beside Bernadette watches her pick at her skin. She tells the group that she is Bernadette's mother and later introduces herself as Eugenia. The order of introduction is relevant. Eugenia began shooting heroin with Bernadette when she was sixteen, and the two have been using together ever since. Their affiliation as kin and as "co-addicts" precedes the establishment of an autonomous self, the premise of personhood that most behavioral and biomedical models of recovery assume, and reveals an ethics of kinship premised on discourses and practices of intergenerational heroin use.

Theirs is not an unusual arrangement among Hispano heroin users in northern New Mexico's Española Valley. Here the biological family is a primary domain of heroin use, and the circulation of the drug therein is described as maintaining kinship ties, if not affirming them. At one point a young woman named Jennifer admits that although she knows how to avoid the bacteria that can lead to the painful skin inflammation, she takes comfort in her heroin-related wounds (and thus presumably induces them). She says she feels as if *coronas* sustain her connections to the family members she has loved—and lost—to heroin overdose.

Such practices and sentiments stand in contrast to popular representations of heroin addicts in which kinship ties are sacrificed by the purported social and moral demands that accompany heroin use.[1] Whether by necessity or choice, the supporting and intimate roles generally attributed to kin are supplanted by the figure of the "running partner," the trusted co-addict who helps score drugs and shares in risky behavior—needles, street crime, and sex. Similarly, many anthropological studies of heroin addicts describe addicts as isolated from biological or "traditional" family ties, a consequence of the fragmentation of social and intimate life that frequently accompanies addiction (Bourgois and Schonberg 2009; Johnson 2006; Reyes 1995).[2]

Indeed, no one at the support group is surprised to hear about Bernadette and Eugenia's relationship. There are always other mother-daughter pairs present—other family jewels etched into flesh.

And yet, over the course of the two-hour meeting, the participants describe in various ways feeling obscured by a local representational economy that remains decidedly male. They express feelings of invisibility and frustration and talk about feeling burdened by the stigmatizing labels associated with being a heroin-addicted woman. A young woman named Marta explains how this representational economy works. Regarding her status as female junkie, she says, "It's like, people think you're already half-dead. They think they know everything about you and there's nothing left to know . . . except you use [heroin]. That's all they think or see."

When the facilitator asks Marta how it is that people know and can see that she is a heroin addict, she gestures to her body. "Look at my arms!" she cries as she rolls up her shirtsleeve to reveal a forearm laced with track marks. "You can tell by the arms. And when you're high or *grifo* [strung out], it's in your eyes, *no*? And I'm skinny, too. *Yo parezco un tecato* [I look like a heroin addict]."

In referring to her body as appearing like that of a heroin addict, Marta relied on the masculine noun *tecato* (junkie), a term that has no feminine equivalent. This *apparent* life of addiction, like the language on which it relies, assumes a certain masculine form. Marta's track marks and thinness and what she refers to as her *"macha"* (masculine) body—gestured in the touching of her flat chest—speak to both the physical and performative dimensions of addicted life.[3]

At this point Bernadette stretches out her arms and boldly announces, "*Me parezco a* ella [I look like *her*]. *She* looks like *me*." Emphasizing her resemblance to her mother and her mother's resemblance to her, Bernadette has begun to rewrite the script of the *tecato*. She has begun to make room for the experiences and relations of and between addicted female kin. Her reinsertion of the feminine and the relational resonates with Luce Irigaray's (1985) claim that although female relations remain caught in a masculine symbolic, that symbolic system is never entirely closed. Irigaray emphasizes the need for a different syntax and politics of discourse so that previously "muted" women, and relations between women, can "speak."

"I look like her. She looks like me."

.   .   .   .   .

This chapter provides an opening to this closed representational economy of addiction by examining the feminine and familial context of heroin use. In the pages that follow, I look at the particular economic, historic, and/or affective burdens that become factors in women's heroin use, and in the use of heroin between generations of women. Focusing on the addictive experience for mother-daughter pairs, I frame addictive experience and the constitution of the addictive subject not through alienation or autonomy, as it is so frequently represented, but in heteronomy—of and between generations of women. This focus on feminine experiences of heroin addiction is a necessary and overdue reworking of the persistent archetypes of heroin addicts that operate on the local level, as well as more broadly. Moreover, by presenting intergenerational addiction as part of the biological, social, and affective mix that is kinship, I show how heroin works through, and provides endurance for, ties of blood and property, of *inheritance*. In doing so, I challenge certain local commitments to notions of kinship, tradition, and inheritance, which are still conceived of as passing in the name of the father. This last point requires elaboration.

In the local idiom, the notion of inheritance—*querencia*—is both material and psychic. It is a value, a practice, and a structure of feeling whose etymological roots blend the notions of heritage, land, and love. *Querencia* is employed in many ways, such as when elder Hispanos describe their emotional connectedness to place or tradition. *It's my querencia,* they might say, speaking of a certain village or agricultural practice. Alternatively, querencia can suggest the transmission of affective traits or material goods from one generation to the next. As an analytic of both kinship and inheritance, *querencia* embraces pragmatic and experiential meanings. And as property still typically passes through the male line, the conduit of *querencia* is similarly conceived of as passing in the name of the father.

In the preceding chapter, I examined disruptions to long-standing forms of inheritance, in particular, property, through processes of economic and cultural dispossession. Nevertheless, while the material basis for *querencia* has been largely lost, the tradition of querencia endures. Indeed, it is in this matrix that younger heroin addicts describe their addiction to heroin as their *"nueva querencia,"* that is, a new practice and ethics of kinship that centers not on inheritance of property but on the heritable experience of addiction. The shifting meaning of inheritance highlights how intergenerational heroin use is a life-affirming project but one that is also tied into injury, loss, and even death.

In seeking to understand the place of heroin addiction in contemporary Hispano kin relations, as well as how ideas and practices of parenting and care are mediated by heroin, I point to this history of dispossession as a possible way to conceptualize the intrinsic connection among history, intergenerational heroin use, and emergent forms of inheritance. In other words, I show how the contemporary practice of intergenerational heroin use, and the thorough integration of addictive experience into the fabric of everyday family life, is inseparable from the region's history of dispossession. And yet it is in part through this history of dispossession, through heroin, that a long-silenced maternal genealogy emerges.

BERNADETTE AND EUGENIA: THE INHERITANCE OF MALADIES

> I was born a heroin addict. It's in my blood.
>
> Bernadette Martinez

Bernadette Martinez's single-wide trailer sits on an acre of hard dirt in the village of Hernández, approximately five miles north of Española. A half-dozen rusted cars flank each side of the trailer, and a trampoline sits in what was once, perhaps, a backyard. Beneath the trailer's underbelly, a dog hides from the punishing sun. He looks at me suspiciously as I approach the pyramid of bricks that forms the staircase to the front door. A red gardenia sprouts from a tin can on each step.

At the sound of my knocking, Bernadette yells, *"¡Pasa!"* (Come in!) Inside, the trailer's wood-paneled walls seem to absorb all trace of outdoor light. As my eyes slowly adjust to the darkness, I notice that the walls are covered with small framed images—mostly landscapes: a field of sunflowers, a farmhouse surrounded by leafy oak trees, a glacier fingering out into an arctic sea. There are a few family photographs, too, one of which is of Bernadette's mother, Eugenia, who squints against the sun. In the faded image, Bernadette, then four, sits in her mother's arms, her head resting in the curve of her neck. Bernadette catches me staring at the photograph when she emerges from the trailer's narrow hallway. She's dressed in cut-off jeans and a tight pink tank top. Her hair is pulled back tight, and her green eyes are lined in black. I point to the picture and ask, *Is this you?* Bernadette smiles a yes and shows me another photo—this time of her own daughter, taken at about the same age. The physical resemblance is striking.

For some reason, Bernadette thinks I've been to her trailer before. When she finds out I haven't, she offers me a tour. I follow her from the tiny kitchenette with its pale green appliances to the furniture-stuffed living room, on to the two small bedrooms (one for her older son, the other for her and her daughter), and, finally, to the bathroom at the very end. There is a water pitcher and wastebasket by the shower, and Bernadette warns me to not throw paper down the toilet. The septic tank is on the outs again, and she can't afford to have it repaired. I tell her I understand the problem, but she demonstrates a flush anyway, just in case.

I first met Bernadette at Nuevo Día's women's support group in spring 2004. She had just been arrested on drug possession charges and was placed on house arrest while awaiting trial. On this day, an electronic monitoring device that Bernadette calls her "leash" is fastened around her ankle. The bracelet emits radio signals through her telephone line when she leaves her trailer. Both her probation officer and the county police read these signals and determine their legality. Bernadette's only "legal" or approved time away from home is to attend the support group and to meet with her drug counselor and probation officer. Still, she steals moments between her approved visits—a trip to Walmart, lunch at Sonic, a quick visit with her children who are under the care of a relative. But these are just moments. These days, nearly all Bernadette's time is spent alone in her trailer, which has been transformed into a "confinement area." It is no longer a home.

It's hot in Bernadette's trailer. We sit in the living room and drink Coke from the can. Bernadette complains that the monitor hurts her ankle, and she shows me her swollen, irritated flesh. I ask if the bracelet can be loosened, and she points out that it's already on the last rung. It's her lupus, she says. She's been feeling lousy lately, and her joints have swelled. She shows me the rash that cuts across her face and chest. "Two minutes in the sun, and this is what I get. And the only thing I can do besides sit in here is sit out there." Bernadette admits that she's come close to cutting the monitor off several times, but the threat of an early jail sentence stops her. And yet sometimes she wonders if jail would be the same as *this*—being stuck inside, alone.

To my surprise, Bernadette tells me I'm her first visitor in almost two weeks. No one comes around anymore, she says, not since "the party ended." She adds that her mother hasn't come by with the groceries she promised. Her pantry is nearly empty, and she asks me if next time I might bring her a few things—some peanut butter and tortillas, some Kotex and maybe a few magazines.

Bernadette asks if I've seen her mother lately. She wants to know if she's showing up at her meetings at the drug treatment center. I don't tell her the rumors that I've heard about her mother's worsening drug use.

"I don't know why she doesn't call anymore," Bernadette says.

Tears

According to the notes kept by Bernadette's drug counselor, Eugenia began smoking heroin when her daughter was twelve years old. At that time the two lived together in a small adobe house in Chimayó. I asked Bernadette about her mother's early heroin use, but she wanted me to know about her mother *before* heroin—when things were, in her words, *all right.*

"I was like in seventh grade," Bernadette says. "She worked at Bealls' [a department store in Española]. She had this car, and it was always breaking down or had no gas. Sometimes she walked to work or got rides, you know, hitched . . . she liked her job and was always bringing me these cute clothes. She got them on discount. She didn't steal. She was so pretty back then, you wouldn't believe it. And she always smelled real nice. It's crazy that I can remember her smell. She had this perfume—I can't remember what its called."

Bernadette described the tempo and texture of her and her mother's life before heroin in great detail. She described the house in Chimayó—the sunflowers that bloomed in the yard and the series of stray dogs that became beloved pets. She recalled events (her first period; the way her mother embraced her) and celebrations (birthday parties and Halloween costumes). When there were photographs that corresponded to memories, Bernadette pulled them out and shared them with me. She painted a scene of her childhood that seemed, for the most part, idyllic—a mother and daughter living alone, without a lot of money but with an abundance of love and dignity.

According to her narrative, men were entirely absent from their lives. I asked Bernadette if she knew or missed her father. She told me no. I asked her if she knew of anything that had happened that might have led her mother to heroin. Again, she said she didn't know. "My mom didn't hang around *tecatos*," she said defensively. "I mean, they were always all around, but she didn't associate. She kept her distance, you know?"

I sensed that it was Bernadette who was keeping her distance—from certain memories and from me. She didn't want to talk about why her mother began using heroin and became increasingly frustrated with my questions. "Look, it's just like things were good and then they weren't," she said. "I don't know what was going on. Sometimes people just do stupid things for no reason and you can't go back . . . can you turn that fucking thing off [gesturing to my tape recorder]?"

I turned the recorder off. Bernadette fished another cigarette butt out of an ashtray; she was out of cigarettes and was tired of smoking butts. She asked me to bring her a carton of Native cigarettes on my next visit and reminded me to get them at the pueblo where they were considerably cheaper. I told her I would.

With the recorder off and after some silence, Bernadette told me that the only thing she could think of was the crying. Her mother cried a lot, and the crying grew more frequent. It got to the point, Bernadette said, where the tears wouldn't stop.

. . . . .

Inactive patient files were kept in a locked basement room of Nuevo Día's main office. The room was stuffed with rusted filing cabinets, the contents of which dated to 1973. Because the files were organized by calendar year and not by patient name, I had to consult hundred of files to locate a specific person. There was little room in the basement to sit and read. When I found a file marked "Eugenia Martinez," I pulled it out and trudged upstairs to a small office space. This was how I began piecing together a narrative for Bernadette's mother.

From these files I learned that between the years 1992 and 2004 Eugenia had either sought or was court appointed to drug counseling or treatment a total of nine times. In one entry Eugenia reports that a boyfriend introduced her to heroin when she was twenty-eight. Another entry says she began using heroin with a female friend at twenty-two and that her habit was "approximately 80 dollars a day." In 1996 she is described as being "physically addicted" and "a danger to herself." In 2001 a municipal judge labeled her "a repeat offender," and, over the years, numerous physicians diagnosed her as either clinically, severely, or manic depressed. And yet, despite twelve years of entries, the files offered little information about Eugenia's life. Not once is there mention of her daughter. Not once is there mention of events that may have contributed to her depression or addiction.

There was, however, a brief note and accompanying police documents describing an event that occurred in 2003: a drug raid at Eugenia's trailer. The details of the raid were piecemeal at best. According to the note, police had been "tipped off" by a concerned neighbor regarding drug trafficking activity. There had been several previous "domestic disturbances," though none of them appears to have been followed up or investigated by the police. The police document lists the date and time of the raid. Six officers were at the scene, including two from the state drug enforcement agency. On entry into the trailer, they discovered approximately three ounces of black tar heroin, which had a street value of approximately $5,000. Small quantities of marijuana and drug paraphernalia—syringes, "cookers," and papers to divide and wrap heroin bundles—were also found. At the time of the drug bust, Eugenia was not home. A woman referred to as "Bernadette Martinez" was present, and she was arrested without incident. Her relation to Eugenia was not noted.

Bernadette was present; Eugenia was not. This would become a major factor in the sentencing of both women when they eventually went to court and appeared before a judge. It is at this point that their blood relation would finally be described: Eugenia, the mother and owner of the trailer; and Bernadette, the daughter and temporary occupant. Of the two, Bernadette would receive the harsher sentence. She was at the scene and high on heroin at the time of the bust.

The Promise

More than a year after the drug raid, while sitting in Bernadette's trailer, I asked her where her mother was the day of the raid. She told me that her mother says that she was in Albuquerque, supposedly looking for work. But Bernadette admitted she sometimes doubts the truth of this story.

I asked why she should suffer the consequences if the trailer and the drugs belonged to her mother. Bernadette lit a cigarette and, after a long pause, described to me the *"conpromiso"* (commitment) she and her mother forged long ago—a commitment to ease each other's pains, to alleviate *las malias* that are produced by and treated with heroin. It was because of this commitment that she took responsibility for the drugs.

"My mom had more to lose than me," she said, her voice trailing off. She explained that Eugenia suffered from depression and had attempted suicide. She worried that the punitive consequences of the drug bust might be too much for her mother to withstand, so she took—via a code of silence—responsibility for the drugs. The silence was intended to protect her mother, who she insisted was then the more vulnerable of the two. But Bernadette was also a mother, was also vulnerable—as were her own children. Watching Bernadette fiddle with her ankle bracelet, it was clear that in caring for her mother her relationship to her own children, as well as to the larger social world, was threatened.

These kinds of ethical transactions are common among addicts, who must continually weigh a sense of obligation and concern for kin against the social and legal implications that accompany heroin use. Bernadette and Eugenia's *conpromiso* offers an alternative frame for thinking about the relation between kinship, law, and care and recalls John Borneman's (1997) formulation, "caring and being cared for," which was part of his project to reframe the assumptions of law and kinship. It is in a similar manner that I understand Bernadette and Eugenia as improvising forms of care amid physical and financial need, the threat of incarceration, individual vulnerability, and family responsibility. I suggest, too, that their ethic of "promise" has led to practices of care that are not always remedial, and which bring unexpected, even dangerous, consequences. The point I want to make is that the complexity of addictive experience, especially as it shared within families, creates new "codes of conduct" (Schneider 1980). Addiction solidifies the relationships between some members while breaking or refusing relationships with others. Indeed, this is the very structure of kinship. Kinship operates as a matrix of forms of inclusion and exclusion, through which we derive a particular sense and practice of being and belonging.

During my visits to her trailer, Bernadette began to weave for me the story of her heroin use (a story that in the clinical setting is called a "drug history"—thus oddly framing the *subject* of history with an object). As she did, it became clear to me that her story hinged on a deeper history, the history of an other—namely, her mother. Her account was hesitant. She spoke in stops and starts, occasionally revising or refuting previous statements. It was as if she had not quite worked out the meaning of certain events: events that involve her, her mother, both of them. Her inability, or unwillingness, to narrate "fully" seems to indicate how she is, from the start, implicated in the life of someone else, a someone else who is implicated in her life, too. This is a point Judith Butler (2005: 64) makes when she writes, "We are constituted in relationality: implicated, beholden, derived, sustained by a social world that is beyond us and before us."

Together, Alone

On one visit, I found Bernadette waiting for me on her trailer's makeshift stoop. Winter was approaching—the air chilled and the sky heavy with clouds. Bernadette wore a thick hooded sweatshirt and tight jeans. While she helped me retrieve bags of groceries from my car, I noticed that she appeared considerably thinner since I had last seen her two months earlier. Bernadette asked me what took so long, why I hadn't come by any sooner. I told her I had been in Texas, where my fiancé worked. "It's not right for him to leave you," she said.

Inside her trailer, Bernadette promptly lit a cigarette from the carton I brought at her request. Between drags, she explained that her sentencing was fast approaching and she was nervous. She was afraid of going to jail and losing her kids for good. "I think this is it," she said.

We made ham and cheese sandwiches and sat down to eat in the living room. The only light in the room came from the reflected images from a television set, which we huddled before, as if it were a fire. Bernadette ate her sandwich quickly and got up to make another. It wasn't that she was hungry, she said, it was that the food in jail was the worst. Bernadette was preparing to go to jail.

As before, Bernadette asked me if I had seen or heard anything about her mother. I hadn't seen Eugenia, but I told Bernadette that it was because she had entered a long-term residential drug treatment program located in the village of Alcalde, about ten miles north of Española. Ironically, the facility was once known as Swan Lake Ranch, a walled adobe compound that was a favorite resort of Hollywood stars in the 1930s and 1940s. Clark Gable, Carole Lombard, and the Barrymores frequently vacationed there, and in many ways the compound still looks like a set from a movie. Within the property, manicured terraces encircle the famous man-made lakes that draw water from the nearby Rio Grande. There are still strutting peacocks and a grand hacienda. Despite the vestiges of a bygone era, the air of leisure and wealth is gone.[4]

Bernadette told me I must not have heard the latest on her mother, who is now living at Española's Church of Our Savior. "She cleans it and has been converted or something. She told me she's being saved. That's why she don't talk to me. The elders won't let her. She says I'm *lost*."[5]

I asked Bernadette if she feels betrayed by Eugenia. She looked at me from across the darkened living room and said that her mom's just doing the best she can.

.   .   .   .   .

From time to time, I visited Eugenia at the church at the request of Bernadette, who was still confined to house arrest. She worried about her mother, fearing that she had sunken into another deep depression. Despite their devotion to each other, there was a gulf between them. They refrained from seeing each other: partly because of the tensions surrounding the drug bust, partly because the church in which Eugenia now lived demanded that she "break relations" with her daughter, and partly because they had been ordered to stay apart by their respective probation officers. In the months before Bernadette's trial, I functioned as a kind of go-between, trafficking messages of worry and love.

On one afternoon, when I visited Eugenia at Bernadette's request, I found Eugenia just as her daughter imagined her to be. Her face was drawn, her voice flat. The church was empty, and Eugenia was dressed in nothing more than a T-shirt emblazoned with the face of Mickey Mouse. She made no effort to cover her bare legs, and I could see that her thighs were heavily scarred from "skin popping," a subcutaneous injection practice common among heroin users who have difficulty accessing their veins. Eugenia guided me through the church's modest congregation room, to a back patio with a fold-out table and chairs. She lit a cigarette and told me that I had awakened her from a nap. She was tired, she said, because earlier that morning her brother had come to pick her up and take her to the Chimayó cemetery. I knew the cemetery well. It was a desolate stretch of land enlivened with colorful plastic flowers and ironwork-bordered plots.

It was the anniversary of her father's death. I told Eugenia that Bernadette had not forgotten the anniversary and handed her a small photo that Bernadette asked me to deliver. The photo depicted an image of a much younger Eugenia, dressed in cut-off jeans and a flannel shirt tied around her slender waist. In her arms was Bernadette. The two posed in front of the house Eugenia inherited from her father. Eugenia studied the photo. After a period of silence, she said, "I was named after him, Eugenio [referring to her father]. It's an old-timey name. Eugenia, Eugenio." Such names and naming practices are common in the Española Valley and seem to bear the symbolism of permanence in changing times.

I asked Eugenia what happened to the house. She set the photo down on a small table that separated us and told me, simply, that it was gone.

·   ·   ·   ·   ·

Unlike with Bernadette, my visits with Eugenia were intermittent and brief. She was more reserved than her daughter, and her weathered face and graying black hair seemed to convey a world-weariness that Bernadette, despite her many troubles, had not yet assumed. I was curious about Eugenia's story and had to glean information about her through conversations with Bernadette and by consulting Eugenia's extensive patient files. On one occasion I cared for Eugenia at the detox clinic, after a probation officer determined that her urine test was dirty for heroin. She stayed at the clinic for a week and remained in bed during most of my twelve-hour shift. Every night she would ask permission to use the telephone, then speak Bernadette's or her brother's telephone number as I dialed the number for her. Like an overseas operator, I established the connection, then handed the telephone to Eugenia, who spoke in low tones, her hand self-consciously covering her mouth. It was through our rare conversations, documents, and moments that I began to piece together something of a narrative for Eugenia—one that seemed to echo and enable the narratives of others.

Take, if you will, the house that Eugenia inherited from her father, the house in Chimayó. I visited that house more than once, drawn there for reasons I didn't quite understand. I would park my car on the road's sloping shoulder and take in the image: the fading pink adobe walls (Eugenia's brother had painted the house for her years ago, when it was still in her possession); the dented tin roof; the neglected apricot trees in the front and backyard that still bore fruit. Someone else lived there now.

I knew that Eugenia's mother died in that house when Eugenia was four years old, leaving Eugenio to raise his three children there: Eugenia, the eldest child and only daughter, and two younger brothers,

Raymundo (Ray) and Johnny. Like many residents of Chimayó in the 1940s, Eugenio worked as a weaver and a farmer, selling his wares out of a street-side shed. Weaving, like agriculture, was a trade he had inherited from *his* father, who had, in turn, also inherited it—and so the story goes, according to Ray, for eight generations.

It was Ray who filled me in on many of the details of Eugenio's life and suggested to me that it was "probably all written down somewhere." I consulted the state archive and, in fact, much of what Ray told me was preserved in its microfiche documents. I learned, for instance, that Eugenio was the first of the Martinezes not to have inherited the land, on which traditional inheritance practices were based: that is, the communal holdings of Nuestra Señora del Rosario Land Grant, established in 1751, to which Eugenio and his children were heirs. Depending on who you talk to, this communal land was either "sold" or stolen. Whatever the case may be, what is undeniable is that with the loss of these lands came a steep decline in family fortunes and community well-being. Each family that had used and cared for the collective land—whether for agriculture, timber, water, or grazing—was now forced to rely on its private holdings, which often were extremely limited. Subsequent to the loss of the communal lands, family livestock holdings decreased sharply, and state assistance programs that provided food were introduced in the region. New tensions to which families were subjected emerged. For example, without access to the ancestral lands, the sheep Eugenio raised, for their milk and wool, lived in the Martinez yard, alongside their shrinking plot of crops. Eugenio was forced to seek work outside his village, and in his absence his children led the sheep through Chimayó and into the hills and steep ravines that surrounded their home. School, Eugenia once told me, felt like a burden. It interfered with the time she needed to help provide for her family.

During my visit on the anniversary of her father's death, I asked Eugenia to tell me more about growing up in Chimayó. She looked at me in frustration and answered that she wasn't from *Chimayó* but from *Los Martinez*. Her response marked an important distinction that I had obscured. One didn't "grow up" or "reside" in a particular village; rather, one lived in Los Martinez, Los Rendones, Los Luceros—communities *within* communities that were composed entirely of kin. Many of the rituals and activities that produced social cohesion in the valley were tied to these kin-based communities. They were the center of social and economic life and the conduit through which land, language, and tradition were transferred and maintained. In tracing her roots to Los Martinez, which has never existed on U.S. or state maps, Eugenia reveals the materiality of places past or unseen.[6] I wondered now about the potentialities of these places, about the multiple and contingent ways they continue to shape the present and the future. How does one trace particular practices and feelings through which people are presently engaged to inherited forms of life that no longer exist?

Toward the end of our visit, Eugenia picked up the photograph from the table. As she stared at the image of her father's house—her house— she asked me about Bernadette. Is she okay? Did I visit her often? Is she afraid? I answered her questions to the best of my ability, even suggesting that she call or visit her daughter (and then regretted this suggestion, fearing the legal consequences). Eugenia shook her head no. She knew better. She looked at the photograph for a few silent moments and then extended her arm toward me. "Here. Give this to Bernadette," she said. "It belongs to her."

.   .   .   .   .

According to Bernadette, the thing I don't understand is that no one wants to end up like this; no one thinks it'll get this bad. And there are moments in between the bad times that make it all worth it. I tell her that *this* is what I don't understand—those moments that offset pain. Bernadette explains:

> When I was a teenager, I don't know, like twelve, that's when I really knew there was something going on with my mom, you know, with drugs. She'd be crying all the time and sick with *las malias*. She didn't go to work no more, and I started staying home from school, you know, to try to take care of her, make sure nothing worse happened. But there was nothing I could do. She'd cry for her *medicina*. That's what she called it . . . It's not that I didn't know any different [the difference between

drugs and "legitimate" medicine]. It's that I wanted her to feel better. That's all that mattered. And I was afraid she was going to die. I was afraid, and the only thing you feel like you can do is help get them high.

It was because of her desire to help ease her mother's pain—to save her—that Bernadette began scoring drugs. At first she simply made what seemed like innocent telephone calls, often to family or friends. "I'd tell them my mom needed *'medicina'* and they knew what I meant, before I knew." According to Bernadette, once Eugenia got her hit of heroin, everything would return to normal. She would stop crying, and they would sit together on the couch and quietly watch TV until they both fell asleep, usually with Bernadette in her mother's arms.

As Eugenia's addiction worsened, scoring drugs became more difficult. Her connections were no longer willing to support her habit. With no job, Eugenia began to sell things—jewelry, dishes, furniture, eventually the adobe house in Chimayó she had inherited from her father and shared with Bernadette. Bernadette remembers:

> Every day it was something else. Something would be gone. She would get rid of things when I wasn't home. I'd say, *Where are the chairs?* and she'd make up some lie, like, *They need to be fixed, Uncle Ray will bring them back,* but nothing ever came back. . . .
>
> Sometimes she would be gone two, three days. Disappear. I was scared when she'd be gone, *no?* I was worried about her, *pero* the only thing I could do was stay with friends or with my *tío.* That's how I ate, you know, how I took baths and stuff. 'Cause we didn't have nothing in the house for normal people. It was all empty.
>
> My mom would come home, and she'd be all upset if I wasn't there. She'd be crying and saying she was sorry. At first I felt sorry for her, and I missed her *también.* We would try again, you know, go buy some food, live together in that house, even though there wasn't nothing there.
>
> I remember it was winter, and we didn't have no heat.

After Eugenia sold the house in Chimayó, she and Bernadette moved to a mobile home park in Española. Eugenia told her daughter that the move would make it easier for her to get a job in town, that it signified a new beginning. In reality, Eugenia's addiction worsened after the move. Then fourteen years old, Bernadette was alone more often than not, and school days were spent sleeping late and watching a borrowed TV. At fifteen, Bernadette dropped out of school altogether and began working as a home aide to a wheelchair-bound widow named Virginia. She earned a small salary by preparing foods, cleaning the house, and bathing her. Bernadette remembered that Virginia complained incessantly about her job performance and appearance, calling her *"poncha"* and *"huevona"* (lazy) and *sin vergüenza* (shameless). Sometimes she would refuse (or was perhaps unable) to pay Bernadette. Still, Bernadette kept the job for nearly a year. "It gave me something to do," she said.

I calculate the years in my head: Bernadette was sixteen in 1994. According to her patient files, Eugenia had sought treatment for her heroin addiction at Nuevo Día in spring that year. I ask Bernadette if she is aware of this, and she tells me she is not. Bernadette grows quiet and lights another cigarette. "That's about when we started using together."

.   .   .   .   .

For the next thirteen years, Eugenia and Bernadette used heroin together. Their worlds were collectively organized around the drug: they shared it, "hustled" for money or drugs when the other was in need, and took care of each other when one was feeling ill. The dependencies produced through heroin became a part of the relational mix that is kinship, and the circulation of heroin became the substance through which care was performed and through which affective ties between Eugenia and Bernadette were reaffirmed. But they were reaffirmed at the cost of further fragmentation, and perhaps even further subjections.

Bernadette received a five-year jail sentence for narcotics possession with intent to distribute. According to her sentence, she was to be immediately transferred to the New Mexico Women's Correctional Facility in Grants, and her two children would be placed in foster care. From my seat at the back of the County Courthouse, I watched Bernadette's stiff back, swathed in a red blouse, as the judge declared that she would have the opportunity to "earn" her children back upon completion of her sentence. "It's up to you, Bernadette," he said wearily. As is customary, the judge asked Bernadette if she had anything she wanted to say. With a shake of her head, Bernadette declined her opportunity to speak. Her *conpromiso* was unflagging.

Point of Departure

During our last visit in her trailer, a week before her sentencing, Bernadette asked me to contact Eugenia at the church and offer to take her to Grants to visit her daughter in prison. This is what Bernadette wanted, and she was quite sure her mother would want it, too. Two weeks after her sentencing, I began making routine calls to Eugenia; the telephone would ring and ring, but no one would answer. Bernadette began to call me collect from the prison pay phone. She wanted to know when her mother and I would be coming to visit. Finally, I drove to the church. It was midafternoon. I walked up the handicap ramp that led to the church's front door. To my surprise, Eugenia answered to the sound of my knocking. I hadn't seen her for some time, and although she wore new clothes and her hair was neatly brushed, her face held the same tired expression.

Before I could speak, Eugenia said she knew why I was there. There was nothing she could do, she said. She stood protectively in the doorframe—the interior of the church visible behind her. Peering past her, I could see rows of metal fold-out chairs facing a plain wooden lectern. I asked Eugenia how she was doing. "I'm in God's hands now," she said. She told me that she prayed for her daughter, but, again, there was nothing she could do.

I left angry. The next morning I called the women's prison to ask if the visitation application I sent in had been approved. Three weeks later I made the three-hour drive west, to Grants.

· · · · ·

Established in 1989, the New Mexico Women's Correctional Facility (NMWCF) is the first privately run women's prison in the United States. It is a sprawling sand-colored structure that sits before the surrounding mesas of Grants. At any given time the prison is filled to capacity with six hundred women. It is the largest employer in the region, and its presence signals what later became a full-blown trend: the privatization of incarceration, both state- and nationwide.

Currently, there are ten "correctional facilities" in the state of New Mexico, half of which are privately run. According to NMWCF correctional officer Betty Ramirez, this is not enough. "New Mexico has the third highest recidivism rate in the country," Betty explains to me on my arrival. "Eighty-five percent of the women incarcerated and released return within five years." I ask Betty why she thinks the rates are so high. She answers with one word: "Drugs." Despite the alarmingly high rate of prisoner return, Betty is proud of the work that the Corrections Corporation of America (which employs her) does at the women's prison. "When I started working here sixteen, seventeen years ago, we had just over 100 women," she explains. "Now it's 600, and we need to expand. Most of them are nonviolent and drug addicted."

A small but commanding woman, Betty gives me a tour of the prison units, or "pods," including the Solitary Pods where up to thirty women are "locked down" in small, dark, solitary confinement for twenty-three hours a day. Betty tells me she worked the Solitary Pod many years ago, admitting that it was stressful and sad. "Most of these women are victims themselves," she says.

Betty also shows me the "God Pod," or the Life Principles / Crossings Program. Here a fundamentalist Christian ministry named the Institute in Basic Life Principles houses women who are willing to be converted to Christian fundamentalism. Established in 2001, the program receives financial support from President George W. Bush's Faith-Based Initiative and is the most structured and institutionalized of the prison's religious offerings. On conversion (usually from Roman Catholicism), women housed in the program are provided with educational and vocational programs. I ask Betty how many women move from the Segregation Pod to the God Pod. "That's a good question," she replies. "I don't know the answer to that, but you'd think it would be incentive."

The classification of inmates in specific identity and housing divisions has always been central to prison management (Foucault 1995; Rhodes

2004). But the rise of religious forms of classifications is fairly new and can be traced to the recent wave of conservative political clout. Some argue that the ability to move from one prison segment to another opens up a space for negotiation in a setting that is, by definition, closed. But the rewards that accompany Evangelical conversion (among them, better housing, educational opportunities, increased family visits) introduces yet another level of control. The increased enmeshment of segregation, "rehabilitation," and religion in the classification system introduces new moral codes for inmate behavior, and the practical rewards for being "saved" are less incentive than coercion.

.   .   .   .   .

After my brief tour of the prison pods and workshops, I am shuttled to the visitation quarters, where I will finally meet with Bernadette. I enter another round of metal detectors and body searches, which seem unnecessary, since I have already been subjected to them once before. A corrections officer orders me to leave my small notebook and pencil before entering the highly guarded visitation center, but I am allowed to bring the clear plastic baggie filled with $20 worth of quarters that Bernadette had requested. No other gifts are allowed—only quarters, intended for the countless vending machines offering sodas, potato chips, and candy that line the prison hallways.

I wait for Bernadette at a small round table. Several minutes pass before she enters through a side door. She is smiling, and I stand to greet her. A female guard stationed against a nearby wall shouts, "No touching!" We sit across from each other, our bodies positioned at a carefully calculated degree of distance. I place the quarters on the table that separates us, and Bernadette begins to cry. Speaking through her tears, this time Bernadette asks me not about Eugenia but about her own children. She asks, "Have you seen them? Are they okay? How is my little girl?"

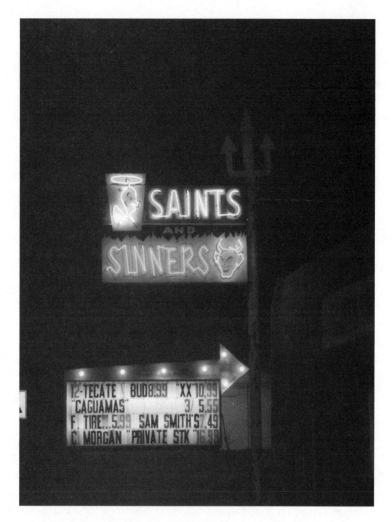

Figure 6.   Friday night. Photo by the author.

WOMEN AND THE CRIMINAL STATE

The number of incarcerated and "criminally supervised" women has increased dramatically in recent decades. In 1990 there were just over 500,000 women in prisons or jails, on probation, or on parole in the United States; by 2000 the figure had risen to more than one million women. Although the rate of incarceration for women continues to be lower than that for men (58 in 100,000 women vs. 896 in 100,000 men), the number of women incarcerated in the United States has increased at a rate double that of men (Bureau of Justice Statistics 2002; National Institute of Justice 1998). Like Bernadette, more than half of these women are incarcerated for what are classified as "nonviolent drug offenses."

This increase is the outcome of larger forces, including the so-called war on drugs and federal and state mandatory sentencing laws, which prescribe simplistic, punitive responses to complex social problems. Both stem from a view that sees addiction and lawbreaking as individual pathology and that too frequently ignores the structural and social causes of addiction and crime (Covington and Bloom 2003). This view feeds into the public's obsessive fear of crime, even though crime—especially violent crime—has been declining for more than a decade. This obsession is fueled in large part by the media, whose "reality-based" dramas such as *CSI* and *Law and Order* are among the most popular TV programs in the United States. Considered together, they present a looming image and experience of crime wherein "theater and fantasy appear integral to the workaday routines of policing" (Comaroff and Comaroff 2004: 802).

Contrary to such criminal "phantom-states,"[7] many criminal justice professionals agree that nonviolent, drug-addicted female offenders like Bernadette pose little risk to public safety. The recent development of the drug court model—which combines the therapeutic sensibilities of substance abuse treatment and the criminal justice system's coercive power to legally evaluate the efficacy of treatment—attests in part to the widely held view that drug addict offenders pose "risk" mainly to themselves (Gregoire and Burke 2004). Betty Ramirez agrees. "The only person she's hurting is herself," she said of Bernadette and, by extension, the hundreds of women like Bernadette who are in her charge. This is little comfort to Bernadette, whose five-year sentence is not a symbolic gesture but a tangible one. It is tangible not only to herself but also to her children, whose lives have changed as a consequence not only of their mother's addiction but also of the institutional responses to it.

Despite the so-called second chance many drug addicts are granted by the drug court system, when offenders fail (or "relapse") multiple times, the only recourse is incarceration. Current sentencing laws remain based on male criminology, for men have historically been viewed as the "normal" subject or perpetrator of crime (Bloom and Chesney-Lind 2000; Covington 2002; see also Campbell 2000). Once again, it is a masculine symbolic that mediates an understanding of female involvement in crime, and the application of sentencing laws that emerge from this symbolic fail to take into account the reality of women's lives, responsibilities, and roles in crime. It is women like Bernadette, who ironically lived her life largely in a world *without* men, who understand all too well the repercussions of this symbolic.

In the end, Bernadette served twenty-two months of her sentence and her children were allowed to remain in the care of her uncle. I visited her twice during her period of incarceration and spoke to her on several occasions on the telephone. During our conversations, Bernadette told me that her mother was in and out of rehab, still "living on the edge" but trying to clean up, if only as a gesture to her daughter. She confided that she worried about Eugenia's emotional health but had faith that her mother would pull through. I asked Bernadette about the source of this faith. She told me that they were writing each other letters, and it was in her mother's words that Bernadette found reason to believe that she would be okay. That is, as long as Bernadette kept writing her back, as long as they both kept their promise—their *conpromiso*—to somehow care for each other.

LISA AND MICHELLE: THE SORROWFUL MYSTERY

> I tattooed her name on my wrist. It's what's left.
> Lisa Archuleta

On a bright but chilly September morning, I received a call from Lisa Archuleta, a forty-five-year-old woman in recovery whom I had met at the detox clinic. *I know I'm not supposed to call staff at home,* she explained, *but I really need a ride.* Before I could ask what was so urgent, Lisa began sobbing. The only words she could mutter were *mi hijta, mi hijta* (my daughter, my daughter), which she repeated in swelling succession.

Without Lisa saying so, I knew that her daughter Michelle, also a heroin addict, had overdosed and died.

Minutes later I sat on the edge of Lisa's bed, my hand on her shoulder. Lisa lay on her side, facing the bare dormitory wall, her tattooed forearm clutching a pillow to her chest. Her roommates—Mary, Rose, and Evangeline—huddled together on an adjacent bed. Their heads were bowed, and they held hands. For what felt like minutes but was probably only seconds, we remained positioned like that, as if carved stone. Then, breaking the stillness, Lisa turned to me and, in a matter-of-fact tone, listed all the things she needed to do: identify the body, call family and friends, "make arrangements." Her swollen eyes belied the calmness of her voice. *Get me the hell out of here,* she finally said.

I drove Lisa to Española Hospital, where "anonymous friends" of Michelle deposited her body when she stopped breathing. Mary, who had grown close to Lisa during their clinic stay, joined us. The two women sat together in the backseat of my car, leaving me alone in the front. I felt strangely intrusive and stared hard at the long stretch of highway in front of me. The drive to the hospital took fifteen minutes, during which Lisa cried and whispered, "It should have been me."

Confusion met us at the hospital. Unsure of where to go, we passed through the double doors of the emergency room entrance. Lisa pushed her way up to the admitting receptionist, cutting in front of a short line of people in various states of injury, all of whom gestured their frustration at Lisa's apparent impropriety. Through a thick security window, the receptionist told Lisa to take her place at the back of the line. Lisa yelled that she needed to find her daughter. There was a rapid crossfire of vulgarities. Finally a young nurse was called in; I overheard the nurse ask Lisa for her daughter's last name and why she was admitted. "OD," Lisa replied, and she and Mary followed the nurse through a door marked, "Do Not Enter."

A row of cracked plastic chairs lined the periphery of the ER waiting room. The chairs were bolted to the floor. I sat in one and looked up at the TV set, which hung precariously from the ceiling. A Spanish-language soap opera played. Avoiding the stares of others, I tried to focus on the story line, which seemed to have something to do with a beautiful woman in a state of amnesia. Two hours passed. Finally Mary returned and said that we needed to drive up to the hospital's main entrance, where we would pick up Lisa. When we pulled up in front of the hospital, Lisa was standing with the same nurse who had taken her to her daughter; they were both smoking a cigarette. There were papers in Lisa's hand. Mary jumped out of the car to gather her friend, and, from my car window, I watched the three women embrace. Lisa and Mary returned to the backseat of my car. We drove back to the clinic in silence.

Three days later a Rosary was held at a funeral parlor in Santa Fe. I again played chauffeur, this time driving Lisa, Mary, Rose, and Evangeline down the familiar stretch of Highway 285. Lisa sat beside me in the front passenger seat. She wore a borrowed black dress, and her hair was neatly pulled away from her face in a thick braid. For much of the hour-long ride, she stared out the window, watching the juniper-dotted hills pass by.

There were a few people, mainly female friends of Lisa, waiting inside the funeral home when we arrived. Michelle's body lay in an unadorned white casket, which was propped open for a traditional viewing. Other than old photographs that Lisa kept in her dormitory room, I had never seen Michelle. She wore a yellow dress. The profile of her face was visible, and her features were, as Lisa had described, delicate. Michelle's still lips were painted red, and her hands were crossed on her chest.

From a back pew I watched Lisa approach her daughter and stand before her body, grieving. I was struck by the contrast of the supine daughter and the standing mother, by the contrast of color, by Michelle's silence and Lisa's quiet weeping.

It was Rose, Lisa's roommate from the detox clinic, who led the small gathering in the recitation of the Rosary—the prayer that, by its movement through the Mysteries and incantatory renditions of Our Fathers and Hail Marys, is meant to mark the rhythms of life, death, and resurrection. Rose, who had recently turned to God in her own recovery from heroin, struggled through much of the prayer; it was still unfamiliar, and, suffering from dyslexia, she had difficulty following the text. Still, Rose recited the Hail Mary with growing conviction, and the gathering of women responded: *Hail Mary, full of grace; the Lord is with thee: blessed art thou among women, and blessed is the fruit of thy womb, Jesus. Holy Mary, Mother of God, pray for us sinners, now and at the hour of our death. Amen.*

.   .   .   .   .

Staff and patients at the detox clinic expected that Lisa would resume heroin use after her daughter's death. It is a familiar and well-documented pattern—recovering addicts "relapsing" after a traumatic event. In sociological and behavioral health literature, this pattern is understood as a consequence of not having yet developed appropriate "coping mechanisms" for life's stressors. But relapse in the Española Valley can also be understood differently. Here, heroin addicts who die from overdose are memorialized by and through heroin. Friends, lovers, and family members who are co-addicts frequently shoot up at the deceased's grave site and, among the votive candles and flowers, pierce the grave's newly turned dirt with syringes filled with heroin. It is a macabre tradition, a variation of the Mexican celebration of Día de los Muertos (Day of the Dead), in which offerings are dedicated to the dead, often at their grave sites.

But Lisa did not relapse—at least not for some time. Instead, she returned to the detox clinic after her daughter's funeral with a renewed committed to "really kick it." Michelle's death became the impetus for Lisa's recovery and for her sudden emotional outpouring—the first, Lisa said, in her entire life. She had so many secrets, she said one evening in the women's recovery group; she felt that if she was going to make it clean, she needed to get them out.

After the initial compassion she received from fellow addicts at the clinic, Lisa felt like she was judged and blamed for her daughter's death, and the women's recovery group in particular proved hostile territory for Lisa's confession. As the group's facilitator, I often was the recipient of patients' private complaints that Lisa monopolized the sessions with her grief. Others expressed frustration that Lisa was treated too gently by clinic staff and was not held more directly responsible for Michelle's death. A few women rather viciously complained that Lisa's intimate relationship with

Figure 7.   Española. Photo by the author.

Mary, who was her girlfriend, was "not right" and that if Lisa had shown her daughter half the care she showed her Mary, Michelle might still be alive.

Michelle's death and Lisa's recovery became the depository for the women's own feelings and experiences of loss. Many of the women in the support group had also lost a child—usually to Child Protective Services—because of their addiction. They felt that there was no outlet for the grief they felt at their loss, which was considered a "legitimate"—not tragic, as in Lisa's case—consequence of their addiction. Others had lost a parent or sibling to heroin, and many, especially the younger women, had ambivalent or hostile feelings toward relatives who introduced them to the drug. Finally, during one of the sessions, a twenty-year-old addict named Margarita told Lisa it was her own fault that her daughter got hooked on heroin and died. "I'm tired of listening to you," Margarita said angrily. "You always say the same thing. You're guilty and sorry, but it's too late."

With her growing sense of alienation from the other women in the program, Lisa began to talk privately to me. Once she completed her thirty-day detox program and moved into a ninety-day residential program, we were able to leave the clinic grounds for more structured interviews. Sometimes we would sit on a picnic table beside a stretch of the Rio Grande, and sometimes we would order lunch at a local taco stand and sit together beneath the shade of a cottonwood. It was during these visits that Lisa told me how and why she herself turned to heroin and how her drug use with Michelle started. Lisa wanted these interviews recorded. She wanted, she said, to get the story straight.

Other People's Houses

From our meetings, I began to stitch together Lisa's life history. This was a difficult endeavor given Lisa's partial knowledge of what she called the "cold hard facts" of her early years, including the exact date of her birth. It was also difficult because Lisa was full of contradictions. The specifics and texture of her recollections shifted constantly, usually according to her mood.

For instance, when she was feeling low or hopeless, Lisa's perspective on her childhood was decidedly grim, and she accentuated her narrative with stories of abuse and extreme hardship, especially at the religious orphanage where she was raised. When she was feeling good, she would paint an entirely different picture of her childhood, one much happier and more optimistic. If during one of her "good moods" I recalled an event she had recounted to me during one of her low points (such as a story about being assaulted at knifepoint by a former male friend, or details about Michelle's father, sometimes one and the same person), Lisa would often not remember or would accuse me of getting her story mixed up with someone else's. "That wasn't me," she would say—though, in the coming weeks, that very incident might very well reappear in her narrative, often with different shades of detail. At other times Lisa would punctuate a certain story with the phrase "No lie," as if she sensed my (or even her own) doubt about the veracity of her narrative. In this way, "getting the record straight"—which is what she insisted she wanted—was an impossible task for both of us. Still, in her vacillation of mood and "truth," perhaps something more telling emerged.

From the few consistencies I could gather regarding her early childhood, Lisa was born around 1960, the daughter of a Native American mother from Cochiti Pueblo and a Hispano father. At the time of her birth, her father was married to another woman and had a family in Santa Fe. The circumstances of her parents' intimate relationship are unclear and a point of contradiction for Lisa; sometimes she claimed her parents were involved in a doomed love affair, and other times she was adamant that her parents were strangers and that her father had raped and impregnated her mother. In either scenario, Lisa was consistent that her conception was not something to be celebrated and that she was born into *"vergüenza,"* shame. "She [her mother] gave me up right after I was born," Lisa told me. "She didn't give me an Indian name. I didn't get my father's name." Being denied an Indian first name and a paternal surname embodies and signifies the *vergüenza* Lisa feels she was born into. This shame is amplified by "the fact" that her present name was given to her by the very orphange where she says she suffered emotional and physical abuse. "They weren't good religious people, no way," Lisa said. "They liked to remind me that I didn't have nobody and it was because of them that I was even alive."

Over the years, the orphanage placed Lisa in several sponsor homes, none of which led to a permanent living situation. At the age of eighteen, she moved to Albuquerque to live with a Navajo man named Jack who she befriended at the orphanage. For a few years the two lived together, forging their own version of family life. It was the first time, Lisa said, that she had any kind of normalcy or routine. "It was the longest I lived in one place, when I lived with him. He was a good man. He treated me with kindness."

Each morning they walked to the same downtown hotel, where Jack worked as a cook and Lisa as a housekeeper. They talked of getting married and starting their own family, maybe moving to Arizona where Jack's birth family was from. But when Lisa was twenty-one, Jack died; he was twenty-five years old. Sometimes Lisa said he died in a car accident; other times she said he died as a result of a fight that occurred at El Madrid, a bar next to the railroad tracks that cut through Albuquerque's downtown. Lisa remembered:

> There was no one to call when he died, no family, I mean. I called the orphanage, and they gave me some money for the burial. That was the one decent thing they did. No one was there [at the burial], just me. And I didn't have nobody for a long time after that. I kept living there, in our house, but I didn't have no one.
>
> I was pregnant with Michelle when Jack died.

Sometimes Lisa claimed that Jack was Michelle's father. But this version is contradicted by her frequent assertion that she and Jack were "only friends" and by her occasional assertion that the man who killed Jack at El Madrid was, in fact, Michelle's father. In either case, Lisa raised Michelle alone. For the first few years, they shared a rented room and bed at a hostel on Central Avenue in Albuquerque, where Lisa remembered cooking meals of beans and rice in the communal kitchen—meals she had to hide from the other hungry residents. She made money for necessities by cleaning office buildings at night. Sometimes at work she imagined what her life would be like if she were one of those people, "you know, office people, the kind with a place to go work in the day and a place to go home to at night."

Living a Decent Life

Lisa began using heroin while living at the hostel, where the drug was readily available. Her heroin use continued when she and her daughter moved north to Santa Fe, a move that symbolized, like Eugenia's move to Española, what she hoped would be a "new beginning." In Santa Fe she found work as a housekeeper at a large hotel catering to tourists, and she was able to rent her own one-bedroom apartment. Despite a full-time job, making ends meet was difficult. Rather than take on an additional job at night and leave her daughter in someone else's care, Lisa moved in with a coworker whose husband had a heroin habit. "That's where it started again," she said, adding that for several years her heroin use was limited to "chipping" (occasional or recreational use).

> I wasn't like one of those people who woke up and all they could think about was getting high. I had my daughter, and I'd take her to school, go to work, and live my life. I didn't waste my days with heroin, *okay*?
> Usually, I'd just use a little at night, when Michelle was asleep. A little poke in the arm. I used it because it relaxed me and I never liked the taste of alcohol or anything else. Heroin was like so calming for me, and I was careful about it, *okay*? I didn't get *malias* or anything. I was careful and I didn't want to be *out of it*.

While I was piecing together her story, I noticed there was a shift in Lisa's drug use—from chipping to habitual heroin use—around 1990. From what I could gather, this was around the time that Lisa had told me she was assaulted (always keeping the details of her assault a mystery). However, when I asked if there is a relation between the two, Lisa doubted that it had anything to do with her increase in drug use. "I think I was just tired," she said. "Tired, like depressed?" "Probably," she replied.

> I didn't feel my life *going* anywhere. I worked hard, but for what? I didn't have nothing to show for my life. I was cleaning other people's messes. Other than Michelle, I didn't have any family, and she didn't need me so much. What did I have?
> All I had was need.
> I needed heroin, and it was there. It made me feel like things were possible. Being high was the only time I felt like things were possible. You think about your future when you're high, and it doesn't look so bad. You even think about quitting. You can't even think about quitting when you're strung out. But when you're high you think, *I can do this. I can do anything*.

Lisa's narrative points to a terrible irony that many addicts I spoke with repeated: the possibility of living another kind of life—what Lisa calls "a decent life"—seems possible only when one is high on heroin. In the absence of heroin, there is nothing but "bad feeling," the collective weight of years of damage: physical, emotional, financial, and familial. In heroin's embrace, the bad feeling dissipates, and the addict is released into feelings of love, serenity, and possibility: the possibility of living clean.

According to her patient file at Nuevo Día, Lisa was in five different recovery programs between 1993 and 2003, before finally enrolling at Nuevo Día in 2004. She also tried to "kick it" on her own with what she called her "home detox program." Lisa would stock up on black market medications such as the narcotic analgesic Darvocet and benzodiazepines (tranquilizers and sleeping pills) to alleviate the pain of withdrawal. She would buy marijuana and the cheapest alcohol she could find, usually brandy. "The only time I drank alcohol was when I was trying to kick heroin," she told me. She bought cookies, water, and plenty of cigarettes and holed up in her room with the goal of getting through seven days without heroin. Lisa recalled home detox:

> I'd try to keep my mind off things by watching TV. You feel at first like you can do it. The heroin hasn't completely gone away yet and when you get uncomfortable, you have a pill or two, or a shot of something. It cools things off for a while. But then it starts to hit you and it fucking hurts. Your temperature goes all crazy, your fingers, your stomach, everything hurts. You can't imagine the pain. You feel like your hands and feet are going to pop off your body. No lie.
>
> I would try to keep it down, be quiet, you know, in case Michelle was home or came by. But this one day, I just started screaming, and she was knocking on my door begging me to shoot up, *Just do it! Just do it!* I can remember her voice. It was a terrible thing.

Having witnessed her mother suffer through the pain and indignity of heroin withdrawal, Lisa had imagined that her daughter would avoid heroin and drugs in general. But she was wrong. When Michelle was nineteen, she and a friend were pulled over for a minor traffic violation. In their car were two grams of heroin. Michelle was arrested and later placed on bail. At the time of her arrest, Michelle told her mother that the drugs were not hers, that she and her friend intended to "cut" and sell the heroin to *tecatos*. "She told me she wasn't one of *them*, someone like me. But I knew better."

"Cutting" or "stepping on" is a process in which other ingredients—such as baking soda or talcum powder—are added to heroin. By means of cutting, a gram of heroin can be converted into a gram and a half, sometimes even two grams. A dealer can thus make back the money to maintain his or her own high by selling the additional amount of heroin. Lisa knew this. She knew that it was unlikely that her daughter was selling heroin without using any herself. "She wasn't in it for the money. Lord knows she didn't have any money," Lisa told me. When I asked Lisa if there were any early warning signs that Michelle had been using heroin, she grew quiet. After some silence, she said, "Yes. But I was living hit-to-hit myself. I couldn't see or do much back then . . . to help her, I mean."

In fact, when Michelle's own drug use was out in the open, mother and daughter began sharing and using heroin together. When we talked about their shared drug use, Lisa's narrative became tentative, full of pauses. She would smoke a cigarette and shake her shoulders, roll her head. "I don't like talking about this," she would say, visibly uncomfortable. She told me she thought it will be hard for me to understand, adding that it's even hard for her to understand, especially in the wake of her daughter's death. And yet when she did talk to me about their drug use, there was something entirely *sensible* about her story—something deeply, and painfully, understandable.

> Look, I knew if she came to me [for heroin] she must be hurting [the pain of withdrawal]. I know what that feels like. Nobody wants to be in that pain or to see it in someone you love. And when it's your child, *fuck*, all you want to do is make it go away. That's all I felt like I could do for her.
>
> I was so fucked up myself.

Bonds of Shame

"Shame attaches to and sharpens the sense of what one is," Eve Kosofsky Sedgwick writes (2002: 4). It is attached to, and constitutive of, one's very being. But as shame comes into being in the face of another, one wonders how shame might also be lessened in the other's presence, even if the "moral codes" are nevertheless still transgressed.[8]

Lisa tells me that for much of her life she felt a deep sense of shame about being a heroin-addicted mother. She describes the many failed attempts to hide or downplay her addiction for the sake of her daughter and reminds me that her attempts to get clean were, ultimately, attempts at being a better mother.[9] But when she failed at these, her feeling of shame was compounded. "When you don't make it [get clean], you know you're not just hurting yourself, you're hurting your kid, too." When Lisa learned that her daughter was also using heroin, the nature of her shame shifted. Yes, she felt shame and guilt for her role in her daughter's drug use, but she also felt a sense of release and understanding. "I didn't feel as bad about my body or my need [to get high]. And I think she felt the same."

In describing her drug use with her daughter, Lisa suggests that the shame she had so long suffered from was somehow eased. There was no way to hide the physical toll of her addiction. It was written on her arms and her neck, in her collapsed veins and tired voice. But with her daughter also a heroin addict, Lisa says of her body, "I didn't have to worry about it as much." She no longer had to hide her "face," as it were, for it was a face that Michelle also shared. Thus, through their bond of addiction and shame, a deep—though destructive—understanding was forged. When Lisa talks to me about her and her daughter's drug use, vestiges of the shame remain. She avoids looking at me directly. She lowers and shakes her head and tells me that, maybe, when I have kids, I'll understand what it feels like to just want to take the pain away. I can't help but wonder whether the pain Lisa is referring to is her daughter's or her own.

Lisa and Michelle used heroin together intermittently for three years. Unlike Lisa (who considers herself "an old-school *tecato*," only using heroin by "mainlining," or injecting), Michelle would use a wide variety of drugs—often simultaneously and usually depending on availability. According to Lisa, her daughter developed "a love of *las pildoras*." Though they could be taken orally, Michelle would inject them because "it was the closest thing to a heroin high." Compared to heroin or tablets (which needed to be finely crushed), preparing capsules for injection is relatively simple: the user merely has to open the capsule and cook the ready-made powder. As such, the common tendency, which Michelle apparently shared, was to swallow the tablets (Percocet, Valium, or Xanax) and shoot the capsules (Darvon, Librium, or Secanol).

Ironically, Lisa describes Michelle's poly-drug use as a means to "cut down on heroin." She used prescription medications as a kind of surrogate, one considered less harmful in its effects than heroin, partly because it was considered (at least in some contexts) medically sanctioned. But Lisa says that her daughter also used prescription drugs, usually Percocet, to ease the physical pain of heroin withdrawal. "I guess over the years I got used to the pain of *malias*. But she never did. She always needed something."

Michelle's poly-drug use worried Lisa, who knew of the heightened risk of overdose when mixing drugs. Indeed, the vast majority of overdoses in the region involve heroin in combination with prescription medications and alcohol. Several of the addicts I spoke with who had experienced overdose claimed they nearly died because they were unable to determine the exact quality or quantity of the products they were mixing. "It's like playing a game of chance," one addict said of mixing heroin and prescription drugs. "You know if you get it right its gonna be beautiful, but if you get it wrong it'll blow up in your face." Lisa says she frequently warned Michelle of this danger and constantly worried about the capacity of her daughter's body to tolerate the variety and quantity of drugs she used. It was because of this worry that Lisa contacted Nuevo Día.

> I called and said my daughter and I have this problem. They said we'd have to be on a waiting list and it was like several months long, but I said okay. It was for the two of us, and Michelle agreed. We thought if we did it together it would be easier. We could help each other through.
>
> We had nothing to lose.

While waiting for openings in the detox program, the women moved to Española, where they lived temporarily with a friend of Michelle's. The plan was to informally begin recovery by attending the weekly women's group for heroin addicts. But in the months preceding their admittance to Nuevo Día, the plan failed, and their heroin use worsened. Lisa described the Española drug scene as a "smorgasbord," one that proved too tempting for Michelle. When the program called with the news that they had two immediate openings, Lisa would be the only one to enter the program. She did so, she says, with the hope that her daughter would eventually join her.

.   .   .   .   .

It took six months for the state Office of the Medical Investigator to confirm that the September 9, 2004, death of Michelle Archuleta was drug related. The toxicology report revealed that the concoction of substances in her blood at the time of her death included cocaine, morphine (metabolized heroin), and prescription drugs. Michelle was twenty-four years old. Her death was labeled accidental and the result of drug intoxication. Michelle was one of six people in Española who died of overdose in the same month.

The following March, after reading Michelle's toxicology report, I drove to the trailer that Lisa shared with Mary. The trailer was located in a small mobile home park in Española, within walking distance of the laundromat where Lisa worked part-time, cleaning the machines and floors at night. On the previous occasion when the two women had invited me over for dinner, I found their home tidy and warm. Fresh flowers were set out on the coffee table, and curtains softened the iron-barred windows. An 8-by-10-inch framed photograph of Michelle and Lisa was perched prominently on a new, wide-screen TV. Lisa and Mary served soft drinks and spaghetti, and they told me they were doing well with their drug- and alcohol-free life and that their only regret was that Michelle wasn't with them.

On this visit, however, I found the trailer in disarray. Cigarette butts littered the walkway, and garbage was strewn about the small yard. For a moment I wondered whether Lisa and Mary had moved, but I recognized the curtains and decided somewhat ambivalently to knock.

Mary opened the door. Her eyes were bloodshot and her pupils big black saucers. She's coming off of something, I thought. At first, Mary didn't recognize me, but when I told her who I was, she forced a smile and offered a hug. I could feel her sweat through her layers of clothes; it smelled like formaldehyde.

From deep inside the trailer Lisa shouted, "Who is it?" She came to the door and stood beside Mary, beneath the trailer's narrow doorframe. Lisa's eyes were the same: big, black saucer eyes. I wanted to leave.

I told them I was thinking about them and, on a whim, decided to stop by. Mary asked me to come inside, but I declined. "I was just thinking about you," I said again—even though, the truth was, I was thinking about Michelle.

Lisa looked at me like she knew that I knew. She rolled up the sleeve of her shirt and pointed. There were fresh track marks on her forearm, but that wasn't what she wanted to show me. On her wrist was a tattoo of Michelle's name. "It's what's left," she said.

A KIND OF SACRIFICE

When I began this chapter, I initially turned to the narratives of these mother-daughter pairs to provide a counterfigure to a representational economy of heroin addiction that marginalizes women through archetypes or ignores them altogether. I wanted to explore a long-silenced feminine genealogy of heroin addiction in what remains a patriarchal context, and I imagined that—by bringing this genealogy into language—I might rectify certain misconceptions. Perhaps I have accomplished this to a certain extent. But I find myself in dangerous territory. In thinking about the narratives that appear in this chapter (and in others that do not appear here), I ask: What does it mean to write a "maternal genealogy" of drug addiction where, in both cases, there is a kind of sacrifice of the daughter? How can a feminist ethics and politics respond to the figure of the sacrificed daughter? What does the incarceration of Bernadette and the death of Michelle signal in terms of the gendered politics of blame and shame in the context of drug addiction? And what is my role, as an anthropologist, in drawing these out?

Judith Butler (2000) returns to the figure of Antigone to examine the sacrifice, resistance, and representation of the feminine. Antigone, the protagonist of Sophocles' play of the same name, is the child of an incestuous union and devoted to her brother. As such, she has long figured in literary, psychoanalytic, and philosophical discourse, usually standing in to represent the dissolution of kinship and moral order. Butler is similarly interested in how Antigone is at once entangled in the terms of kinship but resigned to live outside its norms. She writes that Antigone "represents not kinship in its ideal form, but in its deformation and displacement, one that puts the reigning epistemes of cultural intelligibility into crisis" (24). Antigone thus comes to signify the power and trauma of "blood" relations, for her heritage (which she cannot control) and her transgressive love for her brother (which she presumably can control but does not) condemns her to a kind of living death: "she is already living in the tomb prior to any banishment there" (77).

In her sacrifice, Antigone rewrites the figure of bloodline as a kind of bloodshed and "brings into relief the violent forgetting of primary kin relations" (4). But Butler casts her neither purely as victim nor purely as heroine. Rather, she remains throughout a liminal figure—one that haunts the very field of power that excludes her, and one that is haunted herself. As such, she comes to signify a complex politics of kinship, love, and mourning.

When I reread Butler's analysis of Antigone, I was struck by how Bernadette and Michelle (and Eugenia and Lisa, for that matter) also figure in this trace of kinship. They destabilize certain norms of kinship and of mother-daughter love in particular. They are all, to a greater and lesser extent, "outsiders," culpable of certain "crimes"—some inherited, others of their own making. It is hard to determine who bears a harsher fate—the mothers or the daughters. Bernadette is incarcerated, and Michelle is dead. Eugenia lives in a kind of purgatory, and what is left for Lisa remains etched painfully on her skin.

FOUR Suicide as a Form of Life

My soul is sorrowful even to death. Remain here and keep
watch with me.

Matthew 26:38

THE STRUCTURE OF SURRENDER: THREE SCENES

Scene One: Imagine standing in a field of snow. There is snow falling
everywhere about your body—tiny, white petals of it—hushing, as they
fall, all sound; absorbing, as they fall, all traces of shape and color. You
stand still, mesmerized by how the snow swallows your breath and by
how little breath your body seems to need to stand so quietly alone.
You feel warm, and are grateful for it, even as your skin turns cold.
Gradually, this thickening veil of whiteness obscures your body, until
you disappear altogether from this wintry scene. But you are unaware
of your own disappearance, just as you are unaware of the coldness of
your skin and the tapering of your breath. All that you are aware
of now is the endless falling of snowflakes. Trapped in the thickest of

boundaries, you can't imagine anything else. You can't imagine anything.

Some call it serenity.

Scene Two: The portion of the brain that controls breathing with peripheral input from chemoreceptors becomes flooded with heroin. Opioids inhibit these chemoreceptors, and the message to the diaphragm and lungs to breathe is disrupted. The first apparent symptom is the suppression of respiratory rate and depth. As the respiratory rate declines—often as low as two to four breaths per minute—blood pressure begins to drop and, with it, body temperature. The skin becomes cold and clammy, eventually turning blue-gray. Sometimes the body begins to seize, like epilepsy. The body enters a comatose state, and, usually within twenty to thirty minutes, respiratory failure occurs. The heart stops beating.

Some call it overdose.

Scene Three: She was already gone. It was just a few minutes, but we were all too late. They hadn't even covered her face yet, and her body was still surrounded by machines meant to revive her. It was just a few minutes. She looked familiar, but she was cold. Even her hair was cold. I looked at her lying there and knew that it wasn't an accident. She wanted this—an end to her misery.

Some call it suicide.

. . . . .

I begin this chapter with three scenes of suicide by heroin overdose—the first, an elaboration of an account of a failed suicide told to me by a twenty-seven-year-old heroin addict named Sarah; the second, a physician's rendering of the body's physiological decline as it succumbs to a fatal overdose; and the third, the recollection of a mother whose daughter committed suicide by heroin overdose. All three accounts represent different encounters with suicide. They knit together individual lives and relations that may otherwise seem isolated. This is intentional on my part, for the psychoanalytic and literary portraiture of suicide foregrounds the existential isolation and despair of the suicidal subject.

I have argued throughout this book that the existential status of the self is not so easily given and that there is a complex relation between self and others in the experience of loss, mourning, and addiction. Put differently, I have argued that, even in its most seemingly incommensurate forms, life is not *lived* in the singular. I extend this argument in the consideration of suicide by heroin overdose, where I try to conceptualize how life on the verge of death, or life ended by suicide, is similarly not alone but embedded in a set of intimacies. Many of these intimacies are indeed fragile, such as the mother-daughter intimacies described in chapter 3 and others that I explore here, but they are intimacies nonetheless, and as such they remain fundamental—even in their failed form—in the structuring of subjectivity and everyday life. Suicide from this perspective constitutes, in a critical sense, a "form of life."

In considering suicide as a form of life, I draw from Wittgenstein's later work on language as an evolving practice, where the meaning of a word is not in its objectified form but in its usage (Wittgenstein 2001). Through detailed examples and scenes, Wittgenstein demonstrates the extent to which context informs language use and thus the degree to which language reflects the world of its users. As Wittgenstein puts it, to imagine a language is to imagine a form of life. This embodied notion of language is useful in the conceptualization of an anthropology that is firmly grounded in the subject's local, moral, and psychological world.[1] To consider suicide as a form of life emphasizes the very dependencies that are immanent in that world. It situates suicide as intimately connected to the idea and experience of life, making it a thread in "the weave of our life" and not something external to or reflective of it (Wittgenstein 2001: 157).

My framing of suicide as a form of life thus differs from the familiar sociological view of suicide as a social phenomenon or social fact (Douglas 1967; Durkheim 1997; Giddens 1971; Halbwachs 1978). While this framing has helped us move beyond the consideration of suicide as a merely individualistic phenomenon, I question the continued use of suicide, especially as it is manifested in suicide *rates,* as evidence for the influence of the social over the individual. Durkheim (1997: 214) summarizes this tendency when he argues that when the subject tries to "free himself from the social environment" through suicide, he actually "submits to its influence." The notion that the subject cannot escape, even by taking her own life, the influence of society maintains an artificial boundary between the two realms and places the individual in a subordinate position. It also limits suicide to a descriptive function and ignores the possibility that it helps create the very social world it seems to describe.[2]

In this chapter, I explore the tragic though increasingly common context of suicide by heroin overdose. I conceptualize suicide as it is situated in a complex weave of domestic, physical, and institutional dependencies—not as an event that is an effect or description of them. In the Española Valley, suicide by heroin overdose is now "recognized" as a serious concern. I ask: a concern of what, and for whom?

EXISTENTIAL MURK

"Any death," Veena Das (2006: 193) writes, "raises the question of the obligations of the living towards the dead." At a minimum such obligations include the anthropologist's struggle to discern the circumstances and consequences of suicide in context. But there is also an obligation to think about how to best provide an account of a life that no longer exists, to write of the deliberate surrendering of life without fetishizing this surrender and without abstracting it from its immanent social contexts. And there is an obligation to find meaning in suffering without wishing, seeking, or imposing a redemptive narrative—no matter how much I may wish for one to exist.

I started this chapter with three accounts of suicide: by a young woman who attempted to take her life, by a doctor who tends to fatal overdose cases, and by a mother who lost her daughter to suicide. Absent, of course, is an account of the subject who committed suicide, an absence that nevertheless constitutes a kind of account, an "absent center." I sense in the three accounts I have offered a gesture toward constituting this absent center—toward giving it voice and meaning, no matter how speculative this gesture may be. Indeed, I have found that to think and write of suicide is to think and write speculatively, without a clear moral or political stance toward the lives that I discuss.

In *The Myth of Sisyphus,* Albert Camus (1991: 3) writes, "There is but one serious philosophical problem, and that is suicide." True or not, Camus's remark points to the challenges of thinking and writing about suicide—an endeavor that presents an array of ethical, methodological, and narrative concerns too complex to resolve here. But let me say that to think and write about suicide is to run into the serious question of how to give meaning to a deeply intimate event—an event "prepared within the silence of the heart" and which, by its very nature, excludes me but concerns me nonetheless (4). It concerns me because, in the Hispano milieu, suicide occupies a region of language and experience that is enmeshed in personal histories of heroin addiction, overdose, and death. Suicide by heroin overdose has become an integral part of the devastating cycle of heroin addiction. It is a form of life whose internal structuring lays bare the simultaneous aloneness of the subject and her connections— no matter how fragile—to the world.

It is admittedly difficult to conceive of suicide in this way, especially when one is entangled in the emotional and psychological hurt of suicide's wake. The very immediacy of heroin-related death—concretized by emergency late-night phone calls, the shattering wail of the aggrieved, newly erected *descansos* along country roads, and the litany of heroin-related obituaries in the local newspaper—can paralyze ethnographic analysis. It paralyzes the ethnographer, too, but not through "feeble fictions in the guise of realism," resulting in an "epistemic murk"—as Taussig (1987: 132) writes in relation to doing ethnography in the realm of danger.[3] Rather, it results in the paralysis of the ethnographer as she succumbs to the very force of these signs—the reality of what they do in fact represent: the personal loss of a lover, parent, child, or friend; the failure of kinship, institutions, and friendships; the sense that we are losing, always losing. In my view, this is more of an *existential* than epistemic murk. The question, then, is how to guide oneself through it.

Wittgenstein writes:

> Nothing could be more remarkable than seeing someone who thinks
> himself unobserved engaged in some quite simple everyday activity.
> Let's imagine a theatre, the curtain goes up and we see someone alone in
> his room walking up and down, lighting a cigarette, seating himself etc.
> so that suddenly we are observing a human being from outside in a way
> that ordinarily we can never observe ourselves; as if we were watching a
> chapter from a biography with our own eyes—surely this would be at
> once uncanny and wonderful. More wonderful than anything that a
> playwright could cause to be acted or spoken on stage. We should be see-
> ing life itself. (1998: 8)

I read this passage as a call to attend to the unscripted and the ordinary.
I also read the idea of "seeing life itself"—made visible by the image of ob-
serving a man who "thinks himself unobserved"—as an ethical call to recognize the intimacy and dependency that exists between the observer and
the observed, the ethnographer and her subject. I believe it is through a focused commitment to such moments that one may find a way out of the
existential murk that accompanies the thinking and writing of ethnography of deep suffering. In light of this, I return to the three scenes with
which I opened this chapter. In attending to the details of the three narratives, I attempt to articulate their fullest implications for understanding
suicide as a form of life that *intensifies*, rather than negates, the intimacies
and dependencies that exist in a social world.

SCENE ONE: AS I LAY DYING

Every Tuesday evening, Sarah Montoya joined the dozen or so women
who gathered for Nuevo Día's recovery group for heroin-addicted
women. She was a striking woman, with pale green eyes and dark hair
that she wore in a neat ponytail down her back. Depending on who you
asked, Sarah's attractiveness was obscured or accentuated by her provocative dress. She squeezed her thin body into tight white jeans, showed off
her taut midriff beneath shrunken shirts, and made herself look taller by

wearing brightly colored high-heeled shoes. Given how she attracted attention, I was surprised when I first noticed that she walked with a subtle limp, as if one of her legs were shorter than the other, or one heel a bit too high. But Sarah didn't seem to care. Her appearance drew the ire of women (who whispered behind her back that she should "learn to walk") and the catcalls of men. During the recovery group's fifteen-minute break, when the men's and women's support groups emptied out into the parking lot for cigarettes, Sarah stood deceptively tall and proud.

It was rumored that Sarah was a prostitute and that she attended the recovery meetings not to "work her program" but to meet potential tricks. Several women wondered why else someone would attend the meetings if she didn't have to. In fact, Sarah came to group not because she was court appointed—as were most attendees—but because she wanted to. She rarely spoke during the course of the two-hour meetings, and her apparent aloofness was another detail that the women complained about with bitterness. They asked her confrontationally *why* she was there, insinuating she didn't belong. Sarah responded that the women "didn't know shit" and should just leave her alone.

It came to everyone's surprise, then, when on one Tuesday evening, Jeanie, a heroin addict who attended the women's group, reported that Sarah was seen at the local hospital's emergency department, being treated for a near-fatal heroin overdose. According to Jeanie's cousin, who worked as a medical assistant at the hospital, Sarah arrived at the ER in cardiac arrest. After being stabilized, she was transferred to Albuquerque, to UNM Hospital's Psychiatric Center, for evaluation. Jeanie told the group that her cousin said Sarah's overdose was a self-reported suicide attempt.

Over time, I would slowly learn about the night that Sarah had in fact tried to die. I thus learned something of Sarah's life and, if not exactly the reasons for her suicide attempt, at least some of the context for her despair.

· · · · ·

Once, when I was visiting Sarah at her mother's house where she and her two younger sisters lived, Sarah told me she felt like she was losing control of her life. It was several weeks after her overdose. Although she was dressed in her usual provocative attire, Sarah was visibly distraught. Her delicate hands shook as she spoke, and one side of her face erupted in twitches. Initially, I interpreted these spasms as symptoms of nervousness or as being related to heroin withdrawal. Sarah must have sensed that I was aware of her spasms, because she confessed in a veritable outpouring that her "fucked-up body" was not related to drugs but her worsening multiple sclerosis, which she had been battling on and off since she was a teenager. Now twenty-seven, things were, in her words, *caótico*, spinning out of control. She described her ailing body as being at the center of the chaos, as a kind of negative force from which so many misfortunes seemed to emanate.

Sarah's "attacks" were growing ever more frequent and painful. Her vision was now affected, and the world around her was growing increasingly out of focus. She admitted that she was experiencing a progressive loss of muscle control—a primary symptom of MS—and feared *appearing* disabled. Suddenly, I saw Sarah's body and her dress as a protest against her declining sexuality and health—of her desire to maintain the appearance of health and attractiveness. Sarah was openly worried about her lopsided gait, about being able to find and keep a job, and that Carlos, her boyfriend of two years, would break up with her if her condition got worse.

Carlos didn't know about Sarah's MS. He thought her limp was related to a childhood injury—something based on a story she concocted one night when he told her she "walked funny"—and he defended it as such. But would he defend her disease? Would he remain loyal to her if her condition continued to get worse—for instance, if her speech began to deteriorate, or if she became paralyzed? Sarah imagined the possibilities and suspected that in fact Carlos would leave, adding with bitter irony that she wouldn't blame him. Even her doctors—who were surprised by how quickly her disease was progressing and recently suggested that her family move to Albuquerque or Denver where better treatments might be available—even they were beginning to abandon her. If her doctors couldn't stand by her, Sarah reasoned, why would Carlos?

As we sat in the kitchen, Sarah told me that there were other factors "making life harder than we [her family] deserve." Her mother had recently lost her job working at a nursing home in Los Alamos. She later found work as a home health-care assistant but earned half the salary of her previous job and had no benefits. In fact, everyone in the family was now worried about their ability to make ends meet, especially since they helped to pay for Sarah's costly medical treatments. Somehow, Sarah felt that these misfortunes were all her fault. She suspected that if she *just left* things would improve. I wanted to ask Sarah if her disease and related feelings of responsibility were related to her heroin use; if her desire to "leave" was an impetus for her overdose. (I myself was not ready to call it a "suicide attempt.") But I let Sarah continue with her outpouring of worries, and soon I began to worry, too. I began to worry about Sarah.

Byron Good (1994) notes that in the context of illness narratives, the narrator of the autobiographical story is relating something that is not yet finished—that there is more than one temporality woven into the narrative. This is certainly true in the case of Sarah's narrative. In the context of talking about her MS, she expressed the experience of previous "attacks" (i.e., her history of MS); her current condition, one that she identifies as being worse than before and therefore foreshadowing a grim future; and the potential for further progression of disease (and along with it, a consciousness of what she might lose). Leaving Sarah's house that afternoon, I wondered how her illness, present in all three temporal registers, came to be incorporated into her many worries, her heroin use, and the way she presented her body. I wondered how she imagined herself and her body on the night she overdosed and whether suicide remained a part of her story that was not yet finished.

Under the Skin

Sarah did not consider herself a heroin addict. She would later tell me, yes, she injected heroin, but it was one of the few things she felt like she could control. "I'm not an addict," she said. "I can take it or leave it."

Like many young women I interviewed, Sarah's boyfriend introduced her to heroin. While she described Carlos's heroin use as "more than recreational," she insisted he was not a *tecato*. In her view, the fact that Carlos had a job and a car and had not been in jail meant that he "had it together." By insisting that they were both in control of their drug use, Sarah distinguished herself and her boyfriend from the addicts who attended the group. "They have it really bad," she said. "I'm not like that. I don't, you know, *need* it."

Listening to her, I was curious about why she used heroin at all. I was even more curious about why she attended the women's recovery group if, as she insisted, she was so in control. I asked Sarah why she used. She laughed and asked me if my question was a serious one; I told her it was. After some thought, she answered that being high simply felt good. "It takes all your worries away," she said. She then related her heroin use to treating her MS. "Do you know how they treat MS? You inject yourself . . . under the skin. It's like skin popping . . . I inject every day, on my arm."

Sarah showed me the fleshy portion of her upper arm. Small needle marks, presumably from her MS medications, were still visible. She continued, "With some meds, it's in the muscle, but those don't work for me. There's this new drug my doctor told me about, it's IV, in the vein. But you can't get it here for some reason." Apparently, the regional clinic where Sarah received MS treatment lacked the equipment and support necessary for IV infusion of her medication, which was slightly ironic, given how common and readily available illicit forms of intravenous drug use were in the area.

The disease that she kept secret from Carlos fostered in her a familiarity with needles that made her, in his eyes, unusual and attractive. Sarah described how, when they began to use heroin together, Carlos was impressed that she wasn't afraid of needles. "He thought I'd want to smoke," she said. "That's what most females do at first. But I said, no, give me a hit [in the arm]. Carlos thought I was used to it, or that I had needle fever [an obsession with shooting up]. But I never shot heroin before. I just wasn't afraid."

Sarah described heroin as a "perfect high" for her—not only because she was used to needles but also because the medications for her MS made her jittery, feverish, and achy. They simply didn't alleviate the pain, "even," she said, "if the doctor says you need them—that they will make the disease slow down." Sarah's medications did not ease her pain, and she could not feel the supposed slowing of her disease. But heroin was different. With heroin, "you feel right away, and the relief from *it*."

Sarah continued, "Usually, I prefer heroin under the skin. I don't know why, maybe because I'm so used to injecting that way. Plus, I don't care about a big rush, you know? I'd rather the relief last longer, and it does if it's under the skin or in the muscle. That's where I've always injected my meds all these years."

I began to sense continuity between Sarah's experience of treating her multiple sclerosis and her heroin use. Both depended on the same route of administration—a syringe injecting "meds" beneath her skin. Both were, in their respective contexts, sanctioned. But on either side of the dividing line between these forms of use lay a dangerous silence. Carlos and the staff at Nuevo Día did not know about Sarah's disease, and Sarah's physicians and family did not know about her heroin use, at least not the extent to which she used. Sarah's mother was aware that her daughter "used in the past," and she believed that Sarah was committed to putting heroin behind her. In fact, Sarah admitted that her attendance at the women's recovery meeting was motivated in part by her mother's concern. "I don't want my mom to worry about *that*," Sarah said, suggesting that her mother already had enough to worry about and that she felt some comfort in her daughter's portrayal of herself as being "in recovery." But the truth was, she wasn't. Sarah continued to inject heroin with Carlos, even as she told her mother she was working hard to stay clean. According to Sarah, it was an essential ruse, one meant to protect her mother from the painful impression that her ailing daughter was risking her already fragile life. It was a ruse, Sarah suggested, premised on love.

Adding to this tangle of crossed signals was how Sarah experienced pain. On the few occasions that she felt sick from heroin withdrawal, she blamed her MS. Conversely, when Carlos suspected that something was physically wrong with Sarah, she would suggest that they "party" in order to assuage her pain and his concern. In both instances, Sarah diverted attention away from the shame of her double condition: multiple sclerosis and heroin addiction. She could not reconcile the anguish or shame of either and thus lived a divided life in which she silenced, to her detriment, the pain of her laments.

A Body with a Mind of Its Own

Multiple sclerosis is a curious disease. Surrounding the nerve fibers of the central nervous system is the tissue myelin, which helps nerve fibers conduct their normal electrical impulses. It is believed that MS is an autoimmune disease in which, for unknown reasons, the body attacks its own myelin. This process interferes with the ability of the nerves to conduct electrical impulses to and from the brain, thereby causing the symptoms of MS—from depression and numbness to tremors and vision problems.

The self-afflicting nature of MS was not lost on Sarah. She understood that her body was attacking itself. On one occasion, she said to me, "It doesn't really matter how much you want things to change. It's like *your body has a mind of its own.*"

This statement resonated powerfully with the accounts of many heroin addicts I spoke with who described their addiction and the course of their lives as having their own inevitable trajectory. They surrendered to this inevitability, just as Sarah seemed to surrender to living a divided life in which on the one hand she was a patient suffering from an increasingly debilitating disease, and on the other she was a young woman who liked or needed to get high and forget about her troubles. Sarah tried to keep these domains of her life separate—at least for the benefit of those she cared about and was afraid of losing if the truth of her condition were known. In this way, she lived a fragmented existence, with each fragment having its own social norms and experiences. She moved precariously between these two worlds. Sometimes it seemed that the only things that tied the two worlds together was the ritual of injection and the fear of disappointing those she loved.

·   ·   ·   ·   ·

There were two ways in which Sarah thought she asserted control over her heroin use. The first was to avoid "mainlining"—that is, to avoid injecting the drug directly into her vein and instead inject just beneath the skin (what she describes as injecting *"cautelosamente,"* or gingerly, warily.) The second was to never shoot up alone. In both gestures, Sarah expressed a certain tentativeness or reluctance toward heroin, as if by limiting her exposure to it she implied a certain foreboding. Indeed, she was aware of heroin's deadly power. One of her close childhood friends died from a heroin overdose, and her maternal uncle "lost everything" as a result of his "need." Moreover, Sarah lived in a social world where heroin overdose and its ruinous effects were commonly known—whether by actual events or in the realm of rumor. In controlling her own need, she tried to prevent a scenario in which *she* would be caught in the circulation of stories about "fallen women" that were part and parcel of the local drug discourse. This is perhaps partly why Sarah chose to remain quiet during the women's recovery group. In her words, she didn't want anyone to know—let alone talk about—her "business."

And yet she told me that the practices of separation and secrecy—whether about her drug use or her illness—were difficult to maintain. She wanted to be a survivor in the eyes of her mother and sisters, capable of overcoming heroin and her disease. In the eyes of Carlos, she wanted to be "normal" and physically alluring. Sarah straddled these two versions of herself with increasing difficulty. Her body was giving way, and so was her ability to maintain the illusion of coherence.

In one exchange that I had with Sarah, she tried to explain the context for her overdose. At that point, neither of us directly referred to her overdose as a suicide attempt, but Sarah made clear that it was intentional, thereby implicitly referring to it as suicide. And although she apologized throughout her narrative for "not making sense," she described the events and emotions that led up to her overdose with painful clarity.

"I started feeling like there was no way out, like I was living this big lie," she said. "And the thing that was hardest was that people *liked it*, the lie. They liked me but only a part of me. I kept my feelings bottled up, like my real feelings. This sounds stupid, doesn't it? I feel stupid telling you this stuff."

Sarah broke off into silence and then recalled:

I was sick back then. I was having an attack. My whole left side was hurting, and it spread to my chest. Carlos was complaining that I was no fun
anymore. I was avoiding seeing him and he was like, *you don't like me
anymore? Okay, pues, I'll move on.* But I didn't want to lose him. So one
night I said I'll come over and we'll watch a movie or something. *Pero* the
truth was I was feeling like shit. My medicine wasn't working, and my
mom was stressed about getting me to Albuquerque to see a specialist
because of her job. Everything was getting to me.

   I couldn't drive my car because I couldn't move my legs too good.
They hurt. I told Carlos I was too stoned to drive, and he picked me up
and we went to his house. Before he came over I smoked some weed so I
would smell like it and be more chill. I was used to making everything
look like I said it was, like I was okay, just high. He didn't suspect anything, and when he picked me up he was all happy. It made me kind of
sad actually, that he was happy and didn't know what I was going
through.

During the drive to Carlos's house, Sarah tried to keep her pain secret.
But she was feeling increasingly agitated, and she worried that the marijuana she hoped would veil her pain had in fact amplified it. Things continued to spiral.

When we got to his house he wanted to have sex right away. He was
complaining that it had been so long. But I couldn't. I felt like I was
having a heart attack or something because my chest was all tight and
then it went like still or something and I like couldn't breathe. Carlos
said, *what's wrong with you?* He thought I was having a panic attack, but
I knew it was something else. He was like, *let's get high, that will make you
feel better.* But I had already smoked weed, and I just wanted a Xanax or
something. So I did. I took Xanax, and we tried to watch a movie. The
Xanax helped for a while.

According to several physicians I interviewed, the anti-anxiety medication alprazolam, or Xanax, is the most commonly used prescription
drug in the Española Valley. It is widely prescribed by physicians and is
also sold "on the street."

   Sarah continued:

Carlos wanted to have sex, and I was not into it, but I tried. It didn't feel right. My body was making me nervous. It was twitching. I thought he could see it twitching, and he was like, *what the fuck is wrong with you?* Now I know he didn't mean my body, just my attitude. Maybe he saw my leg spasm, I don't know. . . .

I told him he was being an ass and I wanted to go home. It wasn't true, but that's what I said. He was really pissed. He started calling me names. He called me a fucking retard, and I hit him, not hard, but I hit him. He was shocked. He's not a violent type, you know? Me neither. He didn't hit me back, but he called me names and said, *it's over.* I acted like I didn't care.

Before I left his house I stole some *chiva* from his stash. I wasn't really thinking when I took it. I just did.

When Sarah returned home, her mother and sisters were already in bed, the house dark. She sat in the family room for a while and thought about her fight with Carlos. She told me that the more she thought about it, the more upset she became and the more she wanted to talk. She called Carlos's cell phone, but he didn't answer. She called again and again, and still Carlos did not answer. She assumed he was out partying with friends and deliberately ignoring her calls. The thought of this enraged her. "I was imagining all kinds of things," she said. As her mind raced, her left side continued to itch and spasm. Sarah told me she hated her body. She pounded on her legs in the solitude of the darkened family room.

As Sarah talked to me about the moments preceding her overdose, I was acutely aware of the closeness of the event. Not only were we relatively near in time to it (the overdose occurred only a few months before our interview), but we sat in the very room where she called out to Carlos, where she struck herself in a moment of deep despair. I looked around the family room, taking in its pale blue sofa set and a vase of plastic roses. The room seemed a stage to me, a panoramic theater designed to represent the normal and tragic setting of a profound historical event. But Sarah did not attempt suicide in the family room. Rather, she did so in the privacy of her bedroom—a room she did not invite me to see.

Sarah recalled almost jokingly that she hadn't even remembered the heroin she stole from Carlos, that is, until she went into her bedroom and began to undress. She described seeing the clear plastic baggie that contained the *gorritas* of heroin. It was more heroin than she had ever used, yet she decided to cook it all. She debated about filling three separate syringes—each containing one *gorrita*, which was her usual fix. But she decided to load the entire amount into one syringe and inject it into a vein. Sarah described her decision as being a kind of whim. "I didn't think about it really. It's like, my head went blank and I just acted. I knew it was more than I ever did, but I didn't care. That was, you know, the whole point. I didn't care."

Finding a vein was difficult, perhaps because she was nervous. She described tying and slapping her skin. "I was like, *come on, come on!* When I got one and I could really see it, I just shoved the needle in. I didn't even think twice. I just wanted to get all the *chiva* in me nice and strong, and I did."

I asked Sarah if she had been afraid. After a long pause, she responded, "If I was afraid of anything, it was that it wasn't enough. That I'd just get sick from it and nothing else. That it wouldn't work."

During the course of my research, when I asked addicts what it feels like to inject heroin, I was usually told one of two things: that it feels like heaven or that it's not worth trying to explain since I would never understand. When I asked the same question of Sarah, referring to that summer night, she closed her eyes and said to me, "Snow. It feels like you're surrounded by snow."

Afterlife

The emergency medical technicians who first responded to Sarah and eventually transferred her to the local hospital alerted the attending physician that her overdose was a suspected suicide. This prompted a nurse to interview Sarah the following morning. The nurse asked Sarah whether she knew she had injected a lethal dose of heroin and whether her intention was to die; Sarah answered yes—yes, she was aware that she might die.

But Sarah did not die that night—because of Carlos. On discovering the missing heroin, Carlos became both enraged and concerned. After trying Sarah's cell phone, he called the family's home phone and awakened Sarah's mother. In the confusion of the moment, she said to Carlos that her daughter was certainly with him. But with Carlos still on the line, Sarah's mother went to her daughter's bedroom, where she discovered her lying unresponsive on her bed.

Things fall quickly into place at the sight of a body in the state of overdose. There is a particular orchestration of cries, phone calls, and frantic gestures—always the same. Sitting in Sarah's family room, I could imagine how her house and family moved from absolute stillness to panic. But for the first time I could imagine something else: what it's like to be revived—to come back to the sights and sounds of concerned faces surrounding you. And in this image I found a degree of comfort.

SCENE TWO: STATES OF EMERGENCY

It's three o'clock on a Tuesday afternoon and the emergency room's waiting area is full again. All sixteen seats are occupied—some with patients in varying degrees of distress, others with concerned or bored family members. In one seat, a young mother tries to console her crying baby whose small, round face is red with fever. The mother anxiously offers a breast, but her baby recoils and continues to cry. In another seat, a man tends to his profusely bleeding nose. A stream of blood courses down his tattooed forearm and gathers in a pool on the waiting room floor. A concerned neighbor brings him a wad of toilet paper and tells him that his nose must be broken. Despite the physical awkwardness of the situation, the men engage in easy conversation, while in another seat, an elderly woman who smells strongly of alcohol frantically waves a swollen and purplish arm. A group of children watch in apparent amusement while the old woman cries, "*¡Se quema, se quema!*" (It burns, it burns!).

It is a typical afternoon in the ER waiting room. With only one nurse and one physician on duty, the patients-in-waiting are resigned to a long stay. Many have already traveled a great distance. An eighty-two-year-old sitting next to me says he's from the village of Los Ojos, more than seventy miles away. With watery eyes and a sunken mouth, he explains he waited two weeks for his son to make arrangements to pick him up and drive him to the hospital to attend to what he suspects is a broken ankle. He shows me his makeshift cane, which he has made out of a sturdy branch of pine, and asks in whispery Spanish whether I think the hospital will arrange for a proper crutch so he can walk again.

There are only eighty beds in Española Hospital, whose charge is to serve all of Rio Arriba County. Nearly half the county's forty-two thousand residents are uninsured, and the ER is ground zero for Rio Arriba's sick and injured. Like many hospitals that serve a large uninsured population, much of its caseload is related to primary and urgent care. The hospital's recently opened urgent care unit, adjacent to the ER, was established to reduce the burden of the ER's caseload, so that "true emergencies" could be attended to. In practice, patients—especially those without insurance—wait so long to be seen that they all become "emergencies."

Drug-related hospitalizations account for approximately 500 per 100,000 admissions—more than twice the statewide rate—and nearly 27 percent of all hospitalizations are related to violent injury, homicide, or suicide, much of which is also presumably drug related.[4] All of which is to say that drug-related injury and illness accounts for a significant portion of the ER's hospital admissions.

Beatrice Lopez fetches me from the waiting area, and after wishing the old man with a broken ankle good luck, I follow her through a locked door and into the interior of the ER. Beatrice has worked as a nurse at Española Hospital for more than ten years, during which time she observed a dramatic shift in caseload from alcohol- to heroin-related emergencies. Recently, she has become concerned by a precipitous increase in rates of what she suspects are intentional overdoses, especially among female addicts. "Before," she explains, "we treated all overdoses like accidental poisonings. But I became suspicious of the numbers. Maybe because I am from this community, and I know these kids. I know their troubles. I started thinking, is this accidental? What's going on? Are we sure it's just the purity of the drug? I knew we needed to start asking overdose patients, Did you *mean* to do this?"

On the afternoon of my visit, two of the six beds were occupied by heroin overdoses, and Beatrice pointed out the curtain-drawn stalls that contained these patients. In one lay a nineteen-year-old man whose overdose was considered accidental. In the other was a forty-two-year-old woman; her overdose was "possibly intentional." Both patients, Beatrice says, are lucky to be alive.

Overdose patients are now routinely asked if their overdose was "accidental" or "intentional." But the determination of intentionality by medical staff is by no means straightforward. In rare cases, patients will report having deadly designs when injecting or mixing drugs, acknowledging matter-of-factly their intention to die. But when asked if their overdoses were intentional, most patients respond ambiguously. They might acknowledge feelings of depression or loneliness prior to their overdose or say that they wanted to "just go away." Only on occasion will they go so far as to say that they wanted to die—even if it is clear to the medical staff and loved ones that this was indeed the case. Thus the determination of intentionality is usually one based on judgment and intuition. Beatrice explains:

> You learn to read a particular case. How someone comes in is really important. Were they dropped off anonymously? Usually that rules it out and suggests accidental overdose. You pay attention to how the person responds to being revived. Believe me, it makes a difference whether they are happy or not [about being revived]. If it's a mother and she doesn't ask about her kids, well, I think that's a sign that something's going on, something's not right. If they're still despondent even with good vitals, that's probably a clue. These are things you look for. You have to take all the factors in. You ask questions, but you know you're probably not going to get a straight answer. So you watch for things.

As we tour the ER, Beatrice says it's typical to have overdose cases at this time of day, even midweek. But she adds that if I *really* want to see the ER in action, I should come in the early morning hours when things "heat up." She explains, "What happens is people wait till the last minute to bring overdoses in. They're hoping things will improve without intervention, or they're afraid of getting into trouble. So when we get overdose cases, they're in the worst possible state—unresponsive, not breath-

Figure 8. Wall of prayers. Photo by the author.

ing, low pulse—basically almost dead. In the wee hours, that's who is in these beds right here. Not the sick but the dying."

Not the sick but the dying. I was struck by this distinction and wondered if and how it mirrored determinations of intentionality. What standards of care were in place to attend to "the dying"? Or were those who intentionally overdosed considered, to a certain extent, already dead?

Visible Concealments

Whereas much is known about heroin addiction and suicide as distinct areas of concern, the issue of suicide among heroin users, or heroin overdose as a means to suicide, has received little attention in anthropological or psychiatric literature (Appleby 2000; Darke and Ross 2002). Meanwhile, the few epidemiological studies that have characterized heroin overdose events identify a *perceived* relationship between overdose and suicide; rarely do they demonstrate the prevalence of attempted or completed suicide by overdose among heroin users (Farrell 1996).

One notable exception is an overdose surveillance study of two northern New Mexico hospital emergency departments, one of them Española Hospital (Shah 2006). This study examined the characteristics and intent of overdose events that occurred between July 2004 and August 2005. According to the study, during this fourteen-month period, there were 561 emergency department visits due to drug overdose, representing 506 unique patients. At Española Hospital 48 percent were female and nearly 70 percent were Hispanic, and the median patient age was thirty-five. Overdoses resulting from a combination of over-the-counter and prescription (i.e., benzodiazepine) medications and heroin were the routine presentation in the emergency department. Significantly, nearly half (47 percent) of overdoses were determined to be attempted suicide; female gender was the most significant covariate among those who attempted suicide by overdose.

The study's association between female gender, heroin overdose, and suicide intentionality mirrored findings from my own random review of Nuevo Día's patient intake surveys for 2004. Of the twenty female surveys sampled, nine women reported overdosing within the year. Of these women, five reported that their overdose was intentional—in other words, that they injected a lethal dose of heroin with the intent to die. While the total number of women compared to men was smaller, the percentage of women who reported heroin overdose with the intent to die was approximately three times that of men. Alarmingly, more than half the women who overdosed reported suicide intentionality.

Both the literature on suicide and the experience of local health providers agree that such numbers likely reflect only a portion of actual suicide attempts. The incidence of attempted suicide is estimated to be ten to twenty times that of completed suicide.[5] How many suicide attempts remain unacknowledged?

Underreporting is frequently linked to the persistent stigma associated with suicide, whose effects touch not only the suicidal subject but also his or her survivors. And while suicide-related stigma is likely an impediment to disclosure in some cases, one wonders about alternative framings for understanding the silence that surrounds intentional overdose, especially in a milieu where the family is often at the center of heroin use. Indeed, during my visit to the ER, Beatrice remarked:

> We know that there are people who won't disclose [overdose with suicidal intention]. And why should they? It isn't just a pride thing. It's . . . *¿que vamos hacer para ellos?* [what are we going to do for them?] There just aren't enough services. So patients come into the ER because of an OD and, if they're lucky, survive and are released. But they usually return.
>
> I've been here long enough to know if someone's coming back, and I can sense—ah, this is hard to say—but I can sense if the next time they're gonna be so lucky. I've seen the same person two, three times. *Y la última vez, es muy tarde* [And the last time, it's too late].

Two issues in particular struck me in Beatrice's characterization. First, I was struck by the idea that an unknown number of overdose patients do not disclose their suicidal intentions because of a sense of futility and not because of stigma (characterized as "pride"). When Beatrice asked what the point of disclosure was given the anticipated absence of an effective response, she captured the sense of worthlessness that mirrored feelings addicts described to me about the inefficacy of rehab. These feelings, of course, flow from concrete experiences of what is deemed "drug relapse" or "treatment failure"—impoverished terms that do not accurately attend to the complex phenomenology of addiction and feelings of failure and worthlessness. Over the course of my research, I frequently heard drug counselors, parole officers, health providers, and addicts repeat the dictum "The odds are stacked against you" when describing the likelihood that most addicts would *not* be able to stay off heroin. Combined with the shortage of effective services, such a message contributes to the widespread sense of futility in attempting recovery and has significant moral and practical implications for the suicidal addict.

Second, I was struck by Beatrice's overall sense of the inevitability of overdose and patients' eventual (successful) suicides. At first I understood it as symptomatic of the hopelessness and burnout that many clinicians feel, especially those who work in resource-poor hospitals with high caseloads (see Raviola et al. 2002). Indeed, I had witnessed this among drug counselors and mental health professionals working in the region—the particular kind of moral detachment that one succumbs to after working too long in an environment of mounting need and repeated loss. But Beatrice's account of caring for the same overdose patient multiple times and the particular foreboding she often felt—knowing that the next time would likely be the last time—was not at all "distant" in tone or affect. Rather, her account was morally charged, and she made it clear that her pursuit of the question of suicide intentionality was based on a commitment to *not* let overdose-related deaths be routinely mislabeled "accidental poisonings." She said:

> Each time I see someone come in, I feel kind of like we've failed. Drugs have been our number one issue in this community for twenty years, and we haven't got a grip on it yet. We haven't done anything really as far as I'm concerned, based on what I see here.
>
> I tell people it's not enough to add another bed. Not when you go home and Mom and Dad or your husband or kids are shooting up in the other room. And here [the hospital], it's all triage, you know, put a bandage on the problem and send the patient to another facility. When I started seeing the same ones coming back, I started feeling like it wasn't right to call it "accidental." I started asking questions, you know, to the patients, even before the doctors or administrators knew I was asking them.

Questions like?

Questions like ¿*Usted lo pretendió?* [Did you mean to do it?] And many people, *many people*, you know, they would break down crying. They would tell me, *yes, I meant it.* It really broke my heart. And it made me angry.

What do you do with that information?

You know, it's hard to say, because honestly there's not a lot I can do with it other than make referrals. I know right now there are researchers getting grants for this kind of information, and they say it's to make services better. But I don't have a lot of faith in the system because, like I said, I see the same people over and over. So what I really do is make sure, you know, it doesn't get lost . . . that when someone comes in and they've OD'd we don't just check a box saying it was an accident, because no matter how you look at the situation, there's nothing accidental about it.

While Beatrice worked hard to rewrite the script of the "accidental overdose," she relied on the language of "luck" when attributing survival to overdose patients. She did not see her own care, or the care of others, as constituting the possibility of recovery. Indeed, she said she had little faith in local structures of care and admitted to collecting data on suicide intentionality to ensure that the events were recognized as such, not necessarily to change their outcome. Moreover, in expressing a pervasive sense of the inevitability of patients' tragic return to the ER, Beatrice sullenly suggested that change was unlikely.

Thus, in Beatrice's account, one sees how language and event constitute each other: the overdose is intentional, even inevitable; the recovery is accidental. Emerging from her experience of witnessing too many overdoses and deaths, such a view becomes an essential part of the devastating cycle of overdose and suicide. I wanted to ask Beatrice about this, about the potential consequences of her account. Some months after our first interview in the ER, I returned to the hospital on a whim, hoping to schedule a follow-up interview. When I arrived, Beatrice was standing in the parking lot with a medical assistant. They were smoking cigarettes and talking softly. When I approached, Beatrice shook her head and told me that I had arrived just in time. It had happened again—another life lost.

SCENE THREE: *LA ÚLTIMA VEZ* (THE LAST TIME)

In the previous chapter I introduced Lisa Archuleta, a heroin addict whose daughter Michelle died of a heroin overdose, which I later learned was a presumed suicide. I described the "bonds of shame" that Lisa and Michelle forged in their years of using heroin together—bonds that I argue led Lisa to seek treatment for her addiction and, after her daughter's death, to resume her heroin use. I ended with a scene describing the day I showed up unannounced at Lisa's trailer. Lisa was high. During that brief and awkward visit, she showed me her wrist, which memorialized her daughter in the form of a tattoo. Even today, years later, I can recall feeling angry with Lisa: angry that she was high and her daughter Michelle was dead; that Michelle was etched on Lisa's body like so many other scars. I did not fully understand these feelings, but I swore as I drove home that it would be my last visit with Lisa. It was not.

In fact, following her relapse, Lisa and I saw each other several times before I left the field, and we have talked on the phone since. Unlike the visits and conversations before Michelle's death, these were largely prompted by Lisa and not by me. I admit that I found it hard to listen to Lisa talk about her struggle to regain her sobriety after her daughter's death. But I did listen—even if a part of me shut down.

In January 2007 Lisa called me in California to talk about the death of Alma (see chap. 2). Before I had an opportunity to process the news of Alma's death, Lisa began sobbing on the phone. It was a sound that I was familiar with: the morning her daughter Michelle died, Lisa also called and wept.

As Lisa shared the little information that she had regarding Alma's overdose, I became distracted by the recognition of a particular continuity of feeling that the sound of a weeping woman can bring. On hearing Lisa's familiar crying, I felt—for the first time in nearly two years—the same rush of sorrow and regret that I felt when she called me after *her* daughter's death. Simultaneously, I experienced the same continuity of feeling elicited by the news of an overdose—that terrible mix of anger and dread. The two strands of emotion do not reconcile easily.

As I listened to Lisa talk, I was aware of the way that she wove into her account of Alma's death recollections of her daughter's death—as if, to a degree, the two were interchangeable. In interweaving the two lives, Lisa must have felt her own continuity of events and emotions.

Lisa described the last time she saw Alma. It was a December afternoon. The two women—who met when they were patients at the recovery program—ran into each other at the Española Post Office. They talked briefly about the holidays; neither woman had special plans or felt like celebrating. Alma mentioned feeling tired and stressed out, but Lisa said that there was no indication things were that bad. They hugged each other, wished one another Happy New Year, and said good-bye. The interaction was unremarkable.

Perhaps it was the everyday nature of their interaction and the feeling that she "should have known" (and ostensibly would have been able to do something to alter the course of Alma's future) that led to a subtle shift in Lisa's narrative. In this shift, Lisa recalled her final interaction with her daughter.

On that day, Michelle drove up to Española from Santa Fe with a female friend to visit her mother, who had not yet entered rehab. Lisa recalled that Michelle seemed fine: she was not "strung out" and did not ask for money or drugs. Michelle and her friend drove Lisa to Walmart for groceries. The three women then had lunch. Lisa described the visit as "nice and relaxed." That afternoon, she was able to imagine a future in which her daughter would join her in Española and the two of them would get clean together and start a new life. "That's what makes it so hard," Lisa said, referring to her final visit with Michelle. She felt that she had missed a vital clue that her daughter's life was hanging in the balance. "I still think about it all the time," she said, referring to their last afternoon together.

> Every day I think about it. And I can't think of anything that explains *it*. There was nothing. We didn't argue or nothing. There was no problem . . . nothing I could see. That's why for a long time I didn't believe. 'Cause everything felt good that day . . . that last time I saw her, I mean. So when it came up [that Michelle's overdose was a suicide] I couldn't believe that she wanted it that way. She's my daughter, and I couldn't believe that after all we'd been through together . . . that I didn't know.
>
> Sometimes I don't know if it's true [that she committed suicide]. It's harder to believe than anything else. But that day in the hospital, I knew.

The first talk of suicide occurred the morning that Lisa went to identify her daughter's body at the hospital, which had been anonymously dropped off at the ER. Such a "point of entry" is consistent with accidental overdoses; co-users attempt to solicit medical care for the overdose victim but are afraid of potential legal repercussions. In such cases victims are deposited in the ER waiting room or in the hospital parking lot. In some fatal instances, identifying information that is written on the

Figure 9.   Alone. Photo by the author.

skin or in the form of a note accompanies the victim's person, so that hospital personnel can contact next of kin.

Beatrice was on duty the morning Michelle arrived. Initially, she also assumed that the overdose was accidental. However, a handwritten recitation of the Lord's Prayer was found in Michelle's jeans pocket and suggested otherwise. The hospital knew that it would be important to determine if the overdose victim wrote the note. If so, the fatal overdose would be consistent with other suicide cases where a prayer accompanied the deceased body.

I drove Lisa to the hospital to identify her daughter's body. Some months later I would learn that in addition to being asked to confirm Michelle's identity, Lisa was asked if she recognized the handwriting in the note bearing the Lord's Prayer. With some hesitation, Lisa confirmed both. She recalled:

> I knew when I saw her that it was her, my baby. But I was confused. I wanted to ask her, *Why are you here?* She was living in Santa Fe. What was she doing [in Española]? It took me a minute to put two and two together . . . that she couldn't, you know, tell me . . . that she was gone.

They showed me the letter. They said, *Did she write this?* I looked at it and didn't know. It looked like her writing, but it was long ago [that she'd seen her handwriting]. I told them I wasn't sure. I thought it was. That's what I told them.

It was the only prayer she knew. She didn't know anything else.

I learned [the Lord's Prayer] when I was like ten years old. I remember a foster mom teaching it to me. I thought if I learned it good, I don't know, good things would happen. I prayed it hard. No lie. I prayed it hard, and I taught it to Michelle when she was just a little girl.

Sometimes the whole situation feels like a nightmare, like I'll wake up and it'll all be different. Now when I think of that prayer, I don't know [voice trails off]. It doesn't mean the same thing. Everything's changed.

An Unreliable Witness

Some months after her daughter's death, Lisa tried to make sense of why Michelle was in Española the night she overdosed, as well as of the meaning of the prayer that was found in her pocket. We were sitting in a small, windowless room at Nuevo Día's outpatient services building. Lisa was meeting with a drug counselor, who had invited me to observe the session as a part of my research. The counselor instructed me to sit behind Lisa so that I would not disrupt the flow of the session. But when Lisa spoke of her daughter's death, she turned awkwardly in her chair—her back to the counselor—and addressed me.

During the counseling session, Lisa explained that she still didn't understand the circumstances of Michelle's overdose—that is, why and how Michelle was in Española, who dropped her off at the ER, and whether the person knew that she was already dead. She speculates that the female friend who accompanied Michelle during their final visit may have been present during her overdose, but she cannot recall the friend's name. Lisa reluctantly admitted to being high the afternoon they met.

Even with all the unknowns, Lisa believed that the site of her daughter's overdose was intentional, that Michelle wanted to be near her mother so that she might be easily found. And, reversing an earlier statement, Lisa was convinced that the prayer that accompanied her in death was intended to keep her alive.

She didn't mean to do that. She . . . we had some close calls, both of us [with heroin overdose]. That's what happened. She didn't mean it on purpose. *Con determinación.* She was maybe angry at me for moving away, trying to change my ways. I don't know. She was . . .

Sometimes she would, like, just tell me she wanted peace and quiet. If that means anything . . . I don't know.

All I know. It [the prayer] was supposed to protect her. That's what prayers are for. That's why she had it. That's why. I taught it to her. It would just, like, pop in my head.

Lisa began to slowly recite, misremembering the words:

Our Father whose in heaven, how will be your name. Thy kingdom come, thy will be done on earth as is in heaven. Give us this day. Give us our daily bread. And forgive our trespasses as we forgive those who did it to us. Please lead us not in temptation and deliver us from evil. Thank you, Lord. Amen.

Lisa shook her head in a gesture that conveyed both disbelief and certainty, her words writing and rewriting the script that was hers and her daughter's life.

There's no way I can believe that she really meant to do it, even if that's what people are saying. She just wanted, maybe, I don't know. Tell me something? I mean, she wanted to tell *me* something. She wanted me to find her. That's why. But it didn't work.

I kept telling her, *You can't do that! It's too much!* The thing is, she never knew how to handle it. I would have made sure it wasn't going to go down like this. I would help her. Back then, I mean. I wanted her to be in here with me. In the program. But even if we were on the streets, loaded, this wouldn't have happened.

She'd be okay. I would make sure she'd be okay.

·   ·   ·   ·   ·

At the time of the session, Lisa was shooting heroin again and was obviously high when she met with her drug counselor. Physically, she appeared sluggish: her head and shoulders drooped with the force of gravity, and her pupils, when I saw them, were huge. Vocally, she spoke in an unusually slow drawl, and her thoughts were often disconnected. But the disconnectedness might too easily be interpreted as an effect of her drug-induced state. In my view, it pointed to the kind of disorientation that often accompanies unexpected loss. Indeed, Lisa's movement between states of "knowing" and "not knowing" suggests this. It also suggests her profound desire to understand her daughter's death, and the very limits of such understanding.

Many months after this interview took place, I carefully pieced together Lisa's narrative in the quiet of my home. I was five months' pregnant at the time, and, perhaps because of my pregnancy and the gravity of experience Lisa detailed, I transcribed her recorded thoughts and memories with great care. About to give birth to twin daughters, I felt that it was more important than ever to try to understand—however imperfectly—the meaning of Michelle's suicide. I believed, as Lisa did, that Michelle was trying to tell her mother something and that she did, in fact, want to be found—though I was not convinced she wanted to be found alive. I believed, as I imagine Lisa did, that through her death Michelle was communicating how deeply hurt she was and that her hurt was caused, at least in part, by her mother and their years of heroin use.

It is, of course, impossible to know for certain Michelle's intentions or her emotional and psychological state, just as it is impossible to know why the Lord's Prayer was in her pocket when she died. Perhaps it is even dangerous to rely on speculation and belief when trying to understand the final moments and intentions of the deceased. But, in the absence of Michelle, there was little else to consider.

I turned to the clinical literature on heroin addiction and suicide for clues. Unfortunately, much of it simply attributed the expected "risk factors" to suicide: depression, social isolation, and family dysfunction, factors that could not capture the complexity of Lisa and Michelle's relationship and their struggle of connectedness and alienation. Nor do references to the fatal dangers of "poly-drug use" in the context of heroin overdose account for what Lisa suggested was the reckless nature of her daughter's drug habit.

The closest witness to Michelle's death was Lisa. Listening and transcribing her narrative, it struck me as ironic that I was seeking Michelle's voice through her mother's; that, in her absence, I had to rely on Lisa—high again on heroin—to give meaning to Michelle's actions and intentions. I couldn't help but wonder what Michelle would have thought of this—what objections she might have had to my methodology and Lisa's explanation of events, especially concerning the question of responsibility. Indeed, more often than not, Lisa blamed others for her daughter's death: drug dealers, former boyfriends, and failed social services. She blamed her daughter's poly-drug use and her relative inexperience when it came to shooting heroin. When she finally did speak of her own possible role in her daughter's death, she did so in terms of *not knowing* her daughter was in trouble or in pain. She would ask, "Why didn't I know? Why didn't I ask if everything was all right?" In such questions, Lisa implied that—by knowing—she might have prevented Michelle's death. And each time I heard Lisa utter these words, I wanted to ask her, "How could you *not* know?"

It was a question that I could not ask.

Gesture of Transformation

In her work on Greek mourning rituals, Nadia Seremetakis (1991) demonstrates how the interaction between acoustic, bodily, and linguistic manifestations of lament are able to distinguish between public definitions of the "good" and "bad" death. Lamenting a death through screaming, the presence of kin, and the physical gestures of wailing construct a "good death." A death that is met with silence and the absence of kin constitutes a "bad death." Seremetakis argues that it is the role of women to witness death and that women in particular can transform—through the form of their laments—a bad death into a good one.

Similarly, a kind of transformation took place at Michelle's Rosary, though not necessarily one that converted bad into good (although, in some contexts, Michelle's death might indeed be considered a "bad" death). In this instance, it was not the "value" of the deceased that was to be transformed through the work of mourning but the nature of the relationship between Lisa and Michelle.

Michelle's Rosary was a simple affair. It was attended by a handful of close friends, most of whom were women. There were no decorative

flowers or photo collages that charted Michelle's life, nor was there cel-
ebratory music or speeches. The focal point of the event was Michelle
herself—whose still body, dressed in yellow, lay in a plain white
casket.

Lisa knelt before Michelle. Unlike the hysterical wailings that Seremetakis describes, Lisa wept softly. She remained thus, even while her
friend Rose led the small gathering through the endless recitations of
Our Fathers—the very prayer that accompanied Michelle's body into
death—and Hail Marys. As they were presented, the prayers seemed
like they were just part of the ritualistic order of things.

At the completion of the Rosary, Lisa was embraced by friends who
offered heartfelt condolences and donations to offset the cost of renting
the funeral home for the gathering. (There would be no formal funeral,
as there was no money to pay for it.) As people collected in the parking
lot and prepared to leave, there was no mention of shame or responsibility, or talk about the details of Michelle's death. Instead, the talk was
about Lisa's pain, the pain of any mother who has lost a child.

In a strange way, it seemed a completely normal afternoon. The circumstances of the loss were unimportant. A child had died and people
had gathered around her, and her grieving mother, one last time. That afternoon, all was forgiven, all transgressions absolved.

.   .   .   .   .

I want to end this chapter by returning to the epigraph from the Book of
Matthew with which I began: *My soul is sorrowful even to death. Remain
here and keep watch with me.* The passage comes from the moment in the
gospel when Jesus has asked Peter to keep vigil with him in his hour of
need at Gethsemane; soon, Jesus, abandoned by all his disciples, will
face death alone.

Although I am not a religious person, I have often thought of that
passage in relation to this question of overdose and suicide, wondering,
might things have turned out differently if we were to remain watchful
with one another? How many overdoses might have been prevented, suicides interrupted? Would Alma and Michelle still be alive?

The notion of "watchfulness" is somewhat vague, but to me it suggests an ethics of community and a form of care. To remain watchful *with* one another—not over or against the other—is to offset forms of alienation that accompany addiction and to insist on the persistence of certain intimate ties. It is a practice that opens up the possibility of being-together, which is, in the end, the very heart of social commensurability. In the midst of loss, insecurity, and abandonment, the healing potential of social commensurability, of keeping watch with one another, remains vital.

FIVE Experiments with Care

I had three sets of neighbors during the time I conducted my research, and all were related to each other by blood or by marriage. For the most part, I only talked to the "good ones." I bought my firewood from them, and we exchanged homemade gifts during the holidays. Their dogs played with my dogs. They kept an eye on things when I was out of town, including and especially my *other* neighbors—their relatives—who I worried about and who they agreed I *should* worry about. More than once, they reported that they had to come to my place armed with a shotgun to chase away trespassers. For some time I doubted the truth of these reports, until I offered my house to a friend during one of my absences. My friend confirmed the story about my gun-toting neighbor and swore he would never visit me again.

My other two sets of neighbors were drug dealers. Although they fit the profile of my research, I never considered them subjects—never interviewed them. Early on during my fieldwork, I decided it was too risky. For two and a half years, our conversations were kept to a respectful minimum. But I watched them closely from my attic window, especially at night, when they would appear—fighting and screaming and dealing— in the headlights of the cars that showed up at their houses. I read about them frequently in the regional weekly paper. More than once they were front-page news.

I did not regret my decision to keep a distance from them until, one evening, I read about their latest tragedy from my home in Los Angeles. I was sitting in the living room with my husband, both of us quietly reading the world news on our respective laptops. Rubén gasped, then turned quiet. I looked toward him and saw that his eyes were full of pain. "You have to read this," he said, at the same time shielding his computer from me. Once again my old neighbors, the "bad ones," were headline news. Their youngest son, Danny, had mysteriously died.

I remembered seeing Danny's mother pregnant with him, the sudden presence of a stroller and a playpen in her yard. During this time, things at her house were calmer; there wasn't as much screaming or traffic or tears. Once, when I was outside pulling weeds, I spotted her older son kicking a ball around. I asked him if he was excited to be a big brother. His serious face brightened. Of course he was excited.

His baby brother, Danny, was only two years old when he died. According to early newspaper reports, he had been suffering from a cold. His mother had slept in late after a night of caring for him. When she went to his crib the following day, he wasn't breathing. He was dead.

From the minute I saw the headlines, I knew that it was a drug overdose. It took the state Office of the Medical Investigator three months to confirm this—half the usual time. The local newspaper published the toxicology results—again, on the front page. Danny's system contained a concoction of cold medicine, alcohol, and morphine. Along with the toxicology results, the article reported details of the family's mounting legal troubles.

I would learn from my "good" neighbors that Danny's mother left her sick baby with her husband when she was at work. And he left his son at home so that he could meet a connection by the river. It was only supposed to be a few minutes, but he shot up and time evaporated. When he got home, Danny was crying. He gave him a capful of children's cold medicine. Danny wouldn't stop crying. He rubbed alcohol on Danny's swollen gums. The crying continued. He applied heroin in the same manner, on the gums, on the underside of the lips. Soon the crying stopped.

On my next trip to New Mexico, I visited the cemetery in my old village. The burials there are still conducted as they were generations ago—a mound of dirt marking the grave. I immediately spotted the grave of one of my neighbors who had recently died from a heroin overdose at the age of forty-one. Her grave was decorated with a single wooden cross with the words, "Daughter and mother."

A few plots down was Danny's grave. His small mound was completely covered with toys. Teddy bears and Matchbox cars and cowboys-and-Indians figurines. Little blond angels and superheroes. Dozens of crosses and Jesuses and Virgins and pinwheels that spun in the breeze. I read one of the many handwritten notes his mother—the neighbor to whom I rarely dared to speak—had placed there. Among her promises to her son was this: I will be joining you soon.

A SENTENCE

In August 2006 Nuevo Día's detoxification clinic was forced to close after two years of operation. HealthValue, the private managed care company contracted by the state to administer its behavioral health services, which include drug treatment, determined that the detox clinic was "not credible." Among its chief complaints was the clinic's lack of twenty-four-hour trained medical supervision.

I interviewed a representative of HealthValue soon after the clinic closed. She explained, "This is serious business. People can have seizures during detox. They can overdose on the medications if they are not used properly. The staff at Nuevo Día were not prepared to deal with these issues. They didn't have the necessary medical or counseling training. And the patients—they're not stable. Our records show they weren't stable. There's diabetes, high blood pressure, other diseases. To begin with, those patients don't even qualify for treatment. You have to have a trained medical staff and stable patients. Nuevo Día didn't have this."

I asked, "So, when you say 'not credible,' do you mean 'unstable'?"

"Yes. Yes, you can say that."

The idea that Nuevo Día lacked credibility and that it was, like its patients, "unstable" revealed long-standing cultural assumptions about the Española Valley—that it was essentially premodern and its people irrational and untrustworthy. Such assumptions have been maintained in part by the ever-present reference of Los Alamos, which exemplifies the cultural and technological logics that the Española Valley is deemed to lack. As I discussed in chapter 2, the process by which Los Alamos and not Española became "modern" involved its mobilization and concentration of resources in the name of national security, which came at a great cost, materially and psychically, to the communities in the valley below.

This historically fraught relationship continues to plague the everyday relations between the two communities. On news that the region's only drug detoxification clinic would be closed, an emergency meeting was called to discuss the potential public health consequences. Providers and concerned community members in Region Three—Los Alamos, Rio Arriba, and Santa Fe Counties—attended the meeting. The decision to hold the meeting in Los Alamos, which is a central site of power but on the periphery of northern New Mexico's heroin crisis, is a small but significant example of the continued processes of disinvestment from Española of the very standards and capacities of healing that are demanded of it.

The criteria by which HealthValue determined that Nuevo Día lacked credibility and stability reflected transformations long under way in the arena of health care and social services in the state of New Mexico and the United States more broadly. These centered on the "reform" of the federally funded Medicaid system, which serves the poor, and its transformation into a for-profit managed care model. Embedded in this restructuring are certain ideologies and claims that intensify already existent barriers to treatment access and reinforce the unequal distribution of health care resources. A brief review of the principles and techniques of managed care brings to light the conflict between bureaucratic standard-ization, privatizing interests, and local experience.

MISMANAGED MARKETS

The managed care model of health care is part of a troubled dialectic, a dialectic framed by the dismantling of public institutions of care and the implementation of new and expanding modes of corporate managerial techniques that promote efficiency, transparency, and cost-effectiveness in health care. In the Medicaid arena, the ideology and practices of man-agerialism promise to transform the welfare state from an assemblage of "unresponsive, paternalistic and leaden bureaucracies" into a "healthy" bureaucracy by means of rigorous discipline and oversight (Clarke and Newman 1997: 34; see also Clarke 2004; Rylko-Bauer and Farmer 2002). The wide governmental embrace of managed care in the 1990s paralleled much broader processes of welfare state restructuring, including devolu-tion, or the transfer of federal responsibility for social service provision to the state level as a means of "reform" and privatization.[1] With the highest percentage of its population living below the poverty level of any state in the nation, New Mexico was precisely the kind of setting that the new Medicaid managed care model looked to service.

The state's rationale for adopting a managed care approach for Medicaid recipients was based on opinions regarding the overuse of behavioral health services in particular. State officials worried that un-der Medicaid's fee-for-service system mental health clinicians were not "self-regulating" and were unnecessarily placing mental health patients in institutional environments, including residential treatment for addic-tion, for prolonged and costly periods. Their rhetorical emphasis on self-regulation, unnecessary institutionalization, and purported violation of pa-tient trust echoed arguments for psychiatric deinstitutionalization of public mental hospitals that began in the mid-1950s.[2] Absent from these discus-sions were the historical, social, and economic underpinnings of addic-tion and mental illness among New Mexico's citizens, especially those on the margins.

New Mexico began its experiment with Medicaid managed care in 1997, when three for-profit managed care companies won state contracts to provide health care for its poorest citizens. These companies subcontracted with three behavioral health organizations to manage the state's mental health services. The behavioral health services then contracted with regional care coordinators, who then contracted with front-line service providers. This nesting of administrative hierarchies was intended to bring accountability and transparency to a system deemed wasteful, ineffective, and, at times, unsafe (Willging 2005). In fact, the multilayered architecture of managed care ushered in what one addiction specialist described to me as "total chaos." New Mexico lacked the administrative infrastructure, staff, funding, and "cultural buy-in" to carry out the work the new system—or systems—demanded. This was especially true in the rural areas, where issues of Internet access, transportation, and language proved major barriers in the new system's operation, confirming the findings of several studies that populations in rural areas have been the most disadvantaged under Medicaid managed care (Horton et al. 2001; Slifkin et al. 1998).

The expansion of oversight and authorization processes under the new system led to a proliferation of data and interorganizational miscommunication about their significance. Managerial techniques that were promoted as fostering transparency and efficacy seemed secretive and arbitrary. The centerpiece of HealthValue's methodology, and managed care in general, is an assessment process known as utilization review. Conducted by anonymous reviewers, often in different states, utilization review determines treatment eligibility and is promoted as instilling standardized clinical and market accountability among providers. In practice, it has been shown to be a highly biased technique that decreases overall cost by closely limiting the type and length of treatment provided (Willging 2007). Limitation is promoted as a strategy of "responsibilization" of individuals and communities deemed overdependent on the state. It rests on the claim that the sick can be forced to become like the managed care system itself, "rational" economic actors—unless, like Nuevo Día and its patients, they cannot.

CONSEQUENCES OF CLOSURE

Local and state media reported heavily on the detoxification clinic's closure. Their stories highlighted the many failures of the clinic—from fiscal irresponsibility and lack of staff training to the building's structural problems and troubled history. The stories hinted that the closure was a failure not only of the clinic per se but also of the entire community.

Following HealthValue's determination, patients in residence were allowed to complete their programs, but would-be patients who had been awaiting admission (some as long as four months) were referred to "alternative services," which meant a detoxification facility in Albuquerque, whose waiting list at the time ranged from three to six months. Nuevo Día was permitted to offer a "social detoxification" residency program, based primarily on Twelve Step Fellowship principles. It could continue to distribute over-the-counter medications and certain standing prescriptions, such as SSRIs, as long as these were approved through utilization review. The clinic was strictly prohibited from distributing anti-opioid or narcotic-based medications.

I learned that the clinic was closing while attending a party in the mountain village of El Valle, about twenty miles northeast of Chimayó. The party was being held to commemorate the ten-year anniversary of a community newsletter that had been on the forefront of local environmental politics. It was a late-summer afternoon. A herd of sheep grazed nearby, and the sun was just beginning to set behind the towering stands of ponderosa pine. I was enjoying the beauty of northern New Mexico that afternoon—perhaps because I was preparing to leave it; my fieldwork was coming to an end.

A board member from Nuevo Día was in attendance. We talked about the impending closure of the detox clinic and forecasted the likely consequences: an increase in drug overdoses, a decrease in hope. Then he confided that in his view HealthValue had made the right decision. His twenty-two-year-old niece, a heroin addict, had been a patient and nearly died of an overdose while in residence. He had considered suing the agency on whose board he served.

He asked me, from an "insider perspective," what I thought the biggest problem was with the clinic. I looked around me and answered: life outside it.

.   .   .   .   .

The clinic's closure depressed me greatly. It signaled yet another defeat in local efforts to stem the region's heroin problem. The specific determination that the clinic was "not credible" and "unstable" exacerbated the feeling of hopelessness that permeated the valley—a feeling, I have argued, that ultimately feeds the cycle of addiction itself. The failure of the clinic became a part of the material and symbolic order through which heroin use, overdose, and even suicide are realized as a form of life.

Perhaps what struck me most about the closing of the clinic is how, in many ways, it mirrored the experience of addicts: dismissal by institutions that had the power to remake (or undo) their lives; day-to-day instability; feelings of vulnerability and failure. The clinic, like the addicts themselves, had become a victim of the bottom line of corporate health care restructuring. It was like Christina, who turned to the clinic at a time of extreme vulnerability but was refused because of her indigent status. Or John, whose departure from the clinic was labeled "self-discharge," investing him with full responsibility for his supposed treatment failure. Now the clinic occupied the role of the addict. It was imbued with "choice" but was determined to have failed. The repercussions of its failure would be felt for years to come.

The recent work of anthropologists shows how the supposedly neutral promotion of standardization in health care fails to account for local contexts and legitimizes or delegitimizes certain kinds of interventions (Cohen 1999; Farmer 1999; Petryna and Kleinman 2006). Indeed, in the wake of the clinic's closure, the state continued to exercise its expanded juridical powers, and the processing of addict-offenders through the drug court system continued apace. But in privatizing its health services, the state undercut its power to impose treatment sentences. Caught in this space of contradiction were the addicts themselves—some of whom waited weeks, even months, in the county jail for an available bed at a distant drug treatment facility.

One woman I interviewed—a mother of two young children whose custody rights depended on her recovery—recalled the conundrum presented by her parole officer as he explained her treatment options: she could remain on house arrest at her parents' home, where she had endured abuse as a child, until there was an opening at an Albuquerque facility; or she could immediately attend an extensive outpatient drug treatment program in Denver but would need to find housing. In effect, she was given the choice of being a temporary "prisoner" in her parents' home, which was laden with bad feeling, or leave her children and live in an unknown city while undergoing outpatient care. She chose to remain in Española, under house arrest, but would eventually break the terms of her sentence.

During our one interview, she said, "I felt like I never even got a chance to know how it might be . . . to be clean and live a better life."

In the absence of available services, the central bearer of responsibility for care is the family. Yet, as this work has shown, the family is also often the primary site of heroin use. The addict thus confronts a quandary. She must turn away (or is separated from) her family and toward the institution in the recovery process. But then she is abandoned by the institution and must return to the family, where her addiction resumes. This in itself is like consecutive sentencing: "time" is served inside *and* outside. What to do in the absence of care as it is construed in the traditional sense— that is, the care of a doctor or of a parent?

NECESSARY MEASURES

After the detox's clinic's closure there was a mobilization of "community-based" forms of care for addicts, including an increase in training on the administration of naloxone (Narcan), a drug used to counter the life-threatening effects of heroin overdose, for heroin addicts and their families. Also intensified was the Española Valley's mobile needle-exchange program, which exchanges an average of 55,000 syringes each month. State health officials lauded these recent efforts as a means to scale up the region's treatment infrastructure by "empowering" individuals with life-saving techniques. But locals who used these services eschewed the language of "empowerment" and described them as necessary measures. One father I spoke to after a Narcan training session called learning how to resuscitate his son a "terrible necessity" while questioning its very utility—after all, who knew if he would be around when his child needed him. Holding the two vials of Narcan he was given, he said ruefully, "Learning this stuff, it's just all I can do for him now. It's really all there is to do."

In the context of dismantling the few institutions of care that existed for addiction, such state-sponsored services amount more to methods of containment than methods of care. They highlight how such measures are entangled with macrolevel policies, structural conditions, and competing private interests that limit—even as they extend—residents' capacity to care for the addicted. In this milieu, addicts and their families engage in what João Biehl (2007: 48) calls "local economies of salvation," forms of treatment that are simultaneously necessary and insufficient, sustained and diminished, marginal but reflective of a broader social world. Under such conditions, the cycle of addiction such methods claim to address is not broken, is not even alleviated; rather, it is perpetuated and confirmed.

In 2008, nearly two years after Nuevo Día's detox program closed, HealthValue began to hold community meetings that solicited locals' interested in helping to develop and create a new recovery center in Española that would service a wide range of addictions, as well as mental illness more broadly. Locals perceived this gesture of "inclusiveness" with a mix of suspicion and resentment. They asked: Why would they want to start a new program rather than improve the one that already existed and that they closed? What kind of program will this be? Will they provide *treatment* or just more of the same?

In community outreach materials, which included fliers and advertisements in the local paper, the future program was described as a "Safe, Sane and Stigma free space for people to come and work on their recovery from substance abuse, mental health, co-occurring and other disorders." Aside from the behavioral health jargon and the fact that the materials were English-only, I was immediately struck by two words: "sane" and "work." These were precisely the standards of accountability that Nuevo Día—and the Española Valley generally—was deemed to have lacked.

The materials read like a caricature of a solution for addiction, which I suspected would not go over well locally. And, in fact, when I attended one of the "community" planning meetings to discuss the future program, I was literally the only person present who was not affiliated with Health-Value. The meeting was postponed. Later I was told by several locals that the planned program was a ruse. HealthValue's contract with the state was about to expire. The meeting was a disingenuous effort to look engaged in finding solutions to the addiction crisis in the Española Valley, nothing more. It was material for HealthValue's corporate portfolio, which it would submit to the state with its request to have the contract extended. In the end, the contract was not renewed.

It is well known that the twin processes of devolution and privatization have shifted responsibility for health care from the public to the more intimate domains of family and community, which are expected to perform even larger roles with regard to the provision of care. Overdose prevention training and needle exchange exemplify this shift. As practices of "harm reduction," they represent practical strategies that seek to reduce the negative consequences of heroin use, namely, overdose and dirty needles.[3] But these strategies, while important, are not inclusive forms of care; rather, they are the bare minimum.

The political economy of addiction comes into stark relief when one considers that in the region most devastated by heroin, overdose prevention training and needle exchange perform the duties of "treatment," whereas in the affluent neighboring communities of Santa Fe and Taos there are several exclusive residential treatment centers, with exorbitant price tags to ensure a clientele of the wealthy few. These parallel modes of treatment and profiteering reveal much about the entanglements of neoliberal health care and the dynamics of therapeutic processes, of forms of inclusion and exclusion.

But the exclusion of the poor from the forms of care that only the rich, or the richer, have at their disposal does not eliminate the possibilities of care altogether. Hidden spaces of opportunity take root in the everyday. What I want to do now is to turn to one of those spaces and demonstrate how forms of care emerge, not in spite of, but *through* experiences of loss, marginality, and illegality.

THE COUNTRY DOCTOR

Adela Campos is sixty-seven years old. She is the mother of five children, grandmother of seven, and great-grandmother of two. Since Nuevo Día closed in summer 2006 she has received two or three requests a month for her services. These services can loosely be described as "home detox," usually for heroin addicts. For Adela, helping the addicted get through withdrawal, especially the first few days when the physical pain is at its worst, is more of a calling than a profession. She lost a son and many extended family members, as well as family friends, to heroin overdose, and she sees it as her responsibility to do what she does best: attend to the body in times of crisis. She admits that she would like to stop, but the combined sense of urgency and responsibility keeps her going. Plus, at sixty-seven, it's unlikely she will find another job, and she admits that she needs the income.

From her teens to her fifties, Adela was a *partera*, a midwife. She estimates that she assisted in over two hundred labors, mostly of village women and sometimes of village girls. Until the 1970s, home birth in the rural areas of northern New Mexico was fairly common, not as a choice, but as a matter of course. It was often Adela who was there, holding hands, massaging backs, reaching into one exhausted body to guide another one out. "Things have changed," Adela once told me.

The transformation of Adela from a midwife into a detox attendant began with her youngest son, who started using heroin in the 1980s and continued to use it until his death in the early 1990s. During those long years, Adela cared for him through multiple drug-related sicknesses, not structured detox per se, but the everyday pains related to heroin addiction. Although this was not unusual for mothers of addicts, Adela developed a high tolerance for being in the presence of another body in pain, a "gift" she attributed to her years of working as a midwife. By the time she discovered that her grandson was also addicted to heroin, she had

Figure 10.   La Joya. Photo by the author.

learned enough about heroin addiction to begin concocting treatments to ease its associated pains, many of which mirrored those that women experienced in labor. She brewed osha root tea for nausea and vomiting, prepared warm compresses for muscle spasms, and employed massage to rid the body of toxins. But mostly she just remained in the presence of her grandson, determined not to lose him, too.

When news of her grandson's "cure" spread, other addicts began to seek her services. They brought with them medicines, foods, and techniques that they had used in the past, often while detoxing on their own. Soon Adela began to incorporate over-the-counter pain relievers, sleep aids, alcohol, and prescription medications when they were available. As payment, she received money, vegetables, appliances, animals, and TV sets, as well as leftover prescription medications, which she would use to help future addicts, as well as to ease her own pain stemming from rheumatoid arthritis. *The gifts keep coming,* she once told me, *because people keep using.* And now with the closure of the detox clinic, hers is the only drug detoxification service around.

.   .   .   .   .

Approximately a year after the detox clinic closed, I drive to Adela's house in the village of Córdova, east of Chimayó. Córdova's smattering of adobe and trailer homes cuts through a low and narrow swath of the valley. Despite its presence on the "High Road to Taos," a scenic drive favored by tourists, most people pass Córdova without even knowing it's there. They press on, looking for higher ground and better views. This lack of interference has served Adela's business well. No one really knows, or cares, what she does, unless they are in need of her.

As soon as I arrive at her house, Adela puts me to work. She hands me a basketful of still-warm sheets and towels, which I proceed to fold while she puts another load of laundry into the washing machine. She expresses a sense of urgency: she doesn't have much time until her next appointment arrives. "The girl stayed a whole week," she says of her previous "patient." Most addicts stay at Adela's for three to five days before returning to their homes.

"Isn't that a good sign?" I ask. Based on my experience, the longer someone makes it through detox, especially one that is self-imposed, as this one had been, the more likely they would stick with it.

"No. Not necessarily," she answers. "Sometimes they just don't have anywhere else to go."

Adela operates her detox business in the century-old adobe behind her trailer, where she lives. She explains that the trailer is better for her because it has central heating, whereas the drafty adobe depends on firewood. The adobe is where her husband grew up, where they lived as a married couple, and where they raised their children. It is also where her son died of a heroin overdose. The trailer is better for her for that reason, too.

Carrying the laundry, I follow Adela out the trailer's back door, across a stretch of snowy ground, and into the adobe. It is the kind of house people who take the High Road to Taos expect to see: earth-colored walls three feet thick and window frames a fading shade of blue. Inside, fat vigas, or beams, crisscross the white plaster ceiling. The house is three rooms deep—with contiguous doorways leading from the living room to the kitchen to the bedroom. Except for a cast iron woodstove in one corner, the living room is completely bare. Adela tells me there used to be furniture, but one addict took off with it in the middle of the night—how, she can't imagine. After that she decided to keep the adobe "bare bones," with only the necessary features to carry out her work.

The house is dark and terribly cold. Its few windows are propped open in order to let out the odor of her last appointment. Through them, I can catch a glimpse of the snow-tipped juniper trees outside.

I follow Adela to the kitchen, also almost empty, except for one cabinet, which is filled with rows of prescription bottles and supplements. The cabinet contains aspirin, clonidine, robaxin, codeine, melatonin, and calcium and magnesium supplements. Many of the bottles are expired. Adela opens another cabinet, this one filled with half-empty bottles of cheap brandy, port, whiskey—whatever her patients bring with them.

"I don't like using liquor," Adela says. "*Pero* I know it helps some people with the pain." This is something she learned from her husband, who drank his pains away, contributing, in a sense, to her own pain.

Standing in the center of the mostly bare kitchen, Adela gives me a tour of the house, pointing in one of two directions, like an officer directing traffic. "This is where my son overdosed," she says, pointing. "This is where my children were born," pointing in the opposite direction. "That is where my husband was going to build another room but never did. This is where I used to grow my herbs. This is where I used to sleep. This is where I work now," she says, pointing to her old bedroom—now the detox room.

We go inside.

Against one wall, beneath a deeply set window, is a twin bed. And beside the bed, a chair. I sit on the bed and look at the wall. Etched into the thick adobe are messages written by Adela's patients—profanities and prayers, names that I recognize and names that I don't. The walls of Adela's house remind me of the walls at the detox clinic, which had also been etched by patients. The walls are a palimpsest of different temporalities, longings, and hopes. They express sentiments so distressingly similar—the same, repeated patterns of wounds.

I ask, "Is this it?"

"Yes. That's all you really need."

Adela asks me to help her make the bed. She has another appointment—someone she has seen before and imagines she'll see again.

THE POSSIBILITY OF LOVE

Soon after the detox clinic closed, I drove into Española to do some shopping, which inevitably meant a trip to the Super Walmart. There, I ran into Pauline Ramirez at the cashier's stand. Pauline was a patient at the clinic during my first graveyard shift. She accompanied Lisa, Mary, and me to Michelle's wake. I knew very little about her then; she was quiet, preferring to speak only when spoken to, and briefly at that. What I did know came from the few details contained in her patient file: she was forty-two years old and had used heroin for more than twenty years; she had four grown children and suffered from bouts of depression. I hadn't seen her since she completed her thirty-day program.

At first, I didn't recognize her—perhaps because she was dressed in the bright blue smocks worn by Walmart "Associates" who work in the front of the store, not the black sweat suit she always wore at the clinic. Pauline recognized me and offered a hello while she calculated my purchases. I asked her how she was. She looked around her and asked if I wanted to talk during her lunch break. I agreed to pick her up in half an hour near the loading zone in the rear of the building, which also functioned as the employee entrance. Walmart employees are not permitted to use the same entrance as customers.

I found Pauline waiting for me beside a semi truck emblazoned with the Walmart logo. She had taken off her blue smock and was smoking a cigarette. Working around her were dozens of male employees, none of whom wore the blue smocks of the employees who worked in the front of the store, nearly all of whom were women. The men were lifting heavy loads of goods as they moved in and out of the gaping entryway.

With only thirty minutes to spare, we drove to the nearby Taco Bell and ate in my car. Pauline sipped on her soda but left her bagged meal untouched. She told me that she didn't have much of an appetite these days—not because anything was wrong, but because she was falling in love. She asked me if I remembered Michael.

Michael was also a patient at the detox clinic during the time I worked there. He was in his early thirties, tall, thin, and bald. At the time I met him, his scalp seemed the only visible part of his body that was not covered in wounds from injecting heroin.

Pauline told me that they had arrived at the clinic the same day, both of them in a "bad way." They did not know each other on arrival but would soon establish an intimacy that helped to carry them through the first few days of detox. She recalled how they sat outside and looked toward the river while they battled the intolerable pain that wracked their bodies. She described how she told Michael that she didn't think she could make it; Michael reached out and assured her that she could. He told her that they would get through the pain together.

"No one had ever talked to me like that before," Pauline said.

In the end, it was Pauline who made it; Michael left detox five days after arriving and resumed his heroin use. On the night he departed, he left Pauline a note that read, "Don't go back." Pauline told me that she cried the morning she found out Michael had left.

Pauline worked hard to stay clean but, until recently, had not always been successful. Nearly a year after completing her month of detox she went on a weeklong heroin binge, fueled by a succession of disappointments, including the inability to find work and the loss of a parent. It was during her binge that she reencountered Michael. They were both "looking for a hookup." Pauline described the deep sense of shame she felt when Michael saw her—not because she worried she had disappointed him, but because the encounter reminded her of a "lost chance" for love. Michael, she said, felt the same.

After that difficult night, Pauline and Michael began to see each other—first as friends and then as lovers. Pauline stopped using heroin; Michael continued to use but less. According to Pauline, he hoped to stop altogether one day, and she hoped that he would but added that she would stick with him if he couldn't. "I understand how hard it is," she said. "That's why, even if this relationship doesn't go anywhere, I will never really leave him."

As Pauline re-created the circumstances of her evolving emotions, I realized she was relaying more than a love story. She was describing a kind of care—one based on principles of commensurability, which is ultimately a kind of care that does not, indeed cannot, end.

I drove Pauline back to Walmart. Several other employees—mostly women—were also being dropped off. I watched them file in through the back entrance. Before Pauline joined them, I asked if she had heard about the closure of the detox clinic. She hadn't.

"It's a shame," she said. After a brief pause, she added, "That's where it all started," referring to her love for Michael.

REUNION

I saw Bernadette again during a follow-up research trip to the Española Valley. At that time I thought that she was still incarcerated and had on my agenda a visit to Grants to visit her. Ours was a chance meeting, more than two years after our last visit.

That afternoon, I stopped for lunch at a taco stand located just off the entrance to the tortuous Highway 76, which connects Española to Chimayó. In just a few hours I was expected at a support group for heroin-addicted women. As I quietly enjoyed my lunch, sheltered from the sun by the shade of a massive cottonwood, I noticed the figures of two women making their way across the highway. As they came closer into view I saw that it was Bernadette and Eugenia. I called out their names and watched as they looked around, trying to locate my voice. The sun was blinding white, and I realized I must have been obscured in the shade. I called again, standing this time. Eugenia noticed me first and pointed in my direction. We walked toward each other and embraced.

I immediately knew that they were on their way to score drugs.

They had both grown thinner, but otherwise they looked the same, and so much like each other. Bernadette filled me in on certain details of their lives. She had been released from prison a few months earlier and was in an outpatient recovery program. She and Eugenia were living together again, in the apartment complex just across the highway. The complex was relatively new, and the units were clean and cheap. Bernadette's daughter lived with them, too, and for the first time had a room of her own. (She did not mention her other child, a son.) As she spoke, Eugenia looked away, toward the highway, as if she was waiting for someone—or rather, as if *they* were waiting for someone. When her connection appeared, she took leave of us without saying good-bye. Bernadette remained behind and looked at me closely.

"We're okay," she said, her voice suddenly serious. "Everything is okay."

I asked her if she was using, too. Bernadette considered my question thoughtfully and then said that it wasn't like that. I said that I knew she was using and asked, no, implied, that she should be worried about testing dirty. And then Bernadette told me something I had heard many times before but always felt like the first time. It wasn't a matter of using or *not*, of testing dirty or *not*. This was the life she was born into.

"I can't get rid of it," she said. "Just like I can't get rid of her. She is my mother." At the time, I wasn't sure if Bernadette was referring to Eugenia or to heroin.

.   .   .   .   .

I was surprised when, a few hours later, I saw them again at the women's support group. They were already seated, side by side, when I arrived. As I took my place, they made the same gesture of recognition—a slow, lopsided smile. Although it is standard procedure for a meeting's facilitator to discharge attendees who are obviously high, Bernadette and Eugenia stayed. Initially, I wondered if it was because the facilitator—a young college student placed in the role to gain counseling credentials—did not know what a loaded heroin addict looked like. During the course of the meeting, however, I sensed the facilitator's palpable weariness. Beyond the routine introductions, she seemed not to care which direction the conversation went, or whether or not the participants were high. In fact, she seemed anxious to sign the attendees' probationary paperwork and dismiss the meeting early. Already, she had been at this job too long.

In any event, the conversation—the women's admissions and descriptions—had an unusual energy that evening, and I imagined that this was somehow unleashed by Bernadette's and Eugenia's intoxication. The conversation circled around figures of heroin-induced scars, which were placed on display and which were imbued with familial history. One young woman described a complicated story of how she used to feel like a failure for not being able to kick heroin but had come to determine that this was less a reflection of her own true feelings and more an effect of the way she was regarded, especially in the context of treatment. "I will never be cured," she said, "because there is nothing wrong with me. Because without heroin, I can't really live."

Hispano heroin addicts frequently said that they had little or no chance of recovery, and they would often explain their pessimism in biological terms. Their addiction, they said, was *in the blood, like a virus,* something they could not eradicate or recover from, even if they wanted to. This locally biologized understanding of addiction differs from the medicoscientific view, which points to a neurological and/or genetic basis of addiction, usually described in terms of "adaptive changes" or "habituation." But this young woman seemed to be saying something slightly different. She seemed to suggest that it was not so much a matter of "accepting" life with a chronic, biological "illness"; rather, heroin was her very life source.

"But your mother died from heroin overdose," another support group participant interrupted, to which the young woman responded, "No. She didn't die from heroin. My mother died from a broken heart."

. . . . . .

At the end of the meeting, Bernadette asked if I could drive her and her mother back to their apartment in Española. We piled into my car, Eugenia beside me in the passenger seat and Bernadette in the back. I rolled the windows down to let in the warm summer air. In my rearview mirror, I could see that Bernadette had quickly fallen asleep. We made our way across the county road that cut through the village, toward the highway. As we approached the fork, Eugenia asked me to slow down and then to stop. I pulled to the side of the road, aware of where we were. We were in front of Eugenia's old house, the one she inherited from her father.

There were lights on in the house and a car parked in the makeshift driveway. Someone was home. I asked Eugenia if she knew who lived there, and she shook her head no. We sat there for some moments, staring at the house, until Eugenia gestured forward, and we moved on.

QUESTIONS OF CARE

A central component of this chapter and the preceding ones is the idea that we are inescapably shaped by our dependence on other human beings. In the context of heroin addiction, this dependence, or interdependence, persists in states of apparent isolation. I write "apparent" because I have tried to show that these states—"being high," overdose, and suicide—are not autonomous states or events, or effects of personal or cultural pathology, as they are so often described. Rather, they emerge from a complex set of dependencies that expose something of shared human vulnerability. Such a framing ultimately raises the fundamental question of responsibility. Can such experiences form the basis of responsibility? What might such a call to responsibility look like and mean, especially in the form of care?

Recently, I was an invited to give a lecture on my anthropological research to a group of esteemed clinicians and social scientists. During my lecture, I talked about, among other things, the history of material and cultural dispossession in the Española Valley and the way these injuries have come to shape addictive experience, in particular, the phenomenon of intergenerational heroin use. During the question-and-answer period, a woman suggested to me that although the historical and ethnographic material I had provided was "compelling," health care and public policy had limits. She said that she could not possibly conceive of a way to gather the myriad issues I had described—the history, the loss—into a plan for treatment and prevention. Furthermore, she worried that the painful ethnographic picture I painted would easily induce nihilism in physicians and policy makers. Medicine and policy, she repeated, had limits.

At the time, I did not have a catchy response. But as I weave together the narratives of Adela, Pauline, Bernadette, and Eugenia—and all the other men and women struggling with addiction whose experiences make up this book—I am finally able to formulate a response. It is this. While it may be true that *she* and even I cannot conceive of a plan of care that could incorporate all the history, all the losses, this is precisely what families try to do for one another every day. They conceive of ways to care for one another in a context where their very relations, and the very struggle to maintain the everyday, are at stake. Of course, they often fail, and tragically so. But they keep trying to the very end.

CONCLUSION **A New Season**

What I'm looking for, I mean, what I need, is hope.

Alma Gallegos

One of the issues of researching "home" is that you never really leave, and the research never really ends. Such work is, as Alma said, *sin termina*, without end.

This dilemma makes writing a conclusion especially difficult. Perhaps it is especially difficult in matters such as those this book presents—matters of life and death. For lack of a better term, I want to do "justice" to the lives that I have described here—to tell you how they continue, to introduce you to the lives that I now know, and to mourn the newly departed.

Let me share this.

.   .   .   .   .

In April 2008 I returned to the Española Valley. On the day that I arrived, everything seemed to be brushed in gray: the sky, the Sangre de Cristo Mountains, the retail strip along Española's Riverside Drive, the runoff-swollen Rio Grande. Even the air was gray from chimneys releasing smoke, perfuming the valley with the scent of piñon. It was a typical early spring morning, and this pervading sense of melancholy reminded residents that winter was not over yet—not by a long shot.[1]

I returned to visit old friends. My first stop was Nuevo Día, which had "survived," despite the fact that much of its meaningful programming had been stripped away. After nearly twenty years of directing the region's struggle with addiction and caring for the addicted, Andrés, Nuevo Día's executive director, felt that he was little more than a pawn. He was exhausted—physically and morally. In one moment of self-reflection, Andrés confided that it was time to "hang up my hat" and disappear quietly into his own trailer. He said he had been at the helm of Nuevo Día for too long. He was ready to let go, let someone else give it a try, someone younger. But every time he thought about stepping down, the board of directors, or some well-connected local politician, would ask him to stay: just one more year—and then one year more. Soon two years turn to ten.

Although Andrés dreamed of quitting, he believed there was one more thing that he could do for Nuevo Día, with or without administrative approval from whatever managed care company was in charge. He wanted to grow things: chile, corn, beans, squash, apples, and apricots. The kind of crops that were grown on the valley's land a generation or two ago and that once grew on the land that surrounded the clinic but had withered away with years of neglect.

From the beginning, Andrés envisioned the clinic as a sustainable community where addicts could cultivate the acreage that surrounded it. I must admit that during my years of fieldwork and time working at the clinic, I would assume a quietly derisive attitude when he imagined this. Given Nuevo Día's mounting struggles, and the struggles of the addicts I had come to know, it was hard to imagine the land that surrounded Nuevo Día as anything but the tangle of weeds, another missed opportunity. Fortunately, others saw it for what it was: prime bottomland ripe for sowing and reaping. Plus, Nuevo Día didn't need much money or anyone's permission to begin cultivating what was already there. They had perhaps the most valuable asset—their addicts, many of whom had grown up tending the valley's fertile soil.

On that April morning, when I turned down the rural road that leads to Nuevo Día, I was immediately struck by how naked it looked. Its cloak of weeds was shorn and the earth tilled. I drove closer, my car skidding along the icy dirt road, and saw a tractor-trailer. Resting alone beneath a giant cottonwood, the tractor's yellow hue broke the monotony of the cold gray day. It was a sign of spring, a sign of hope.

I returned again a few months later, during the typically hot and bright month of July. In Española, roadside stands selling peas and corn beckoned. I stopped at my favorite stand, across from the Super Walmart, and purchased a pint of fava beans, which I ate in the car as I drove up the highway, toward Nuevo Día. I was eager to see what, if anything, the garden produced.

I turned once more down the familiar dirt road and headed toward the banks of the Rio Grande. Row upon row of bright yellow squash blossoms spread before the clinic, and cornstalks reached a few feet high. The clinic, which housed so much anguish and frustration, looked like a scene from van Gogh. It was, in a word, beautiful.

.   .   .   .   .

That afternoon, I toured the garden with Roberto, a retired farmer who worked as the garden manager. Under Roberto's supervision, Nuevo Día's patients worked the land as part of their recovery process. I followed Roberto through the rows of peas, squash, corn, and native chile. "This land was a mess when I first got here," Roberto said. Someone with little to no experience had tried in the past to plow the uneven fields into submission. Whoever it was eventually gave up but not before tearing large segments of the land into worse shape than they had been.

The clients Roberto were told would be his willing labor force were, in fact, not so willing. Roberto pointed out the fresh scars on a cottonwood where clients took out their frustration with gardening tools. The work crews were quickly segregated along gender lines. It became clear that the good workers were the ones from families who still farmed, and among them, the women excelled. Roberto thought the women were more committed to farming. "They're used to this kind of work. To growing things," he explained.

To encourage their interest in farming, Roberto plowed a separate plot for the women to plant whatever they liked. We walked to the women's garden. Tiny corn shoots the size of pencils peeked out of the dirt. It was native white corn, which would be dried for *chicos*, a regional staple that is stewed alone or with pinto beans. "They get all excited," he said, pointing to the corn. "First thing the women do in the morning when they come outside is check in on them."

Based on my experience at the clinic, I had a hard time reconciling the idea of the women running out of the clinic each morning to check on their tiny corn shoots. I remembered the days when I worked the graveyard shift, how hard it was to convince patients to get out of bed, let alone work. I went into the clinic and met with a group of patients to discuss the role of gardening in their recovery process. I knew that they would talk up the program, especially the garden, in order to be in the counselor's good graces.

We sat around a table. The patients fidgeted with sunglasses, coughed cigarette coughs, and laughed and smiled. Sometimes they seemed natural doing so and sometimes not. The room was familiar to me, but the patients were not. It was strange to be back at the clinic purely in the role of researcher and not as a member of the staff. As I described my past affiliation with the clinic in order to establish confidence among the patients, I felt as if I was recalling events from deep in my past. It was as if so much, and so little, had changed.

They all told me which drugs landed them at Nuevo Día, how many days they had been there, and how many days remained. They told me where they were from and where they hoped they would be going next. The stories were familiar.

Luz, a thirty-something patient, said, "When I got to Nuevo Día and found out I had to garden I was like, I don't want to do this again!" Growing up in Chimayó, she sowed, weeded, irrigated, and picked crops on the land gardened by her family for generations. "I did this work all my life," Luz said—that is, until she got hooked on heroin.

Luz told me that she couldn't even count the number of family members and friends from Chimayó she has lost to heroin—again, too many to recall. The other patients shared similar stories. Their stories weren't just about losing other people. Andy said he lost all sense of who he was because of his addiction to drugs and alcohol. But more than a month into his program, he was now growing the very food he eats. He was helping to build a *temescale*, or sweat lodge, on the property. Andy proudly showed me the blisters on his hands. "Energy goes into these hands," he said. "These hands are making something."

In the absence of medications, the staff at Nuevo Día tried to keep patients so busy that they wouldn't have time to crave drugs. In addition to the gardens and *temescales*, there were chickens and llamas to tend to. Eventually, there would be murals, orchards, and pigs, maybe even buffalo. In the meantime, the clients were selling their crops at the weekly Española Farmers' Market. Beto, the counselor I had worked with years before, laughed, "Imagine, Angela. The last thing you expect around here is to see a *tecato* at a farmers' market! You'll see 'em on the street, or at a casino or the bar, but a farmers' market, selling vegetables? No way." But there they were, on a hot Monday afternoon, sitting proudly behind a table exhibiting squash, corn, and melons.

Toward the end of my visit, I accompanied Luz to a private herb garden that the women were planting. It wasn't much yet—just a circular patch of dirt with a *yerba buena,* or mint bush, at its center. Luz said she wasn't sure what the future holds for the garden, or for her. She was going to be leaving the clinic in a couple of weeks, she hoped to another residential program, if she could get into one. In the sunlight, I saw the track marks that lined her strong, brown arms. She told me that Nuevo Día and its gardening program had helped her in ways she never expected. "I didn't expect I'd be doing this again," she said, gesturing to the land that surrounds the clinic. But she was worried about the prospect of returning to Chimayó, where she would be surrounded by memories and by heroin.

Luz had already inquired about a program in Santa Fe but learned she qualified only if she "failed" Nuevo Día's program. She said the waiting lists for halfway houses were too long, and they were in areas where drugs were rampant. Private residential programs were out of the question. Luz asked me if I could help her get into a program somewhere, somewhere far away from *here*. "I've been down this road too many times," she said of the endless cycle of treatment and relapse—a cycle that, in this context, is precipitated by other forms of return: the return to family, to history, to lands that are no longer one's own.

As Luz talked to me in that garden, her voice so full of worry and hope, I remembered Alma. Like Luz, Alma struggled to find a way *out* of all that which was made to cohere through a multiplicity of losses, memories, injections, and institutions. This multiplicity produced new bodily, moral, and social dimensions of endlessness, to which Alma felt irrevocably tied. Still, Alma struggled to find a way out, first through the work of recovery and then through the promise of rebirth. But her struggle was undermined by the powerful presupposition of inevitable return: a return to certain historically situated pains, a return to heroin, a return to the clinic.

I looked at Luz, standing in a landscape of such deep and troubled beauty. It was land she loved but felt she needed to leave in order to save her life. She asked me again if there was any other place she might be able to go, to continue her recovery. "I just can't go back anymore," she said.

Notes

1. Given the potential legal ramifications of my research, it has been necessary for me to change the names of people and certain places—including the name of the clinic—in order not to disclose identities. However, when Hispano friends, including many of the staff at the clinic, read some versions of this book, they quickly located their stories and even elaborated on them.

2. The term *patients* refers to heroin addicts receiving residential treatment at the detoxification clinic. I avoid the increasingly common terms *consumers* and *clients* because they imply that recovering addicts have purchasing power in their care, which in this case they did not. I also avoid these terms because they miss the nuances of clinical work and the differential power relations that exist between those giving and receiving treatment.

3. In her book, *Ghostly Matters* (1997), Avery Gordon describes the haunting by the ghosts of modernity that are a constitutive aspect of contemporary social life. Often unseen, ghostly matters point to the traces of power on subjects and their social world and are an entry point for discussing the challenges of rendering the complexity of social life.

4. For a discussion of doing anthropology "at home," see Visweswaran 1994; Peirano 1998; Das 1996. See also Clifford 1997.

5. Patients often said they felt that time expanded or slowed and that they were unable to establish normal patterns of existence because of this temporal alteration. Such feelings are physiologically linked to the process of heroin detoxification. They are also related to the structure of clinical time, which is filled with long stretches of inactivity and waiting. For more on the temporal perspectives of addicts in drug treatment programs, see Klingemann 2001. See also Desjarlais 1997.

6. Jake Kosek has written an important work on similar processes of political and cultural sedimentation in this region but with a focus on environmental politics. See Kosek 2007.

7. I draw here on the rich body of work on experiential aspects of "place." For studies of the phenomenology of place, see Bachelard 1994; Tuan 1977; Casey 1993; Jackson 1996; Buttimer and Seamon 1980. For studies connecting power, place, and perception, see Williams 1975; Moore 2005; Moore, Pandian, and Kosek 2003.

8. I am influenced here by Nancy Scheper-Hughes's (1992: 30) call that ethnography be both a "moral reflection on a human society forced to the margins" and a political text that "indicts a political economic order that reproduces sickness and health at its very base."

9. Here, I am indebted to Arthur Kleinman's use of the term *moral* to designate a realm of local and engaged experience that is thoroughly intersubjective. See Kleinman 1999.

10. The adjectives used here are culled from a variety of sources, including local and national media covering the region's heroin problem, as well as commentators on my research findings, including fellow anthropologists and providers. Several state police officers I interviewed suggested that surveillance of households and graveyards was necessary to effectively "crack down" on the region's heroin problem.

11. The field of public health, in particular, has advanced a primarily quantitative understanding of the "burden of care" family members and friends bear in the context of economic precariousness. Extending this research, anthropologists working on mental illness in the setting of economic scarcity have documented how, in neoliberal regimes, the family has increasingly become "the medical agent for the state" (Biehl 2005: 22). See Han 2004; Das and Das 2006.

12. My discussion of dispossession is informed by Marx's claims regarding "primitive accumulation" as described at the end of *Capital*. At its most basic, primitive accumulation is a transformation of social relations where the "historical process of divorcing the producer from the means of production" transforms "the social means of subsistence and of production into capital; and the 'imme-

diate producers into wage laborers'" (1967: 714). The means of this divorce described by Marx are varied but violent and include both individual and institutional acts of robbery that ultimately consolidated the "pigmy property of the many into the huge property of the few" (762).

13.   In his work on the problem of philosophical knowledge, Stanley Cavell differentiates between the failure of knowledge and the failure of acknowledgment. He writes, "A 'failure to know' might just mean a piece of ignorance, an absence of something, a blank. A 'failure to acknowledge' is the presence of something, a confusion, an indifference, a callousness, an exhaustion, a coldness" (1976: 264). The failure to acknowledge is, for Cavell, an avoidance, which is rarely a matter of innocent ignorance of the reality of the Other but an active denial of the Other. In this work, I have tried to prevent my failures of knowledge from transmuting into failures of acknowledgment.

14.   In the vast literature on ethics, I have benefited in particular from the work of Emmanuel Levinas, whose conception of ethics involves the orientation of, and commitment to, the self toward the Other. See Levinas 1969.

15.   For more on the synergy of pain and addiction, see Garcia 2008; Savage 2008.

16.   The American Psychiatric Association's standard reference work, *Diagnostic and Statistical Manual of Mental Disorders* (DSM), exemplifies some of the controversies surrounding the changing terminology of addiction. The current edition, DMS-IV, uses the term *dependence* in an attempt to avoid the purportedly "pejorative aspects" of the term *addiction*. However, by emphasizing the physiological aspects of "drug dependence," the DSM criteria miss the psychological, social, and affective elements of dependent states. Ironically, while recovery programs increasingly adopt a diseaselike paradigm for treating addiction, there is a growing movement within the psychiatric community to use *addiction* for the upcoming edition of DMS and to recuperate the nonphysiological aspects that the term evokes. See Obrien, Volkow, and Li 2006.

17.   In the course of my fieldwork, I interviewed 37 heroin addicts—22 men and 15 women. Thirty-two of them reported having quit using heroin for a period of time, and more than half resumed heroin use within a year. Twenty-nine addicts reported having been arrested for a drug-related offense, and at least 12 were incarcerated two or more times.

18.   Generally, periods of abstinence from heroin were self-imposed or occurred while in drug treatment, though not necessarily while incarcerated. Several reported getting hooked on heroin while in prison.

19.   The popular "crash and burn" scenario in which a person falls deeper and deeper into addiction and eventually dies because of it or finally recovers after hitting a "rock bottom" was rare. Instead, addicts were more likely to describe a series of rock bottoms and attributed drug relapse or worsening addictions to

these. Many of these contributing events involved an experience of loss: of family or a loved one (often to addiction), of an intimate relationship, or of livelihood or land. Without fail, each narrative situated heroin addiction more in terms of personal experiences of loss than in terms of psychosomatic distress or need.

20. In the past, front-line staff evaluated the ASI, as they were considered in the best position to determine patient needs. However, under the new, managed care model, responsibility for monitoring the instrument was contracted out in a process known as "utilization review." While expressly intended to instill professional accountability among service providers, utilization review limited expenditures for care by limiting length of residential treatment stays and counseling visits (Willging 2005). The determination of severity of addiction and need was in the hands of complete "strangers."

21. For the development of liberal ideas and policies in drug treatment, see Fraser and Valentine 2008.

22. For material on the neurobiology of drug addiction, see Hyman 2005; Chao and Nestler 2004. For the socioeconomic factors of drug use, see Andrade 1999; Bourgois 1995; Bourgois and Schonberg 2009; Rhodes 2004; Singer 2007.

23. See Office of Applied Studies, U.S. Department of Health and Human Services, Treatment Episode Data Set (TEDS): 2002 (2005); Discharges from Substance Abuse Treatment Services (DASIS Series S-25, DHHS Publication No. (SMA) 04–3967), Substance Abuse Mental Health Services Administration, Rockville, MD. www.dasis.samhsa.gov/teds02/2002_teds_rpt_d.pdf. Accessed October 10, 2007.

24. In *On Escape* (2003), Levinas undertakes a phenomenological analysis of experiences (i.e., nausea, pleasure) that can be interpreted as an attempt to escape not only the "world-weariness" and "the disorder of our time" but also the very burden of existence (51). "The identity of Being," Levinas writes, "reveals its nature as enchainment, for it appears in the form of suffering and invites us to escape" (55).

25. For more on the Pueblo Revolt and early colonial New Mexico, see Gutiérrez 1991; Simmons 1991.

26. U.S. Census Bureau 2003a, 2003b.

27. Substance Abuse and Mental Health Services Administration, Office of Applied Studies, 2004 National Survey on Drug Use and Health. www.drugabusestatistics.samhsa.gov/nsduh.htm#NSDUHinfo. Accessed October 15, 2007.

28. See Chaisson 1987; Cohen 1985; DiClemente and Boyer 1987; Feldman 1985; Watters et al. 1986.

29. See Egan 2002; Conan 2004; Hartman 2004.

30. DEA, 8–12–2004.

31. For works on meth in the rural heartland, see Pine 2007; Weisheit 2004.

32. Since the early colonial period, Catholicism has had an important public and cultural role in the representation of Hispano life. However, there is a historic and strong presence of Protestant Christianity, stemming from Protestant missionaries whose religious education stressed education and Americanization. The more recent presence of Evangelicals in the region mirrors the contemporary rise of evangelicalism among Latinos more broadly. The recent wave of conversions derives from evangelicalism's emphasis on local Hispano culture, its specific appeal to the dispossessed, and its promise of *"la nueva vida,"* the new life.

33. These early ideas were influenced by scholarly work on "religious treatments" for addiction. See Hansen 2005; Meyer 2004.

34. Again, to protect the recovery program, its staff and patients, I have altered the name of the program.

35. See, e.g., Burns 1989.

36. For more on New Mexico's colonial history, see Mitchell 2005; González 1999; Gutiérrez 1991. For Hispano land grants in northern New Mexico, see Gonzales 2003; Ebright 1994; Briggs and Van Ness 1987.

37. See de Certeau 1988.

CHAPTER ONE

1. Many anthropologists have explored how trauma narratives enable us to grasp events that we can never directly know. These narratives allow us to enter into spaces of violence, trauma, and tragedy and can act as forms of "evidence" through which truth, authority, and dissent are produced (Briggs 2004; Daniel 1996; Das 2006).

2. Many variations of La Llorona exist, but the traditional version describes a woman, abandoned by the man she loves, who is left to raise their children alone. The desire for revenge compels her to murder her children and throw their bodies into a river. Despair ultimately contributes to her death, and she is condemned to wander crying for all eternity, until the bodies of her children are recovered. For gendered aspects of this moral tale, see Saldívar-Hull 2000.

3. U.S. Senator Pete Domenici of New Mexico conducted a series of congressional hearings on drug-related problems in northern New Mexico. The hearings were inspired by a study conducted by the New Mexico Department of Health that showed the state led the nation in numerous substance abuse–related sicknesses and in mortality, including heroin overdose.

4. *Mental health* and *mental illness* are now such standard terms that they seem self-evident. In the context of addiction, the standard term *dual diagnosis* or

multiple diagnosis refers to individuals who suffer from major mental illnesses, such as bipolar disorder and depression, and addiction. Although these conditions are generally understood as co-constitutive, their treatment usually happens independent of each other.

5. During my research, many addicts I interviewed questioned my ability to apprehend or respond to crises. I was often told that I "couldn't handle" certain events, such as the ones James described or those that occurred in the past. Over time I came to understand such statements as a way for addicts to express the gravity of their experiences, as well as a means to gain representational authority for them.

6. See Pud et al. 2006; White 2004.

7. The concept of incommensurability, that state in which two worlds cannot be compared without distorting "the truth" of either world, has long been the domain of philosophy and literary theory. More recently, anthropologists are employing the concept in the attempt to make sense of the emergence and maintenance of radically different social, moral, and political worlds. For a discussion of the historical use of incommensurability, see Kuhn 1962; Biagioli 1990. For more recent anthropological uses of the concept, see Cohen 1999; Povinelli 2001; Daniel 1996.

8. Freud understood *primal scene* as an originary trauma that is at the root of childhood and, later, adult neuroses. The trauma comes in the figure of a troubling "scene" that the viewer cannot fully comprehend. The term first appeared in Freud's "Wolf Man" case (1918 [1914]), wherein a young child stumbles upon the figure of his parents having intercourse. The child cannot understand what is happening, interprets what he sees as the violent castration of the mother, and represses the scene into memory. Freud persistently questioned whether the primal scene was fantasy or something actually witnessed.

9. Institutions—whether medical, penal, or welfare, etc.—have become important grounds for anthropological explorations of the application of techniques and norms and their effect on personhood. For recent ethnographies of institutional life, see Rhodes 2004; Desjarlais 1997. For a provocative examination of how recent developments in biomedicine have politicized human life, see Fischer 2003; Rose 2006; Fulwilley 2007.

10. The work of Henri Bergson (2000) is illuminating in this regard. His example of the simultaneity of fluxes in which, while sitting on a riverbank, the flow of water, the flight of a bird, and the "uninterrupted murmur of our deep life" can be treated either as three distinct things or as a single one resonates with this project (36). The significance of Bergson's example is that it motivates us to think of experience in a manner that depends on the multiplicity of time.

11. This analysis used patient files and Addiction Severity Index surveys of patients who received treatment during 2004. It assessed treatment success rates,

number of times a current patient had previously been treated, and rates of relapse between 2004 and 2006.

12. The correct translation for "Ángel died" is *Ángel estaba muerto*. The instability of Lucretia's tense structure symbolically reflects her personal instability, as well as the instability of the clinic.

13. I asked the clinic's executive director about this policy, which he supported: "If addicts can pay money for drugs, they can come up with $50 for treatment. It shows that they are serious and want to positively invest in themselves and our community."

14. Numerous studies have shown that buprenorphine is extremely effective for short-term heroin withdrawal, with greater retention, less discomfort during withdrawal, and increased postwithdrawal treatment retention compared to symptomatic medications.

15. See Willging, Trujillo, and La Luz 2003.

CHAPTER TWO

1. Nietzsche's conception of eternal recurrence is less a claim about the repetition of certain facts or events and more an expression of the continual recurrence of existence more broadly. My concern here is to provide an ethnographic rendering of the lived sense of eternal recurrence in the context of addiction in the Hispano milieu. See Nietzsche 2006 for more on his conception of eternal recurrence.

2. The counselor was one of the few monolingual English speakers at the clinic. Patients, most of whom were bilingual, often spoke Spanish in her presence to safely express secrets and frustrations or to establish a sense of community or cultural difference.

3. New Mexico has alarmingly high rates of driving while intoxicated, ranking eighth in the United States in 2006. Rio Arriba County, where Española Valley is located, ranks second among the state's thirty-three counties for alcohol-related crashes (DWI Resource Center, www.dwiresourcecenter.org/; March 2006).

4. Sacks (1985) suggests that the reiterative structure of elegy mirrors one of the psychological responses to trauma, whereby the psyche repeats the traumatic event in order to retroactively alleviate the initial shock it caused.

5. One such critical intervention is from Julia Kristeva (1989) . In *Black Sun* she suggests that the very instability of loss and melancholia's continuous engagement with it speaks to the limitless capacity for representing what is lost. The melancholic's ability to express several overlapping losses at once and the affective, material, and aesthetic domains of loss all become, for Kristeva, potential

sites for discursive exploration. In this vein, mood is "language" (21), and melancholia is less pathology than discourse.

6. In this regard, I have found the work of Eric Santner especially illuminating. Santner provides a critical intervention to the discursive embrace of the melancholic concept by arguing that the experience of loss and bereavement to which language brings us is not comparable to the actual experience of loss itself—in particular, the concrete loss of loved ones. He worries that the focus on the linguistic aspects of mourning displaces us from the "particular, historical task of mourning" and leads us to "reducing historical suffering . . . to a series of structural operations depleted of affect" (1990: 29). Santner insists, rightly I believe, that historical or concrete losses far exceed those initiated through language and thus raises fundamental questions regarding the political limits of mourning that is tied to language.

7. For work on the temporal perspectives of patients in drug treatment programs, see Klingemann 2001.

8. Herein lies my problem with Freud, and with the very idea of "the lost cause," so often invoked by counselors at the clinic.

9. Judith Butler's (1997a, 1997b) work on interconnection between the psyche and the social is helpful in this regard. By emphasizing the historicity of psychic life, Butler demonstrates how constraint (which may be experienced as loss) is constitutive but not fully determinative of subjectivity. "Agency begins where sovereignty wanes," Butler writes. "The one who acts . . . acts precisely to the extent that he or she is constituted as an actor and, hence, operating within a field of enabling constraints from the onset" (1997a: 16). Such a concept foregrounds the indeterminacy inherent in most structures of constraint and provides space for the subject to negotiate these structures. In other words, no matter how burdened the subject may be, the flow of history and sociality prevents him or her from being permanently locked into a particular state.

10. For more on Tijerina, land grants, and the Courthouse Raid in Tierra Amarilla, see Nabokov 1970; Gardner 1970. For more on Hispano land grants in northern New Mexico, see Gonzales 2003; Ebright 1994.

11. Cited in Kosek 2004: 344.

12. In recent years the movement has claimed some legislative victories and has the sympathetic ear of Governor Bill Richardson.

13. The Latin root is re, "to repeat," and cordis, "heart," as in "to pass through the heart again."

14. Alma's description echoes the findings of Ed Preble and John Casey, whose classic article, "Taking Care of Business: The Heroin User's Life on the Street," details the mundane and repetitive activities that fill the lives of minority men in New York City. Arguing against the popular and scholarly view of heroin users as lazy, pathological, or retreatist, they argue that the problem was not the

heroin user but the lack of opportunities for living a "legitimate" and meaningful life; see Preble and Casey 1969. Similarly, Philippe Bourgois's *In Search of Respect* analyzes crack dealing in Spanish Harlem as an economically and historically mediated phenomenon; see Bourgois 1995.

15.   My use of the notion of cultural and temporal rootedness is indebted to Kosek's (2006) discussion of the rootedness between people and place. The metaphor of roots, Kosek argues, "can represent a nurturing force but can also represent stubborn, steadfast attachment to a place. This bleaker dimension of belonging underscores a major theory of northern New Mexico's overwhelming social problems" (113).

16.   For example, while a 1934 study of the region rather angrily maintains that "the Spanish planted their institutions so firmly that the trace of the Spaniard and his Mexican successor can never be beaten out of the land," another study from the same period celebrates the region's "cultural indelibility" and declares that Hispano New Mexico is "the most cohesive Hispanic population in the United States . . . and the most faithful to long and uninterrupted traditions" (both cited in Kosek 2006: 107). Central to both readings is the idea that Hispano New Mexico, because of its territorial isolation, exists as an utterly distinct cultural space rooted in enduring land-based traditions and agrarian values.

17.   An alternative reading is that what lures the tourist is the idea that this vestige of what life was like before the closing of the frontier is on the verge of extinction and should be seen now, before it is gone forever. For an excellent analysis of the effects of Hispano tourism on persistent struggles over control of land and water, see Rodriguez 1987.

18.   Frantz Fanon (1963) describes these kinds of tensions in the context of "the colonial situation." For Fanon, colonialism went beyond political and economic exploitation. He determined that the conflictive, subjective state of the colonized is a crucial battleground for the maintenance of imperial control.

19.   The idiom *querencia* is local to the region. It derives from the Spanish verb *querer*, "to love," and the noun *herencia*, "heritage." It is used to describe love and connection to one's place and culture.

20.   Much like the valorization of the "thug life" that is associated with urban hip-hop, there is a valorization of the *tecato* in the valley, especially among youth.

CHAPTER THREE

1.   Such representations include Nelson Algren's gritty novel, *The Man with a Golden Arm,* published in 1949 and the basis of Otto Preminger's 1955 movie of the same title. Frank Sinatra's portrayal of the heroin-addicted ex-con Frankie

Machine depicts a version of a masculine and illicit street economy that, at least in the realm of popular representation, retains currency (see Algren 1999). Or the film *Panic in Needle Park* (1971), in which Kitty Winn's portrayal of Helen, the love interest of heroin-addicted Bobby (played by Al Pacino), fulfills a female archetype—namely, that of a homeless girl who turns to heroin and eventually to prostitution. This was among the first films to explore a distinctly gendered moral economy of heroin addiction—one that also remains largely unchanged.

2. Families, of course, take many forms. Here, I refer to the "traditional" biological family.

3. Judith Butler's work on gender identity has been central to formulating a theory of the performative. She argues that gender is not a role that speaks to a preexisting interior self but an effect of performative acts. See Butler 1997a.

4. At any given time, thirty to forty Hispano drug addicts live on the sprawling property, visible only if one gains entrance to the compound. Addicts are subjected to a "boot camp" regime of group counseling, exercise, and skills training. Few addicts who attend manage to complete the three-year program.

5. According to the church's view on biblical salvation, people who do not obey the gospel or who choose to sin willfully rather than obey God and his law are "lost." Many members of the church believe that the "lost" will be condemned to an eternity without God. A vast majority believe in a literal hell, while others believe it is a metaphorical eternity outside the light of God. A few believe in some version of annihilationism, which holds that the fires of hell consume sinners.

6. Cori Hayden (2003), in her work on Mexico, notes that the juridical reconfiguration of private property erased indigenous claims to territory, materials, and knowledge. A similar dynamic can be seen among Hispanos in New Mexico and the "absence" of kin-based communities such as Los Martinez on legal maps is indicative of these processes of dispossession.

7. See Derrida 1994: 8.

8. The self-reflective emotion of shame involves the painful awareness of the self as less good than hoped for or expected. It is the "negative experience of self," an "implosion," that comes from the "vicarious experience of the other's negative evaluation of oneself" (Lewis 1971: 108). Shame is manifested on the face and body, through articulations of speech and gesture. Perhaps among the most important efforts to recast shame in social terms is Erving Goffman's (1967) work on the centrality of shame in social relations. In Goffman, the individual is always concerned about his image in the eyes of the other. What interests me about shame is its relation to subjectivity.

9. For an exploration of the gendered dimensions of shame, see Bartky 1990; Lehtinen 1998; Dillon 1997.

CHAPTER FOUR

1. Veena Das has written extensively on the uses of Wittgenstein in anthropology. See, e.g., Das 1998.

2. This is a point Ian Hacking also makes. See Hacking 1995.

3. According to Taussig (1987), amid the "murk" of the violent field of inquiry, it is difficult for the ethnographer to locate the violence beyond the fictions (i.e., the bodies and weapons) that are used to accomplish the violent act itself. The bodies and weapons are thus "distractions" that lead the ethnographer away from the subtext of the violence. See also Nordstrom 1997; Feldman 1995.

4. Rio Arriba Department of Resource Development 1997: 11.

5. See Diekstra and Gulbinat 1993; Borges, Walters, and Kessler 2000.

CHAPTER FIVE

1. Commercialization of the health care system took place throughout the 1990s—a consequence of the Clinton administration's 1993 Health Securities Act, which aimed to manage the competition of managed health plans so as to provide universal health coverage. Although the act failed to pass Congress, corporations and policy makers increased their use of managed care organizations as a cost-cutting strategy.

2. For more on the history of deinstitutionalization, see Grob 1995.

3. Nancy Campbell and Susan Shaw show how harm-reduction strategies were simultaneously advanced through "bottom-up" tactics of health-oriented social movements and administered through an institutionalized and standardized set of beliefs. See Campbell and Shaw 2008.

CONCLUSION

1. This chapter grew out of "Digging Deep: Hispano Heroin Addicts Get Back to the Land," an article I wrote for the regional environmental magazine *High Country News* (2008).

Bibliography

Agamben, Giorgio. 1998. *Homo Sacer: Sovereign Power and Bare Life*. Stanford: Stanford University Press.

Agar, Michael. 1973. *Ripping and Running: A Formal Ethnography of Urban Heroin Addicts*. New York: Seminar.

Algren, Nelson. 1999. *The Man with a Golden Arm*. New York: Seven Stories Press.

Andrade, Xavier. 1999. "Drug Sniffers in New York City: An Ethnography of Heroin Markets and Patterns of Use." *Journal of Drug Issues* 29 (2): 271–98.

Appel, P. W., and Joseph H. Kott. 2000. "Causes and Rates of Death among Methadone Maintenance Patients." *Mount Sinai Journal of Medicine* 66: 444–51.

Appleby, L. 2000. "Drug Misuse and Suicide: A Tale of Two Services." *Addiction* 95: 175–77.

Augé, Marc. 2004. *Oblivion*. Minneapolis: University of Minnesota Press.

Avelar, Idelber. 1999. *The Untimely Present: Postdictatorial Latin American Fiction and the Task of Mourning*. Durham, NC: Duke University Press.

Bachelard, Gaston. 1994. *The Poetics of Place*. Boston: Beacon Press.

Bartky, Sandra. 1990. *Femininity and Domination: Studies in the Phenomenology of Oppression*. New York: Routledge.

Bergson, Henri. 1991. *Matter and Memory*. Cambridge, MA: Zone Books.

Biagioli, M. 1990. "The Anthropology of Incommensurability." *Studies in the History of Philosophical Sciences* 21 (2): 183–209.

Biehl, João. 2005. *Vita: Life in a Zone of Social Abandonment*. Berkeley: University of California Press.

———. 2007. *Will to Live: AIDS Therapies and the Politics of Survival*. Princeton, NJ: Princeton University Press.

Blanchot, Maurice. 1986. *The Writing of Disaster*. Lincoln: University of Nebraska Press.

Bloom, B., and M. Chesney-Lind. 2000. "Women in Prison: Vengeful Equity." In *It's a Crime: Women and Justice*, edited by Rosylyn Muraskin. Upper Saddle River, NJ: Prentice Hall.

Boltanski, Luc. 1999. *Suffering and Distance: Morality, Media, and Politics*. Cambridge: Cambridge University Press.

Borges, Guilherme, Ellen Waters, and Robald Kessler. 2000. "Associations of Substance Use, Abuse, and Dependence with Subsequent Suicidal Behavior." *American Journal of Epidemiology* 151 (8): 781–89.

Borges, Jorge Luis. 1998. *Collected Fictions*. New York: Penguin Putnam.

Borneman, John. 1997. "Caring and Being Cared For: Displacing Marriage, Kinship, Gender, and Sexuality." *International Journal of Social Science* 154 (December): 623–35.

Borneman, John, and Abdellah Hammoudi, eds. 2009. *Being There: The Fieldwork Encounter and the Making of Truth*. Berkeley: University of California Press.

Bourgois, Philippe. 1995. *In Search of Respect: Selling Crack in El Barrio*. New York: Cambridge University Press.

———. 1998. "Just Another Night in a Shooting Gallery." *Theory, Culture, and Society* 15 (2): 37–66.

———. 2000. "Disciplining Addictions: The Bio-Politics of Methadone and Heroin in the United States." *Culture, Medicine, and Psychiatry* 24: 165–96.

———. 2002. "Anthropology and Epidemiology on Drugs: The Challenges of Cross-Methodological and Theoretical Dialogue." *International Journal of Drug Policy* 13: 259–69.

Bourgois, Philippe, and Jeffrey Schonberg. 2009. *Righteous Dopefiend*. Berkeley: University of California Press.

Brewer D. D. 1998. "Drug Use Predictors of Partner Violence in Opiate Dependent Women." *Violence Vice* 13 (2): 107–15.

Briggs, Charles, and Clara Mantini-Briggs. 2004. *Stories in the Time of Cholera: Racial Profiling in a Medical Nightmare*. Berkeley: University of California Press.

Briggs, Charles L., and John R. Van Ness, eds. 1987. *Land, Water, and Culture: New Perspectives on Hispanic Land Grants.* Albuquerque: University of New Mexico Press.

Bureau of Justice Statistics. 2002. *Women Offenders.* Washington, DC: U.S. Department of Justice, Office of Justice Programs.

Burns, Sarah. 1989. *Pastoral Imaginations: Rural Life in 19th-Century American Art and Culture.* Philadelphia: Temple University Press

Butler, Judith. 1997a. *Excitable Speech: A Politics of the Performative.* New York: Routledge.

———. 1997b. *The Psychic Life of Power: Theories in Subjection.* Stanford: Stanford University Press.

———. 2000. *Antigone's Claim: Kinship between Life and Death.* New York: Columbia University Press.

———. 2004. *Precarious Life: The Powers of Mourning and Violence.* London: Verso.

———. 2005. *Giving an Account of Oneself.* New York: Fordham University Press.

Buttimer, Anne, and Deavid Seamon. 1980. *The Human Experience of Space and Place.* New York: Palgrave Macmillan.

Camí, Jordi. 2003. "Drug Addiction." *New England Journal of Medicine* 348 (10): 375–86.

Campbell, Nancy. 2000. *Using Women: Gender, Drug Use, and Social Justice.* New York: Routledge.

———. 2007. *Discovering Addiction: The Science and Politics of Substance Abuse Research.* Ann Arbor: University of Michigan Press.

Campbell, Nancy, and Susan Shaw. 2008. "Incitements to Discourse: Illicit Drugs, Harm Reduction, and the Production of Ethnographic Subjects." *Cultural Anthropology* 23 (4): 688–717.

Camus, Albert. 1991. *The Myth of Sisyphus: And Other Essays.* New York: Vintage.

Canguilhem, Georges. 1991. *The Normal and the Pathological.* New York: Zone Books.

Carsten, Janet. 2004. *After Kinship.* Cambridge: Cambridge University Press.

Casey, Edward S. 1993. *Getting Back into Place: Toward a Renewed Understanding of the Place-World.* Bloomington: University of Indiana Press.

Castoriadis, Cornelius. 1987. *The Imaginary Institution of Society.* Cambridge, MA: MIT Press.

Cavell, Stanley. 1976. *Must We Mean What We Say.* Cambridge: Cambridge University Press.

Certeau, Michael de. 1988. *The Writing of History. Heterologies: Discourse on the Other.* New York: Columbia University Press.

Cheng, Anne Anlin. 2000. *The Melancholy of Race.* New York: Oxford University Press.

Chao, J., and E. J. Nestler. 2004. "Molecular Neurobiology of Drug Addiction." *Annual Review of Medicine* 55: 113–32.

Cioran, Emil M. 1992. *Anathemas and Admiration.* London: Quartet Books.

Clarke, John. 2004. *Changing Welfare, Changing States: New Directions in Social Policy.* Thousand Oaks, CA: Sage.

Clarke, John, and Janet Newman. 1997. *The Managerial State: Power, Politics, and Ideology in the Remaking of Social Welfare.* Thousand Oaks, CA: Sage.

Clifford, James. 1997. "Spatial Practices: Fieldwork, Travel, and the Disciplining of Anthropology." In *Anthropological Locations: Boundaries and Grounds of a Field Science,* edited by Akhil Gupta and James Ferguson. Berkeley: University of California Press.

Cocteau, Jean. 2001. *Opium: The Diary of His Cure.* London: Peter Owen.

Cohen, Lawrence. 1998. *No Aging in India: The Bad Family, and Other Modern Things.* Berkeley: University of California Press.

———. 1999. "Where It Hurts: Indian Material for an Ethics of Organ Transplantation." Special issue "Bioethics and Beyond." *Daedalus* 128 (4): 135–65.

Collier, Stephen, and Andrew Lakoff. 2005. "On Regimes of Living." In *Global Assemblages: Technology, Politics, and Ethics as Anthropological Problems,* edited by Aihwa Ong and Stephen J. Collier. Malden, MA: Blackwell.

Comaroff, Jean, and John Comaroff. 2004. "Criminal Obsessions, after Foucault: Postcoloniality, Policing, and the Metaphysics of Disorder." *Critical Inquiry* 30: 800–824.

Courtwright, David. 2001. *Forces of Habit: Drugs and the Making of the Modern World.* Cambridge, MA: Harvard University Press.

———. 2009. "The NIDA Brain-Disease Paradigm: History, Resistance, and Spinoffs." Paper presented at the conference "Addiction, the Brain, and Society," Emory University, Atlanta, GA.

Covington, Stephanie. 2002. *A Woman's Journey Home: Challenges for Female Offenders.* Washington, DC: Urban Institute.

Covington, Stephanie, and Barbara E. Bloom. 2003. "Gendered Justice: Women in the Criminal Justice System." In *Gendered Justice: Addressing Female Offenders,* edited by Rosylyn Muraskin. Durham, NC: Carolina Academic Press.

Daniel, E. Valentine. 1996. *Charred Lullabies: Chapters in the Anthropology of Violence.* Princeton, NJ: Princeton University Press.

Darke, Shane, and Joanne Ross. 2002. "Suicide among Heroin Users: Rates, Risk Factors, and Methods." *Addiction* 97: 1383–94.

Das, Veena. 1996. *Critical Events: An Anthropological Perspective on Contemporary India.* New Delhi: Oxford University Press.

———. 1998. "Wittgenstein and Anthropology." *Annual Review of Anthropology* 27: 171–95.

———. 2006. *Life and Words: Violence and the Descent into the Ordinary.* Berkeley: University of California Press.

Das, Veena, and Renu Addlakha. 2001. "Disability and Domestic Citizenship: Voice, Gender, and the Making of the Subject." *Public Culture* 13 (3): 511–31.

Das, Veena, and Ranendra K. Das. 2007. "How the Body Speaks: Illness and Lifeworld among the Urban Poor." In *Subjectivity: Ethnographic Investigations,* edited by João Biehl, Byron Good, and Arthur Kleinman, 66–97. Berkeley: University of California Press.

———. 2006. "Pharmaceuticals in Urban Ecologies: The Register of the Local." In *Global Pharmaceuticals: Ethics, Markets, Practices,* edited by Adriana Petryna, Andrew Lakoff, and Arthur Kleinman. Durham, NC: Duke University Press.

Derrida, Jacques. 1985. *Margins of Philosophy.* Chicago: University of Chicago Press.

———. 1994. *Specters of Marx: The State of the Debt, the Work of Mourning, and the New International.* New York: Routledge.

Desjarlais, Robert. 1997. *Shelter Blues: Selfhood and Sanity among the Homeless.* Philadelphia: University of Pennsylvania Press.

De Man, Paul. 1979. *Allegories of Reading: Figural Language in Rousseau, Nietzsche, Rilke, and Proust.* New Haven, CT: Yale University Press.

Diekstra, R. F., and W. Gulbinat. 1993. "The Epidemiology of Suicidal Behavior: A Review of Three Continents." *World Health Statistics Quarterly* 46: 52–68.

Dillon, Robin. 1997. "Self-Respect: Moral, Emotional, Political." *Ethics* 107: 222–49.

Douglas, J. D. 1967. *Social Meanings of Suicide.* Princeton, NJ: Princeton University Press.

Durkheim, Emile. 1997. *Suicide: A Study in Sociology.* New York: Free Press.

Ebright, Malcolm. 1994. *Land Grants and Lawsuits in Northern New Mexico.* Albuquerque: University of New Mexico Press.

Eng, David L., and David Kazanjian, eds. 2003. *Loss: The Politics of Mourning.* Berkeley: University of California Press.

Fanon, Frantz. 1963. *The Wretched of the Earth.* New York: Grove Press.

Farmer, Paul. 1999. *Infections and Inequalities: The Modern Plagues.* Berkeley: University of California Press.

Farrell, M. 1996. "Suicide and Overdose among Opiate Addicts." *Addiction* 91: 321–33.

Feldman, Allen. 1995. "Ethnographic States of Emergency." In *Fieldwork under Fire: Contemporary Studies of Violence and Survival,* edited by Carolyn Nordstrom and Antonius Robben. Berkeley: University of California Press.

Fischer, Michael. 2003. *Emergent Forms of Life and the Anthropological Voice.* Durham, NC: Duke University Press.

Foucault, Michel. 1978. *The History of Sexuality.* Vol. 1. New York: Pantheon Books.

———. 1982. "The Subject and Power." *Critical Inquiry* 8 (4): 777–95.

———. 1995. *Discipline and Punish: The Birth of the Prison*. New York: Vintage.

———. 1999. *Abnormal*. New York: Picador.

Fraser, Suzanne, and Kylie Valentine. 2008. *Substance and Substitution: Methadone Subjects in Liberal Societies*. New York: Palgrave Macmillan.

Freud, Sigmund. 1918 [1914]. "From the History of an Infantile Neurosis [the 'Wolf-Man' Case]." In *Standard Edition*, 17:1–122.

———. 1960. *The Ego and the Id*. New York: W. W. Norton.

———. 1989. "Mourning and Melancholia." In *The Freud Reader*, edited by Peter Gay. New York: W. W. Norton.

———. 1997. *The Interpretation of Dreams*. London: Dover Publications.

———. 2004. *Studies in Hysteria*. London: Penguin.

Fulwilley, Duana. 2007. "The Molecularization of Race: Institutionalizing Human Difference in Pharmacogenetics Practice." *Science as Culture* 16 (1): 1–30.

Garcia, Angela. 2008. "The Elegiac Addict: History, Chronicity, and the Melancholic Subject." *Cultural Anthropology* 23 (4): 718–46.

Gardner, Richard. 1970. *¡Grito! Reies Tijerina and the New Mexico Land Grant War of 1967*. New York: Harper Colophon Books.

Giddens, Anthony. 1971. *Sociology of Suicide*. New York: Frank Cass and Co.

Goffman, Erving. 1961. *Asylums: Essays on the Social Situation of Mental Patients and Other Inmates*. Garden City, NY: Doubleday.

———. 1967. *Interaction Ritual*. New York: Anchor.

González, Deena. 1999. *Refusing the Favor: The Spanish-Mexican Women of Santa Fe, 1820–1880*. Oxford: Oxford University Press.

Gonzalez, Phillip. 2003. "Struggle for Survival: The Hispanic Land Grants of New Mexico, 1848–2001." *Agricultural History* 77 (2): 293–324.

Good, Byron. 1994. *Medicine, Rationality, and Experience*. Cambridge: Cambridge University Press.

Gordon, Avery. 1997. *Ghostly Matters: Haunting and the Sociological Imagination*. Minneapolis: University of Minnesota Press.

Gregoire, T., and C. Burke. 2004. "The Relationship of Legal Coercion to Readiness to Change among Adults with Alcohol and Other Drug Problems." *Journal of Substance Abuse Treatment* 26: 337–43.

Grob, Gerald. 1995. *The Mad among Us: A History of the Care of America's Mentally Ill*. Cambridge, MA: Harvard University Press.

Gusterson, Hugh. 1996. *Nuclear Rites: A Weapons Laboratory at the End of the Cold War*. Berkeley: University of California Press.

Gutiérrez, Ramón. 1991. *When Jesus Came, the Corn Mothers Went Away: Marriage, Sexuality, and Power in New Mexico, 1500–1846*. Stanford: Stanford University Press.

Hacking, Ian. 1995. *The Taming of Chance*. Cambridge: Cambridge University Press.

Halbwachs, Maurice. 1978. *The Causes of Suicide.* New York: Free Press.

Han, Clara. 2004. "The Work of Indebtedness: The Traumatic Present of Late Capitalist Chile." *Culture, Medicine, and Psychiatry* 28 (2): 169–87.

Hansen, Helena. 2005. "Isla Evangelista—A Story of Church and State: Puerto Rico's Faith-Based Initiatives on Drug Treatment." *Culture, Medicine, and Psychiatry* 29: 433–56.

Hayden, Cori. 2003. *When Nature Goes Public: The Making and Unmaking of Bioprospecting in Mexico.* Princeton, NJ: Princeton University Press.

Horton, Sarah, Joanne McCloskey, Caroline Todd, and Marta Henriksen. 2001. "Transforming the Safety Net: Responses to Medicaid Managed Care in Rural and Urban New Mexico." *American Anthropologist* 103 (3): 733–46.

Huyssen, Andreas. 2000. "Present Pasts: Media, Politics, Amnesia." *Public Culture* 12 (1): 21–38.

Hyman, S. E. 2001. "Addiction and the Brain: The Neurobiology Compulsion and Its Persistence." *National Review of Neuroscience* 2: 695–703.

———. 2005. "Addiction: A Disease of Memory and Learning." *American Journal of Psychiatry* 162: 1414–22.

Irigaray, Luce. 1985. *This Sex Which Is Not One.* Translated by Gillian C. Gill. Ithaca, NY: Cornell University Press.

Jackson, Jean. 2005. "Stigma, Liminality, and Chronic Pain: Mind-Body Borderlands." *American Ethnologist* 32 (3): 332–53.

Jackson, John B. 1996. *A Sense of Time, a Sense of Place.* New Haven, CT: Yale University Press.

Johnson, Holly. 2006. "Drug Use by Incarcerated Women Offenders." *Drug and Alcohol Review* 25 (5): 433–37.

Kim, David Kyuman. 2007. *Melancholic Freedom: Agency and the Spirit of Politics.* Oxford: Oxford University Press.

Kleinman, Arthur. 1995. *Writing at the Margin: Discourse between Anthropology and Medicine.* Berkeley: University of California Press.

———. 1999. "Experience and Its Moral Modes: Culture, Human Conditions, and Disorder." In *The Tanner Lectures on Human Values,* vol. 20, edited by G. B. Peterson. Salt Lake City: University of Utah Press.

———. 2006. *What Really Matters: Living a Moral Life amidst Uncertainty and Danger.* Oxford: Oxford University Press.

Kleinman, Arthur, and Joan Kleinman. 1997. "The Appeal of Experience, the Dismay of Images: Cultural Appropriations of Suffering in Our Times." In *Social Suffering,* edited by Arthur Kleinman, Veena Das, and Margaret Lock. Berkeley: University of California Press.

Klingemann, Harold. 2001. "The Time Game: Temporal Perspectives of Patients and Staff in Alcohol and Drug Treatment." *Time and Society* 10: 303–28.

Kondo, Dorinne. 1990. *Crafting Selves: Power, Gender, and Discourses of Identity in a Japanese Workplace*. Chicago: University of Chicago Press.

Kosek, Jake. 2004. "Deep Roots and Long Shadows: The Cultural Politics of Memory and Longing in Northern New Mexico." *Environment and Planning D: Society and Space* 22: 329–54.

———. 2006. *Understories: The Political Life of Forests in Northern New Mexico*. Durham, NC: Duke University Press.

Kristeva, Julia. 1989. *Black Sun: Depression and Melancholia*. New York: Columbia University Press.

Kuhn, Thomas. 1962. *The Structure of Scientific Revolutions*. Chicago: University of Chicago Press.

LaMothe, Ryan. 1999. "The Tragic and Faith in Pastoral Counseling." *Journal of Religion and Health* 38 (2): 101–15.

Lehtinen, Ullaliina. 1998. "How Does One Know What Shame Is? Epistemology, Emotions, and Forms of Life in Juxtaposition." *Hypatia* 13 (1): 56–77.

Levinas, Emmanuel. 1969. *Totality and Infinity: An Essay on Exteriority*. Pittsburgh, PA: Duquesne University Press.

———. 1998a. *Entre Nous: Thinking-of-the-Other*. New York: Columbia University Press.

———. 1998b. *Otherwise than Being: Or Beyond Essence*. Pittsburgh, PA: Duquesne University Press.

———. 2003. *On Escape*. Stanford: Stanford University Press.

Lewis, Helen. 1971. *Shame and Guilt in Neurosis*. New York: International Universities Press.

Lovell, Anne. 2006. "Addiction Markets: The Case of High-Dose Buprenorphine in France." In *Global Pharmaceuticals: Ethics, Markets, Practices,* edited by Adriana Petryna, Andrew Lakoff, and Arthur Kleinman. Durham, NC: Duke University Press.

———. 2002. "Risking the Risk: The Influence of Types of Capital and Social Networks on the Injection Practices of Drug Users." *Social Science and Medicine* 55: 803–21.

Martin, Emily. 2007. *Bi-Polar Expeditions: Mania and Depression in American Culture*. Princeton, NJ: Princeton University Press.

Marx, Karl. 1967. *Capital*. Vol. 1. New York: International Publishers.

Masco, Joseph. 2006. *The Nuclear Borderlands: The Manhattan Project in Post–Cold War New Mexico*. Princeton, NJ: Princeton University Press.

Matta, A., and J. Jorquez. 1994. "Mexican American Intravenous Drug Users' Needle-Sharing Practices: Implications for AIDS Intervention." In *Needle-Sharing among Intravenous Drug Abusers: National and International Perspectives,* edited by Robert Battjes and Roy Pickens. Research Monograph 80. Washington, DC: National Institute on Drug Abuse.

Mbembe, Achille. 2003. "Necropolitics." *Public Culture* 15 (1): 11–40.

McLellan, J. 2000. "Drug Dependence: A Chronic Medical Illness: Implications for Treatment, Insurance, and Outcomes Evaluation." *Journal of the American Medical Association* 284: 1689–95.

Merleau-Ponty, Maurice. 1996. *Phenomenology of Perception.* London: Routledge.

Meyer, Birgit. 2004. "Christianity in Africa: From African Independent to Pentecostal-Charismatic Churches." *Annual Review of Anthropology* 33: 447–74.

Mitchell, Pablo. 2005. *Coyote Nation: Sexuality, Race, Conquest in Modernizing New Mexico, 1880–1920.* Chicago: University of Chicago Press.

Mol, Annemarie. 2002. *The Body Multiple: Ontology in Medical Practice.* Durham, NC: Duke University Press.

Moore, Donald S. 2005. *Suffering for Territory: Race, Place, and Power in Zimbabwe.* Durham, NC: Duke University Press.

Moore, Donald S., Anand Pandian, and Jake Kosek. 2003. "The Cultural Politics of Race and Nature: Terrains of Power and Practice." In *Race, Nature, and the Politics of Difference,* edited by Donald S. Moore, Anand Pandian, and Jake Kosek. Durham, NC: Duke University Press.

Moore, J. W., and A. G. Mata. 1982. *Women and Heroin in a Chicago Community: A Final Report.* Los Angeles: Chicano Pinto Research Project.

Morales, A. 1994. "Substance Abuse and Mexican American Youth: An Overview." *Journal of Drug Issues* 14 (2): 297–331.

Muñoz, José E. 1997. "Photographies of Mourning: Melancholia and Ambivalence in Van Der Zee, Mapplethorpe, and Looking for Langston." In *Race and the Subject of Masculinities,* edited by Harry Stecopoulos and Michael Uebel. Durham, NC: Duke University Press.

Nabokov, Peter. 1970. *Tijerina and the Courthouse Raid.* Palo Alto, CA: Ramparts Press.

National Institute of Justice. 1998. *Women Offenders: Programming Needs and Promising Approaches.* Washington, DC: U.S. Department of Justice, Office of Justice Programs.

Nead, Lynda. 1992. *The Female Nude: Art, Obscenity, and Sexuality.* New York: Routledge.

Nestler, E. J. 2001. "Total Recall: The Memory of Addiction." *Science* 292: 2266–67.

Nietzsche, Friedrich. 1997. "On the Uses and Disadvantages of History for Life." In *Untimely Meditations.* Cambridge Texts in the History of Philosophy, edited by Karl Ameriks. Cambridge: Cambridge University Press.

———. 2006. *The Gay Science.* New York: Dover Publications.

Nordstrom, Carolyn. 1997. *A Different Kind of War Story.* Philadelphia: University of Pennsylvania Press.

Nussbaum, Martha. 1980. "Shame, Separateness, and Political Unity." In *Essays in Aristotle's Ethics*, edited by Amelie O. Rorty. Berkeley: University of California Press.

Obrien, Charles, Nora Volkow, and T.-K. Li. 2006 "What's in a Word: Addiction versus Dependence in DSM-V." *American Journal of Psychiatry* 163: 764–65.

O'Nell, DeLeane Theresa. 1996. *Disciplined Hearts: History, Identity, and Depression in an American Indian Community*. Berkeley: University of California Press.

Owusu-Darkara, Lily Nana Amena. 2001. "Wild Hunger: Crack Cocaine and Heroin Dependency in Postcolonial Ghana." Ph.D. dissertation, University of California, Berkeley, with University of California, San Francisco.

Pandolfi, Mariella. 1991. "Memory within the Body: Women's Narrative and Identity in a Southern Italian Village." In *Anthropologies of Medicine*, edited by Beatrice Pfleiderer and Gilles Bibeay. Heidelberg: Vieweg.

Pandolfo, Stefania. 1998. *Impasse of the Angels: Scenes from a Moroccan Space of Memory*. Chicago: University of Chicago Press.

Peirano, Maria G. S. 1998. "When Anthropology Is at Home: The Different Contexts of a Single Discipline." *Annual Review of Anthropology* 27: 105–28.

Peperzak, Adriaan. 1997. *Beyond: The Philosophy of Emmanuel Levinas*. Evanston, IL: Northwestern University Press.

———. 1998. *Before Ethics*. Amherst, MA: Humanity Books.

Petryna, Adriana. 2002. *Life Exposed: Biological Citizenship after Chernobyl*. Princeton, NJ: Princeton University Press.

Petryna, Adriana, and Arthur Kleinman. 2006. "The Pharmaceutical Nexus." In *Global Pharmaceuticals: Ethics, Markets, Practices*, edited by Adriana Petryna, Andrew Lakoff, and Arthur Kleinman. Durham, NC: Duke University Press.

Povinelli, Elizabeth. 2001. "Radical Worlds: The Anthropology of Incommensurability and Inconceivability." *Annual Review of Anthropology* 30: 319–34.

———. 2006. *The Empire of Love: Toward a Theory of Intimacy, Genealogy, and Carnality*. Durham, NC: Duke University Press.

Preble, Ed, and John Casey Jr. 1969. "Taking Care of Business: The Heroin User's Life on the Street." *International Journal of the Addictions* 4 (1): 1–24.

Pud, D., D. Cohen, E. Lawental, and E. Eisenberg. 2006. "Opioids and Abnormal Pain Perception: New Evidence from a Study of Chronic Opioid Addicts and Healthy Subjects." *Drug Alcohol Dependency* 82 (3): 218–23.

Rabinow, Paul. 1999. *French DNA: Trouble in Purgatory*. Chicago: University of Chicago Press.

Raviola, Giuseppe, M'lmunya Machoki, Esther Mwaikambo, and Mary-Jo DelVecchio Good. 2002. "HIV, Disease Plague, Demoralization, and 'Burnout': Resident Experience of the Medical Profession in Nairobi, Kenya." *Culture, Medicine, and Psychiatry* 26 (1): 55–86.

Rawls, John. 1971. *A Theory of Justice.* Cambridge, MA: Harvard University Press.

Reichelt, Lauren. 2001. "Substance Abuse, Culture, and Economics in Rio Arriba County, Northern New Mexico: An Analysis of Impacts and Root Causes." Rio Arriba Department of Health and Human Services.

Reyes, R. 1995. *An Ethnographic Study of Heroin Abuse by Mexican Americans in San Antonio, Texas.* Austin: Texas Commission on Alcohol and Drug Abuse.

Rhodes, Lorna. 2004. *Total Confinement: Madness and Reason in the Maximum Security Prison.* Berkeley: University of California Press.

Rio Arriba Department of Resource Development. 1997. "Report: The Impact of the Los Alamos National Laboratories upon Economics and Culture in Hispanic Northern New Mexico." Rio Arriba County, New Mexico.

Rodriguez, Sylvia. 1987. "Land, Water, and Ethnic Identity in Taos." In *Land, Water, and Culture: New Perspectives on Hispanic Land Grants,* edited by Charles L. Briggs and John Van Ness. Albuquerque: University of New Mexico Press.

Rose, Nikolas. 2001. "The Politics of Life Itself." *Theory, Culture, and Society* 18 (6): 1–30.

———. 2006. *The Politics of Life Itself: Biomedicine, Power, and Subjectivity in the Twenty-first Century.* Princeton, NJ: Princeton University Press.

Ruti, Mari. 2005. "From Melancholia to Meaning: How to Live the Past in the Present." *Psychoanalytic Dialogues* 15 (5): 637–60.

Rylko-Bauer, Barbara, and Paul Farmer. 2002. "Managed Care or Managed Inequality? A Call for Critiques of Market-Based Medicine." *Medical Anthropology Quarterly* 16: 476–502.

Sacks, Peter. 1985. *The English Elegy: Studies in the Genre from Spencer to Yeats.* Baltimore, MD: Johns Hopkins University Press.

Saldívar-Hull, Sonia. 2000. *Feminism on the Border: Chicana Politics and Literature.* Berkeley: University of California Press.

Sánchez, George. 1996. *Forgotten People: A Study of New Mexicans.* Reproduction of 1940 edition. Albuquerque: University of New Mexico Press.

Santner, Eric. 1990. *Stranded Objects: Mourning, Memory, and Film in Postwar Germany.* Ithaca, NY: Cornell University Press.

Savage, Seddon. 2008. "Challenges in Using Opioids to Treat Pain in Persons with Substance Abuse Disorders." *Addiction Science and Clinical Practice* 4 (2): 4–25.

Scheper-Hughes, Nancy. 1992. *Death without Weeping: The Violence of Everyday Life in Brazil.* Berkeley: University of California Press.

Schneider, David. 1980. *American Kinship: A Cultural Account.* Chicago: University of Chicago Press.

Sedgwick, Eve Kosofsky. 2003. *Touching Feeling: Affect, Pedagogy, Performativity.* Durham, NC: Duke University Press.

Sennett, Richard, and Jonathan Cobb. 1973. *The Hidden Injuries of Class.* New York: Vintage Books.

Seremetakis, Nadia. 1991. *The Last Word: Women, Death, and Divination in Inner Mani.* Chicago: University of Chicago Press.

Shah, Nina. 2006. "Overdose Surveillance in Hospital Departments in Northern New Mexico: A Pilot Study." *New Mexico Epidemiology* 3.

Simmons, Marc. 1991. *The Last Conquistador: Juan de Oñate and the Settling of the Far Southwest.* Norman: University of Oklahoma Press,

Singer, Merrill. 2007. *Drugging the Poor: Legal and Illegal Drug Industries and the Structuring of Social Inequality.* Prospect Heights, IL: Waveland Press.

Slifkin, Rebecca T., Sheila D. Hoag, Pam Silberman, Suzanne Felt-Lisk, and Benjamin Popkin. 1998. "Medicaid Managed Care Programs in Rural Areas: A Fifty-State Overview." *Health Affairs* 17 (6): 217–27.

State of New Mexico Department of Health. 2003. *Drug Mortality: Illicit and Prescription, 1992–1993.* Santa Fe: State of New Mexico Department of Health.

Strathern, Marilyn. 1999. *Property, Substance, and Effect.* London: Athlone Press.

Taussig, Michael. 1987. *Shamanism, Colonialism, and the Wild Man: A Study in Terrorism and Healing.* Chicago: University of Chicago Press.

Taylor, Gabriele. 1995. "Shame, Integrity, and Self-Respect." In *Dignity, Character, and Self-Respect,* edited by Robin Dillown. New York: Routledge.

Trujillo, Michael. 2005. "Land of Disenchantment: Transformation, Continuity, and Negation in the Greater Española Valley, New Mexico." Ph.D. dissertation, University of Texas at Austin.

Tuan, Yi-Fu. 1977. *Space and Place: The Perspective of Experience.* Minneapolis: University of Minnesota Press.

U.S. Census Bureau. 2003a. "Hispanic or Latino by Type: 2000. Census Summary File 1 (SF 1)." Available at http://factfinder.census.gov/servlet/.

———. 2003b. "Race and Hispanic or Latino: 2000. Census Summary File 1 (SF 1)." Available at http://factfinder.census.gov/servlet/.

Visweswaran, Kamala. 2004. *Fictions of Feminist Ethnography.* Minneapolis: University of Minnesota Press.

Volkow, N., and T.-K. Li. 2005. "The Neuroscience of Addiction." *Nature Neuroscience* 8: 1429–30.

Wacquant, Loïc. 1993. "Inside 'the Zone': The Social Art of the Hustler in the American Ghetto." In *The Weight of the World: Social Suffering in Contemporary Society,* edited by Pierre Bourdieu et al. Stanford: Stanford University Press.

Weiser, Sheri. 2006. "Gender-Specific Correlates of Sex Trade among Homeless and Marginally Housed Individuals in San Francisco." *Journal of Urban Health* 83 (4): 736–40.

White, J. M. 2004. "Pleasure into Pain: The Consequences of Long-term Opioid Use." *Addictive Behavior* 29 (7): 1311–24.

Willging, Catherine E. 2005. "Power, Blame, and Accountability: Medicaid Managed Care for Mental Health Services in New Mexico." *Medical Anthropology Quarterly* 19 (1): 84–102.

Willging, Catherine E., Michael Trujillo, and W. Azul La Luz. 2003. *Final Report: Ethnography of Drug Use, Help-Seeking Processes, and Behavioral Health Needs.* Santa Fe: State of New Mexico Department of Health.

Williams, Bernard. 1993. *Shame and Necessity.* Berkeley: University of California Press.

Williams, Raymond. 1975. *The Country and the City.* Oxford: Oxford University Press.

———. 1977. *Marxism and Literature.* Oxford: Oxford University Press.

Willis, Deborah, and Carla Williams. 2002. *The Black Female Body: A Photographic History.* Philadelphia: Temple University Press.

Wittgenstein, Ludwig. 1998. *In Culture and Value: A Selection from the Posthumous Remains,* edited by G. H. Von Wright in collaboration with Heikki Nyman. Oxford: Blackwell.

———. 2001. *Philosophical Investigations.* Oxford: Blackwell.

Young, Allan. 1995. *The Harmony of Illusions: Inventing Post-Traumatic Stress Disorder.* Princeton, NJ: Princeton University Press.

Zizek, Slavoj. 2000. "Melancholy and the Act." *Critical Inquiry* 26: 657–81.

Index

Pages in italics refer to photographs.

abscesses, 44, 93, 112
"accidental" poisoning, 90, 147, 167–68,
  172–73, 176
acequias (irrigation ditches), 102
acequias (labyrinth of irrigation ditches), 5,
  96, 100
Adams, Ansel, 30, 104
addict: aloneness, and solitude of, 32, 49–50,
  154; archetypes of, 112, 114, 219–20n1; attire and appearance of, 155–56; biological
  terms for, 202; "co-addicts" and, 112, 137;
  inevitable trajectory of life of, 15–16, 72,
  73, 161, 173, 201, 202, 210; moral life
  connectedness to addict and, 9–10, 34,
  88, 110, 171, 212n9; patient-prisoner life
  script of, 8–9, 11–12, 19, 52–53; performative dimensions of, 113, 220n3; physical
  characteristics of, 44, 113; as rational economic actor, 188; representational authority of, 42, 44, 216n5; representational

economy of, 113, 148, 219–20n1; shame
  and, 140, 144–45, 160–61, 199, 220n8;
  "shooting up" the grave of, 9–10, 137;
  statistics, 16, 28–29, 213n17; *tecato*, use of
  term, 24, 67, 105, 108, 113, 219n20; "vital
  experimentation" of drugs by, 15. *See also*
  care; melancholy; mother-daughter pairs;
  overdose; patient; relapse; suicide; withdrawal *(las malias)*
addiction: ASI and, 17, 214n20, 216–17n11;
  behavioral and biomedical research in,
  14–17, 72, 76, 112; causality and, 13, 14,
  15; as chronic illness, 13, 15, 18, 70, 88;
  chronic illness-care model and, 14–15, 88;
  chronicity model of, 13, 15–18, 90–92;
  discourses of, 14, 16, 18, 23, 72, 162; economics of, 9, 10, 13–14, 32, 53, 107,
  187–88, 193; embodiment of, 10, 30,
  58–60, 70, 79; etiology of, 14; everyday
  life before, 117–19, 123–26; historically

237

Text: 10/14 Palatino
Display: Univers Condensed Light 47 and Bauer Bodoni
Compositor: Westchester Book Group